Think a Second Time

DENNIS PRAGER

Think a Second Time

Semi
educated

ReganBooks
An Imprint of HarperCollins*Publishers*

HarperCollins books may be purchased for educational, business, or sales promotional use. For information please write: Special Markets Department, HarperCollins Publishers, Inc., 10 East 53rd Street, New York, NY 10022.

Designed by C. Linda Dingler

Library of Congress Cataloging-in-Publication Data
Prager, Dennis, 1948–
   Think a second time / Dennis Prager. — 1st ed.
     p. cm.
   ISBN 0-06-039157-X
   1. Conduct of life. 2. Ethics, Modern—20th century. 3. United States—Moral conditions. I. Title.
   BJ1581.2.P725 1995
   170'.44—dc20   95-37478

96 97 98 99 ❖/HC 10 9 8 7

To Jessica DeBoer,
Danny Warburton ("Baby Richard"),
and the DeBoer and Warburton families

One day, because of you, society will understand that children are not property and that love is infinitely more important than blood.

CONTENTS

PART TWO

LIBERALISM: WHAT HAPPENED TO A GREAT IDEOLOGY?

THE STRUGGLE FOR AMERICA'S SOUL

IDEALISTS CAN BE VERY DANGEROUS

PART THREE

THERE IS A SOLUTION TO EVIL

IS THIS LIFE ALL THERE IS? THOUGHTS ON GOD

INTRODUCTION

I have written *Think a Second Time* because most people don't think a second time. Most of us form opinions about life's great issues at a young age and retain them forever. The reasons are not hard to discern: It isn't comfortable to think through every issue; serious thought is as strenuous as serious exercise, and as we age, most of us become preoccupied with other matters. Family and livelihood problems alone can take up all of one's attention, and if they don't, there is always television or sports or hobbies or some other diversion.

This is sad, because unclear thinking is a major source of social and personal problems.

Take, for example, the question of whether human nature is basically good. Differing views on this question alone explain much of the liberal-conservative divide in our society. If you think people are basically good, you probably blame socioeconomic conditions for the evil people do (generally the liberal position); if you think that evil comes from within people's nature, you are more likely to blame people for the evil they do (generally the conservative position).

Your views on this issue can even profoundly affect your own happiness. Those who believe that people are basically good may have set themselves up for repeated disappointment in people, while those who have a more sober view of human nature (neither basically good nor evil) will, instead, celebrate their good fortune every time they meet a good person. In Chapter 1, I discuss why the belief that people are basically good is wrong.

Who am I that you should want to read my thoughts on forty-three subjects?

It is hardly an author's place to sell himself to a prospective reader—his writings have to earn your respect and attention. But since you have either already purchased (or been given) this book, or are reading this at a bookstore, I'd like to briefly introduce myself.

I am a highly passionate moderate. In fact, I am so passionate and so moderate that I am even passionate about being moderate.

I love life and goodness, and I hate cruelty. I want to hug every kind person and to inflict hurt on bad people (I believe in just revenge). I am religious and believe in God, but I readily acknowledge how much harm religious people have done, and I have a tough time praying to Him.

What makes me tick is a desire to see good conquer evil, as corny as this may sound. I have been preoccupied with good and evil ever since, as a child, I saw kids bully other kids. This preoccupation permeates every chapter of this book.

I have always believed that if offered a choice between clarity and happiness, I would choose clarity (though I have come to believe that clarity in fact enhances happiness). These essays represent my yearning for clarity. Very different versions of some of these essays were published in my quarterly journal, *Ultimate Issues*, others in the *Wall Street Journal* and the *Los Angeles Times*. A word, therefore, about my journal. I began writing *Ultimate Issues* to stay in touch with people who attended my lectures (after three thousand lectures, that's a lot of people). Speeches are like one-night stands—pleasurable and intense at night, but you never see each other again. By my fifteenth year of lecturing, I was looking for a long-term relationship. In 1985, I decided to write and publish a personal quarterly journal. Since then, through a divorce and remarriage, three children, changes in my professional life, and personal crises, I have published this journal every quarter, save two. My readers have followed my life and my thinking on everything from God's existence to having a national television show to male sexual nature. This is, therefore, not only a book of thoroughly revised essays, but the culmination of ten years of writing on these subjects.

I would be very pleased if every reader of this book agreed with every word in it, but if thirteen years as a talk radio host are any indication, few readers will always agree with me, and few will always disagree. Many liberals, for example, will probably love my chapter on how religion can lead to cruelty but be annoyed with my essay on how liberalism can lead to cruelty ("Blacks, Liberals, and the Los Angeles Riots"). Religious readers will love my vigorous defense of God- and religion-based ethics but probably be troubled by my defense of men who attend a striptease show. But my primary goal is not agreement; it is to provoke the reader to think a second time.

I wish to thank George Hiltzik of N. S. Bienstock and Richard Pine of Arthur Pine and Associates for bringing me to Judith Regan. My greatest desire is to bring my ideas to as many people as possible, and who can better help me do so than Judith Regan? I don't know if Judith and I share political views, but I do know that we share a passion that overrides politics—that children be regarded as human beings, not as the property of parents. Perhaps our next book . . .

Deep appreciation goes to my capable and dedicated staff at *Ultimate Issues*, Pat Havins, Rochelle Leffler, and Joanne Starks. Led by Pat, who has worked with me since 1976, their superb work has made it possible for me to write my journal without ever having to worry about anything except getting each issue out on time (which I rarely do anyway).

My assistant, Laurie Zimmet, is more than my right arm; she is a source of ideas, a proofreader, and a one-person support system.

The readers of my journal throughout North America and elsewhere and my KABC Radio listeners in Southern California cannot really know how important they and their ideas and challenges have been to me. But I know, and I thank you for years of support.

Thanks also to Mark Wilcox for his work at Micah Center for Ethical Monotheism, the nonprofit organization I founded. The center has made a remarkable video on goodness, based on many of the ideas to be found in this book, directed by David Zucker and starring some of the best-known actors in America. The center's latest project is "Dinners With a Difference," to encourage people of every racial, ethnic, and religious background to have dinners at one another's homes.

One day, I will write an ode to the importance of friends. I view having close friends as the only way to make it through life without going crazy. Throughout my life, I have been blessed with such people. Along with my wife, they make my happiness possible. In addition to their love, I have also received their considered thought on virtually every issue raised in the book. They are Stephen and Ruth

Marmer, Allen and Susan Estrin, Izzie and Rita Eichenstein, Robert and Amy Florczak, and other friends whom Fran and I simply cannot see as often.

I have saved Joseph Telushkin for special mention. My close friend since our second year at the Yeshiva of Flatbush High School in Brooklyn, this book would not exist without his help. His editing ideas, questions, and challenges were right every time (almost). In our twenties, we coauthored two books on Judaism. Working on this book brought back memories of those wonderfully creative times. His associate, David Szonyi, was also of great help, particularly because of his frequent challenges to my thinking.

Years of dialogue and friendship with John Alston, Father Gregory Coiro, Rabbi Leonid Feldman, Pastor Kapp Johnson, Michael Nocita, Jesse Peterson, and Rabbi David Woznica have also made this book possible.

Finally, only parents can know how true it is that we learn (or at least should learn) an immense amount from our children. Anya, David, and Aaron, each in utterly unique ways, have taught me as much as I hope that I have taught them. To come home to children whom you love and who love you is a joy I wish upon every good person.

As for my life partner, my wife, Fran, every word in this book reflects her wisdom. She has taught me so much—about courage, patience, authenticity, women, and being a father—that I can date a significant part of my intellectual and emotional life as Before Fran and After Fran. This book would be dedicated to her were it not for our mutual passion about children being taken from every person they have ever known and ever loved because some judges still believe in the primacy of blood. It is typical of Fran that she insisted that this book be dedicated to those children and the families from whom they were legally taken.

Dennis Prager

Los Angeles, California
July 1995

PART ONE

HUMAN NATURE

1

WHY THE BELIEF THAT PEOPLE ARE BASICALLY GOOD IS WRONG AND DANGEROUS

The belief that people are basically good is one of the most widely held beliefs in contemporary society. Yet it is both untrue and destructive.

WHY IT ISN'T TRUE

The most frequent objection I encounter when I argue that human nature is not basically good is: Aren't babies born good?

The answer is no. Babies are born *innocent* and they are certainly not born evil, but they aren't born good, either. In fact, babies are the quintessence of selfishness: I want Mommy, I want milk, I want attention, I want to be played with, I want, I want, and if you don't do everything I want, I will ruin your life.

To be sure, this is normal behavior for a baby, but on what grounds can it be characterized as morally *good*?

As for older children, having been a camp counselor and camp director for ten years, I know that few things come more naturally to many children than meanness, petty cruelty, bullying, and a lack of empathy for less fortunate peers. Visit any bunk of thirteen-year-olds in which one camper is particularly fat, short, clumsy, or emotionally or intellectually disadvantaged, and you are likely to observe cruelty that would shock an adult. The statement, "I have never met a bad kid," like "People are born basically good," is simply wishful thinking.

To believe that human nature is basically good—after Auschwitz, the Gulag, Rwanda, Armenia, and Tibet, just to mention some of the horrors of the twentieth century alone—is a statement of faith, as nonempirical as the most wishful religious belief. Whenever I meet people who persist in believing in the essential goodness of human nature, I know that I have met people for whom evidence is irrelevant.

How many evils do humans have to commit to shake a person's faith in humanity's essential goodness? How many more innocent people have to be murdered and tortured? How many more women need to be raped?

There is no number. Just as no contrary evidence will shake the faith of many religious believers, so none will shake the faith of many of those, especially the secular, who believe in humanity's goodness. Faith in humanity is the last belief that a secular individual can relinquish before utterly despairing. The less religious a person is, the more he or she needs to believe in humanity. To believe neither in religion nor in humans is to conclude, as does the protagonist in Woody Allen's *Crimes and Misdemeanors*, that life is a cesspool.

WHY THIS BELIEF IS DESTRUCTIVE

If the falseness of the belief that man is basically good does not suffice to move a person to abandon it, perhaps this will: It is a belief that has particularly destructive consequences.

The first of these consequences is the attribution of all evil to causes outside people: Since people are basically good, the bad that they do must be caused by some external force. Depending on who is doing the blaming, that outside force could be the social environment, economic circumstances, parents, schools, television violence, handguns, the devil, or government cutbacks.

As a result, people are often not held responsible for the evil they commit—a notion that has become commonplace in America.

A second consequence is the denial of evil: *If good is natural, then bad must be unnatural, or sick.* Moral categories have been replaced by psychological ones. There are no longer good and evil, only normal and sick.

Third, parents and teachers who believe that people are basically good will not feel the need to teach children how to be good: Why teach what comes naturally? Only when you truly acknowledge how difficult it is to be a good person do you realize how important it is teach goodness.

Fourth, those who believe that evil comes from outside people work on changing outside forces rather than on changing the evildoers' values. It is the dominant view among academics, policy makers, social workers, and psychotherapists that society must focus on the environment that produces rapists and murderers, not on their values and character development. For example, when irresponsible young men impregnate irresponsible young women, it is not better values that they need, but more sex education and better access to condoms.

Fifth and perhaps most destructive, the belief that people are basically good leads to the conclusion that people need to feel accountable for their behavior only to themselves, not to a God or religious code higher than themselves.

My argument with those who believe that people are innately good can be succinctly summarized. Those who believe in innate human goodness view the battle for a better world as primarily a struggle between the individual and society. I believe that, especially in a free society, the battle is between the individual and his or her nature. There are times, of course, when the battle for a better world must concentrate on evil emanating from outside the individual, as, for example, under a totalitarian regime. But in a free society such as our own, the battle for a moral world is waged primarily through the inner battle that each one of us must wage against our nature, against weakness, addiction, selfishness, ingratitude, laziness, and evil. It is a much more difficult battle to wage than one against social policy.

A society can survive the collapse of its economy, but not of its citizens' morality. An America that emphasized character development in its public and private spheres was able to survive the poverty of the Great Depression. A vastly wealthier America that neglects character development is steadily sinking. And this neglect can be attributed in large part to the widespread belief that people are basically good and the destructive beliefs that accompany it.

2

DON'T JUDGE MOTIVES

I hereby offer a simple proposal that could profoundly enhance the quality of all our lives: a one-year moratorium on assessing other peoples' motives.

Assessing motives is usually pointless, and often destructive.

It is pointless because motives are almost impossible to determine. We often don't know our own, let alone others', and it is destructive because we almost always exaggerate the purity of our own motives and assign nefarious motives to others.

The solution to this problem, in fact the solution to much of humanity's problems, is this: We should judge *actions*—our own and those of others—not motives.

When we discover that we have hurt someone's feelings, our first reaction usually is "I didn't mean it." And because few of us do consciously set out to hurt another person, we feel that this exonerates us. By judging our motives rather than our actions, we can assuage guilt over any action or inaction.

What we *do*, not what we *intend*, is what counts.

On the global level, assessing motives rather than actions has led to serious moral distortions. Take, for example, the differing assessments of capitalism and Communism.

Communism resulted in the loss of freedom by more nations, and the deaths of more individuals, than any other doctrine in history. Yet because it was perceived by many people as emanating from good *motives*—abolishing poverty, achieving greater equality, etc.—many people refused to accord it the revulsion that its *deeds* deserved.

On the other hand, capitalism has enabled more people to experience freedom and prosperity than any other economic doctrine. It should therefore be widely admired. Yet it is often vilified. The reason? It is based on selfish motives—profit.

Defenses of Communism and opposition to capitalism have emanated from the same flawed logic—judging motives, not deeds.

Nearly all of us fall into this trap. Like most people, I long tended to judge negatively the motives of people with whom I disagreed. Only after years of hosting a radio talk show in which I speak daily with people whose views oppose mine did I learn the great lesson that people with whom I disagree are just as likely to have the same good conscious motives that I ascribe to myself.

In addition to enabling me to mature, this attitude had an enormous unforeseeable benefit—people who disagree with me listen to what I have to say. When you belittle your opponents' motives, they can only become defensive. But when you ascribe to them moral conviction, they only have to defend their views, not themselves.

The practice of ascribing bad motives to one's ideological adversaries can be found throughout the political spectrum. Many conservatives have ascribed the foulest of motives, even murderous conspiracies, to one of their adversaries, President Bill Clinton. But I have been particularly saddened by how often liberals ascribe mean or selfish motives to their opponents. For example, voting Republican means voting with your pocketbook, whereas voting for a Democrat is voting idealistically.

During the Cold War, those of us who supported a large defense budget and the building of nuclear weapons were accused at various times of loving war, having a psychological need for enemies, hating Russians, supporting the military-industrial complex, having a Rambo mentality, and suffering from missile envy. The possibility was rarely considered that we were motivated by love of peace and justice.

Yet we who supported a strong defense during the Soviet Union's heyday believed that our motives—ensuring peace by remaining strong, protecting democracy, opposing Communist tyranny, and helping small nations survive against Soviet imperialism—were quite idealistic.

So, please, no more assessments of motives. In matters of public policy, let's debate results, not motives. And in interpersonal relations, let's assess ourselves and others by actions, not intentions.

3

WHY FRIENDS DISAPPOINT US

Are you frequently disappointed by the conduct of people you expected to be finer, kinder, or more decent? If your experiences are similar to those of many individuals with whom I have spoken, you'll probably answer yes.

This was brought home dramatically one night on my radio talk show. A twenty-one-year-old woman called to speak about her girlfriend, who had been raped and murdered by a male friend.

I asked the caller, who suffered the additional trauma of having been the discoverer of her friend's battered body, whether she was completely shocked by the man's conduct. So shocked, she answered, that she was no longer going out with men. If that man could do such a thing, she said, how could she ever know what man she could trust?

After reassuring her that virtually any man would be as horrified as she was by what the murderer did, I tried to answer her question. I told her that I have been rather fortunate in having rarely been disappointed, let alone shocked, by the behavior of my friends. I have a simple two-rule system, I told her, that is of great value in identifying people one can trust.

1. Do not choose friends, that is, people in whom you place your trust, on the basis of personality, chemistry, or enjoyment alone.
2. Know people's character before you fully trust them, meaning know their values.

Ask yourself why you are friendly with certain people, or why you trust those you do. Quite possibly, you never have asked yourself this question. You may just like them or enjoy their company, or they might simply be fun to be with. But do you know their values?

I believe that most people do not know their friends' values, and that this is the primary reason people are so often hurt and disappointed by others, including friends. Of course, values are not enough to ensure trusting, enduring friendships. Two fine people, holding similar values, can still drive each other crazy or simply bore each other because they have different tastes, conflicting personalities, or personal habits that get on each other's nerves.

But while values are not enough to ensure a good friendship, they are indispensable in determining whom to trust. People who rely only on similar tastes, on personalities that mesh, or on the right chemistry, and who ignore character and values, are setting themselves up for great disappointment.

How is one to ascertain the values and character of another person? How does one know if this nice person is really nice?

There is no foolproof answer, but three additional guidelines will help:

1:   Find out what the other person's values are.

I mean this literally. Dialogue with, even grill, the person about his or her values. How important is goodness, honesty, unselfishness to the person? What, if anything, is more important to the person than personal happiness? Not only are the person's answers to these questions important, but it is also revealing if the person gets annoyed when such issues are raised.

Finally, ask yourself: If you had to prove to someone who never met your friend how decent a person he or she is, what concrete evidence could you submit?

2:   Pay at least as much attention to how the person treats others, especially people from whom he or she needs nothing, as to how the person treats you.

Watch, for example, how your prospective friend treats a waiter or waitress. Does the person treat the server as an inferior human being to be ordered around?

People generally treat decently those from whom they want something—friendship, approval, sex, money, or marriage. That someone treats you well may therefore reveal nothing about character (and therefore may not indicate how that individual will treat you later).

A person's employees or the janitor where the person works can often tell you more about an individual's character than the person's friends can. Waitresses can sometimes better know a person's character in ten minutes than acquaintances of many years.

3:   Know your own values.

If you don't have strong values yourself, or you do but cannot clearly articulate them, the two previous suggestions may not be very helpful. How can you inquire or talk about values that you yourself either don't hold or can't identify? Thus, the stronger and more focused your values become, the less likely are you to befriend people with poor values.

Ethical values are usually associated with selflessness. And to a real extent, they are and ought to be. But in the final analysis, having the right values also serves a selfish purpose. Those who live by values that are higher than themselves tend to bring such people into their lives. And such people are a great deal less likely to disappoint us.

4

■

THE MISSING TILE SYNDROME

Look up at a tiled ceiling in which one piece is missing. If you are like most people, your eyes will gravitate to the missing tile. In fact, the more beautiful the ceiling, the more likely you are to focus on the missing tile—and let it undermine your enjoyment of the rest of the ceiling.

When it comes to ceilings or to any other form of work, such obsession with missing details may be quite desirable. We don't want a physician to overlook the slightest detail or a builder to overlook a single tile. But what may be desirable or necessary in the physical world can be quite destructive when applied to personal happiness. When people focus on what is missing, they make themselves chronically unhappy because while ceilings can be perfect, life cannot be. In life, there will *always* be missing tiles—because even when there aren't, we can always *envision* a more perfect life, and then find that something is missing.

A bald man ruefully confided to me, "Whenever I enter a room, all I see is hair." Poor fellow. When he is around people, all he sees is the hair on other men's heads; when alone, he feels and sees only the unadorned skin on his own head. He doesn't realize how little his baldness means to most of us. He was shocked to learn that most of us who have all our hair rarely notice which men are balding. If, after meeting five men, I was asked which was bald, I probably wouldn't remember (unless the man had no hair at all, which is often quite appealing to women). Since I have my hair, I don't think that having all my hair is nearly as important as the balding man thinks it is. He looks in the mirror, sees only a large mass of skin on his head, and believes that that is what everyone else sees, too.

If you are overweight, you see only flat stomachs and perfect physical specimens. If you have pimples, all you notice is flawless skin.

I first realized the importance of the missing tile in a dialogue with my lifelong friend, Rabbi Joseph Telushkin. As we were both single until our thirties, we talked for years about women and dating, and the most recurrent theme was our, especially my, obsessive search for the elusive Most Important Trait In A Woman (MITIAW).

Often, after a date, I would call Joseph to announce that I had finally discovered the elusive MITIAW. "Joseph," I would say with great certitude, "last night I finally came to realize the most important thing to look for in a woman." After some dates, I announced that it was personality; after others, sexiness; after others, intelligence; and after still other dates, I was sure that the MITIAW was good values.

One night, after years of this juvenile search, Joseph opened our eyes. I was about to tell him what the MITIAW consisted of when he interrupted me with "Dennis, don't tell me, I know exactly what you'll say."

"How can you possibly know?" I asked. "You don't even know who I was out with."

"It doesn't matter," he replied. "You're about to announce that the most important trait in a woman is whatever trait last night's date didn't have."

I was stunned at how right he was. For years, I had been declaring that the Most Important Trait In A Woman was the trait that I missed in the woman I went out with that night. No wonder I couldn't find a woman to marry. Since no human being can possess all traits in a perfect way, every woman, by definition, was missing the MITIAW. In valuing precisely that which I thought was missing in a woman, I was in a permanently self-destructive cycle.

We do this constantly. The one trait our child or spouse lacks or seems to lack becomes an all-important trait that can sabotage our ability to be happy with the person, while, at the same time, we keep seeing that trait in other children or spouses. That is how we make ourselves, not to mention our loved one, miserable.

If something is missing from your life, my suggestion is: Find it or drop it. If you cannot live without it, do whatever you can to find it. If you cannot find it, stop thinking about it and celebrate what you do have.

5

###

LEGISLATING GOODNESS:
THE STOREKEEPER LAW

There is a law in the Talmud with which even few Jews are acquainted. Yet it is among the most ethically beautiful laws in Judaism. When properly understood and practiced, this law can have a measurable impact on a person's character and a society's quality of life.

The law reads: One is not permitted to ask the storekeeper the price of an item if he knows he will not purchase it (*Bava Mezia* 58b).

When a person asks a storekeeper the price of an item that he or she has no intention of buying, the person is deceiving the storekeeper, and actually robbing the storekeeper (of time).

I need to explain that the law does *not* say that in order to be permitted to ask the price of an item, you must purchase it. The law allows comparison shopping. You can inquire about an item's price from as many stores as you need to. *Only if you know that you will not buy the item from that particular store* are you forbidden to inquire about its price.

This law is as applicable today as when it was first formulated.

A number of years ago, a friend who leased many cars for his business told me that he could arrange for his car leasing company to lease me a car at cost. When I responded that I didn't know what make of auto I wanted, he told me to go around and test various car models, and then tell him which I wanted.

His idea was a practical one, but it is precisely the type of practice forbidden by the Storekeeper Law. I could not test-drive a car
at a dealer from whom I knew that I would not buy or lease the car.
By test-driving a car at a dealer, I am implying that there is a possibility that I will buy the car from that dealer. Otherwise, why on
earth would the dealer give up precious time for me?

To cite another way in which this law is violated, some women
go to a store to try on dresses, knowing that they have no intention
of buying any dresses at that store. Or even worse, some women
purchase a dress, knowing that they will return it for a refund after
wearing it to a specific function. Many men, planning to buy photo-
graphic equipment, will visit a retail camera store, take up the
store's time deciding which equipment they want, then order that
equipment from a less expensive mail-order house. And they knew
that they would order by mail the entire time.

The most obvious reason the Talmud forbade such activity has
already been noted: A seller's hopes have been raised in vain. But
the reason goes deeper than that: Those who violate this law are
deliberately misleading people about one of the most important
concerns in their life—their income.

We should not delude ourselves into thinking otherwise. Whenever we try on a dress, or ask the price of a camera, we are implying the possibility of buying the item, and this is precisely what the
salesperson infers.

If you doubt this is true, the next time you go to a store, tell the
salesperson, "Miss, I want you to know at the outset that though I
will be trying on some dresses here, I won't buy any of them *here*.
I'm only here to see what's available and to get your advice."

Obviously, if we said this, the salesperson would cease working
with us. Stores do not exist in order to show items for people to
buy elsewhere.

There is yet a third level to this law. It makes us keenly aware
that we have obligations even toward people we generally regard as
beyond our obligation. Ever since I learned of this law as a college
student, I have never regarded people who work in stores the same
way as I did before. Whenever I enter a store, I am forced to recall
my obligations to those working there. And I know this to be true
for the many others to whom I have taught this law.

This in itself makes the Storekeeper Law particularly useful in
contemporary society. Our society is obsessed with personal rights,
but it will survive only if we each adopt personal obligations. Amer-

icans are frequently made aware of consumer rights, but this law makes it clear that there are also consumer obligations.

The Storekeeper Law also forces those who practice it to see salespeople in a different light, transforming them in our minds from individuals whose sole function is to answer our questions into individuals with feelings and hopes for earning a living.

The ultimate genius of this law is that it forces us to establish something of an I-You relationship with the person behind the counter, rather than retaining the usual I-It relationship that we have with people whom we meet only in a service capacity.

Finally, this law can and ought to be applied to other areas of life. There are powerful ramifications to the principle that if you know that you are not going to buy, don't imply that you might, i.e., don't raise expectations you know you won't meet. One such ramification was made clear to me when a young woman, who had heard me speak about this law in a speech, told me how she wished the men whom she dated would live by the Storekeeper Law—so often, men imply interest that is, in fact, not there.

For men, therefore, one application of this law would read: Do not sleep with a woman if you know that you have no intention of committing to her, or unless you have made that absolutely clear to her. To most women, sexual intimacy implies the possibility of the man making a lasting commitment. If a man disagrees with this assessment, let him then simply state the truth: "I want to sleep with you, but honesty demands that I tell you that I am doing so only because I like your body. I have no intention of making a permanent commitment to you."

The Storekeeper Law keeps you honest.

MEN, WOMEN,
AND *THELMA AND LOUISE*

6
-

CAN A GOOD MAN GO TO A
STRIPTEASE SHOW?

During the 1992 primaries, I sent readers of my quarterly journal, *Ultimate Issues*, my first and only political fund-raising letter. It was on behalf of Bruce Herschensohn, a close friend and someone whom I have admired for over a decade. He was running for the Republican Party nomination for U.S. senator from California. He won the nomination, but lost to Democrat Barbara Boxer in the general election.

On the weekend before the election, with the race extremely close, Bob Mulholland, political director of the California Democratic Party, announced to the press that he had proof that Bruce had attended a strip show in Hollywood.

A widespread outcry against this further debasing of American politics ensued, prompting the California Democratic Party to suspend Mr. Mulholland. When Barbara Boxer won the election— perhaps owing to this revelation about Herschensohn—Mulholland was immediately reinstated, and he announced that he planned to publicize the private lives of future Republican candidates.

After the election, I received the following letter from an evangelical Christian reader, a math teacher from Laguna Niguel, California. It raises such an important issue that I respond to it at length.

Dear Dennis,

It has been bothering me for some time. Some time ago I received a letter from you requesting that I vote for and support Bruce Herschensohn. You mentioned that you had never done this before and that Bruce was of upstanding moral character. Well, the newspapers reported that Bruce had frequented nude girl shows. I have never heard Bruce deny it. Did you know this about Bruce? Or is it untrue, or did it surprise you?

Dear Sir:

I don't know about "frequented," but as Bruce and I are very close, I did know that he has been to a strip show.

So have I, and so has just about every man that I know. Indeed, given the ubiquity of such shows in Las Vegas, and the number of people I know who have seen a show there, I suspect that most of the *women* I know have been to a strip show. That includes my mother and my wife, two people whose characters I also vouch for.

The real issue here is not Bruce Herschensohn's character; it is one's own views and one's religion's views regarding the sinfulness of sexual acts, or even thoughts, outside of marriage.

As an evangelical Christian, you are heir to a religious tradition that has placed great emphasis on sexual sin. As heir to the Jewish religious tradition, I, too, believe that there is sexual sin. But in part owing to my religious tradition's attitudes toward sex, and in part owing to my belief that there is a major distinction between evil and unholiness, in only some cases does sexual sin play the role in my thinking that it does for many Christians.

Let me explain by briefly analyzing three issues.

1.   The nature of sexual sin.
2.   The distinction between public and private behavior.
3.   Sexual sin and moral character.

THE NATURE OF SEXUAL SIN

In sex, as in all other areas of life, there are gradations of sin.

>*The Ideal*: Monogamous heterosexual marital sex.
>
>*Less Ideal*: Premarital heterosexual sex.
>
>*Lower Ideal:* Promiscuous nonmarital heterosexual sex.
>
>*Sinful* (in alphabetical order): Adultery, bestiality, incest between adults. (As homosexuality deserves its own extended discussion, I omit reference to it here.)
>
>*Evil:* Rape; all adult-child sex.

I recognize that this isn't how many Christians might draw up their list.

First, many Christians do not accept the notion of degree with regard to sin, sexual or otherwise. Nearly every Protestant minister (and an occasional Catholic priest) said to me during the ten-year period when I conducted a weekly interreligious dialogue on radio, "A sin is a sin."

I disagree. Just as human beings distinguish between jaywalking and murder, so, too, God distinguishes between sins. To argue otherwise is to argue that humans are more just than God.

Second, while the New Testament repeatedly condemns fornication, which is taken by Christians to mean any sexual conduct outside marriage, the Hebrew Bible (Old Testament) doesn't mention fornication. Its condemnations of sexual sin are reserved for adultery, homosexuality, incest, and bestiality. With regard to premarital sex, the concern is legal. If a man seduces a virgin, he is obligated to marry her, and if she doesn't want to marry him, he must pay her father the price of virginity. That is it. For the Hebrew Bible, the loss of something valuable, virginity, is the issue, not premarital sex.

The Torah (the five books of Moses) and New Testament differ even more with regard to the sinfulness of sexual thoughts. The Gospel of Matthew cites Jesus as saying, "If a man lusts after a woman, he has committed adultery with her in his heart" (Matthew 5:28). There is nothing analogous expressed in the Hebrew Bible; its concern is with sinful *actions*, not *thoughts*.

The one major exception is the Tenth Commandment, which prohibits coveting. But even though it specifies that one should not covet one's neighbor's wife, it never claims that lusting is a form of adultery or of coveting. Coveting is yearning *to steal* something or someone belonging to another. The issue is not sexual, but preoccupation with taking away that which is my neighbor's— that is why "covet" is also used with regard to our neighbor's house and ox and everything else he owns. If the issue were sexual lust, different verbs would be used for the desire for our neighbor's wife and for his house. And finally, if the Tenth Commandment were interested in prohibiting sexual lust, it would have prohibited coveting *any woman*, not only our neighbor's wife.

As Judaism developed, sexual sin became more of a concern— so much so that, in some ways, Jewish law became stricter than Christian doctrine. For example, it ultimately came to prohibit a person of either sex from merely *touching* a member of the opposite sex other than a spouse or immediate family member. Nevertheless, the revelation that a candidate had attended a nude show would cause very few Orthodox Jews to change their vote. In the case of Bruce Herschensohn, the majority of Orthodox Jews voted for him despite the last-minute Democratic announcement. They probably felt that while a religious Jew shouldn't do such a thing, Bruce Herschensohn was not a religious Jew, and that such a sin would not reflect on his ability to be a political leader.

THE ESSENTIAL DISTINCTION BETWEEN PUBLIC AND PRIVATE BEHAVIOR

Regarding sexual matters, it is essential to distinguish between public and private behavior.

For example, sexual modesty in the public sphere is crucial to the soul of a society. That is why I am opposed to the use of sex in advertising (as on billboards, and in magazines and newspapers), sex on free television, gross talk on radio, and visible covers of pornographic magazines at newsstands.

At the same time, the availability of explicit sex videos, magazines, and the like for *private* use does not necessarily damage society.

This distinction between public and private behavior is not hypocritical. In fact, it is one of the most important value distinctions we can make for the sake of society.

We make distinctions between public and private behavior all the time. There is a world of difference between using four-letter words in intimate private conversation and employing them publicly. The same holds true regarding bodily functions: We all urinate, yet we regard a person doing so in public as harming society. We would hold the same view about a billboard or magazine photograph of a person relieving himself.

The difference between what we do publicly and what we do privately is essential to civilization's development. I believe that we can measure civilization in two ways. One is moral—how decent are a society's laws and how much do its members observe those laws? The other is in terms of holiness—the amount of distinction between the society's behavior and that of animals; the closer a society's behavior is to the animal kingdom, the less developed it is. One such distancing characteristic is the distinction that humans draw between public and private behavior. Animals rarely draw such a distinction, e.g., they relieve themselves and have sexual relations in public.

Thus, I share with religious people an aversion to public indecency. In fact, indecency is almost by definition doing something *publicly* that should be restricted to the private realm. That is why it is possible to be *evil* in private, but more or less impossible to be *indecent* in private. Murder is evil whether done in public or private. But while a married couple making love in private is beautiful, the same couple making love in public is indecent.

Ironically, this is one of those issues about which many religious and many secular individuals agree—there is little difference between public and private behavior. To many religious people, if you shouldn't do something in public, you shouldn't do it in private, while to many secular people, if you can do something in private, you should be able to do it in public (e.g., using expletives).

I find myself in the middle. We should allow all kinds of private sexual activities, but restrict what is aired on free television and radio.

This distinction is in keeping with my religious tradition, which strongly distinguishes between public and private behavior. In the Talmud, Judaism's most important work after the Bible, Rabbi Ilai observed about fifteen hundred years ago (Hagiga 16a): "If a man sees that his urge is prevailing upon him, let him go to a place where he is not known, and put on black garments and let him do what his heart desires, but let him not profane the name of God publicly."

SEXUAL SIN AND MORAL CHARACTER

It is also essential to distinguish between holiness and morality. While an immoral act is always unholy, not every unholy act is immoral. For example, murder is immoral, and therefore also unholy. But premarital sex between consenting adults, while unholy according to all major religions, is not immoral.

The identification of morality with holiness has seriously hurt both religion and morality. Religion has been hurt because identifying morality with sexual behavior has alienated many modern people from religion. Many modern people, like myself, identify morality with goodness, justice, compassion—how we treat other human beings—not with issues of consensual sex. And morality has been hurt because identifying immorality with consensual behavior undermines the battle against real immorality—cruelty and other forms of evil. This is tragic because standards of good and evil—morality—should be society's overwhelming concern.

But, you might ask, isn't it true that by going to a strip show a man is supporting women working as strippers? After all, how would I feel if my daughter became a stripper? As it happens, my wife and I certainly have much greater hopes for our daughter, but I would be more disappointed in my daughter if she worked for Bob Mulholland of the California Democratic Party. The Hebrew Bible depicts prostitutes as capable of great character (e.g., Rahab in the Book of Joshua, chapter 2), while it is unsparing of those in respectable positions who lack integrity. All the strippers in America do less harm than one bad politician.

I regard a man who visits a nude show the same way I regard a man who visits a casino. Neither act says anything about the person's character—unless he speaks out against such behavior, claims not to do it, and then engages in it (e.g., televangelist Jimmy Swaggart, who repeatedly condemned prostitution and other sexual sin while visiting prostitutes). Otherwise it is harmless, though certainly not ennobling, behavior. The argument that women who strip are being hurt is just another way of saying that one is opposed to strip shows. It also is sexist. If a woman candidate had gone to a male striptease, no one would argue that she had harmed the men who were stripping.

It is sexist for another reason. Women do not generally enjoy watching anonymous men strip as much as men enjoy watching anonymous women undressing. It is therefore easy for a woman to condemn behavior to which she has little temptation. But that does not mean that many women do not engage in their own forms of unholy voyeurism and titillation.

For example, women, more than men, spend millions of dollars on sexual, gossip-filled tabloids that do more damage to more reputations and lives than any strip show. And every morning and afternoon, millions of women, not men, watch television talk shows that are, quite simply, women's soft porn. Typical shows feature transsexuals, cross-dressers, adulterers, and every other variation on a sexual theme. Indeed, on one of the few occasions that I have watched Phil Donahue, his guests were female strippers who went through part of their act *in front of their fathers*. I found this far more objectionable—because of its incestuous overtones, because it was broadcast on national television, and because it was broadcast when children could watch—than stripping before adult strangers in a private club.

There is little question that such programs on daytime television talk shows have played a far greater role than striptease clubs in diminishing American public life. We have always had voyeurism, but never before on national television and certainly never implicitly sanctioned for children.

Does attending a strip show, then, reveal anything about a man? Probably not. It may reveal only a person's lack of consistency in religious conduct. If Bruce Herschensohn had been a candidate for chief rabbi of Tel Aviv or cardinal of the Roman Catholic Church, I could understand taking cognizance of his attendance at a nude show. But he was running for the secular position of United States senator.

The Mulholland tactic therefore only revealed what I have long known: Many kind, honorable, and honest men sometimes go to strip shows, sometimes use curse words in private, sometimes play poker or go to a casino, and sometimes buy sexually explicit material; and the truly dishonorable men and women are those who pry into the lives of honorable people to ruin their good names.

There is one other, very important, issue here. Most people need an occasional place and way to express the lower parts of their nature. And, providing it is done innocuously, it probably does some good. True, some people rise above their lower nature every day of their lives and cause harm neither to themselves nor to others as a result of having bottled up or channeled all their lower urges. But they are so rare, so beyond what the rest of us can relate to, that they may not be models for the rest of humanity. In vice, as in most other areas, I hold a moderate position. That is why I like the Talmud's response to the question "Is it permitted to gamble?" While a minority forbids it, the majority ruling says, "Yes, it is permitted to gamble, but only as long as one does not do so for a living, because then one is not engaged in making a better world."

In other words, indulge your innocuous lower urges if you wish, but do so sparingly, because a noble person devotes his or her life to higher causes than sating one's appetites.

That I feel this way is in large part due to my father, Max Prager, who has led a life of particular integrity, and who, during a period of time that included the presidency of an Orthodox synagogue, purchased *Playboy*. He provided a model of integrity, religiosity, and common sense, one that I hope I provide for my children. Indeed, it is a model that our society, with its penchant for the extremes of religious self-denial and hedonism, desperately needs.

7

■

ADULTERY AND POLITICIANS

Members of the American media now deem it important to ask presidential candidates whether they have always been faithful to their spouses. Americans seem to have ambivalent views about this new practice: Most Americans seem to believe that this is inappropriate questioning, yet they also believe that a candidate who has committed adultery is unfit for the presidency.

Those who hold the latter view generally offer at least one of three arguments.

The first, and most frequently offered, is: If a man can't keep his promise to his wife, how can we expect him to keep his promises to the country?

The second argument, offered especially by Christians, is: Since adultery is a grievous sin, a man who commits it is immoral and unfit to be president.

The third argument, offered by many feminists, is: A man who has an affair shows contempt for women and is less likely to be sensitive to women's issues.

Though adultery is wrong and it is important to know the moral values of presidential candidates, none of these arguments is valid. The evidence is overwhelming that whether a man or woman has had an extramarital affair tells us nothing about his or her ability to be a good, *even moral*, leader.

ARGUMENT ONE:
ADULTERY SHOWS A MORAL INCAPACITY TO LEAD

The argument that a man who cannot keep his vow of fidelity to his wife cannot be trusted as a political leader is the easiest of the arguments to prove or disprove.

A generally accepted list of the most effective American leaders of the last half-century includes Franklin D. Roosevelt, John F. Kennedy, and Martin Luther King, Jr. Each committed adultery, and in the cases of Kennedy and King, with numerous women.

Now consider presidents whom most Americans would list as less effective leaders: Richard Nixon, Gerald Ford, Jimmy Carter, and George Bush. To the best of our knowledge, these men were always faithful to their wives.

The argument is historically so weak that if we had to find a link between moral fidelity and good leadership, the evidence would point to a *negative* one—from King David to Franklin Roosevelt, men who committed adultery were *more* likely to be great leaders than men who had always been faithful. To imply such a causative connection is, of course, absurd. But it is no more absurd than concluding that men who have committed adultery are less likely to be good leaders.

The argument that a man who can't keep his promise of fidelity can't be trusted as a leader is a non sequitur. It is the product of wishful thinking—particularly among three groups: women who are angry at adulterous men, religious people who regard sexual misconduct as particularly sinful, and members of the media who want to draw attention to their revelations.

ARGUMENT TWO:
ADULTERY IS A GRIEVOUS SIN

The second argument holds that a man who commits adultery has violated one of the Ten Commandments, and is therefore morally unfit for national leadership.

Although I am religious and deeply devoted to the Ten Commandments, I do not equate sexual misconduct with poor moral character, though they may be related. I think, for example, of one of the few morally great men to emerge from the Holocaust, Oskar Schindler, who saved over eleven hundred Jews destined to be murdered. He was also a serial philanderer.

I recognize that many religious people regard sexual sins to be among the worst kind. But this preoccupation with sexual sins has had many unfortunate consequences—both for religion and for the religious. It has enabled many religious people to overlook or even engage in major evils while concentrating on sexual sin. (I recall that the Islamic terrorists who hijacked an Air France jet that they planned to blow up over Paris, segregated the passengers by sex and covered the women passengers' hair in accordance with their religious beliefs about sexuality.) Also, this preoccupation has given innumerable people unnecessary guilt, e.g., over masturbation. And it has alienated many modern people—people who regard sins of cruelty as much worse than sins in the sexual arena—from taking religion seriously. Now this obsession with sexual sin is helping to undermine the choosing of appropriate leaders. Good men are being disqualified from, or not bothering to run for, higher office.

ARGUMENT THREE:
ADULTERY SHOWS CONTEMPT FOR WOMEN

The argument that a man who commits adultery reveals contempt for women is also untenable. For one thing, it is sexist, since women who cheat on their husbands are never accused of having contempt for men.

Both men and women commit adultery for any number of reasons—anger at a spouse, little intimacy and/or sex with a spouse, some other source of marital discord, a momentary loss of self-control, or a chronic loss of self-control. *None* of these, however, necessarily implies contempt for the opposite sex.

There certainly are male politicians who have contempt for women, but I believe it is impossible to discern who they are by whether they have been faithful.

Women who believe that infidelity shows contempt for women should also realize that the men most identified with commitment to marital fidelity and with antagonism toward adultery are usually the more religious and conservative men, precisely the men whom many feminists regard as least sympathetic to their concerns. Meanwhile, some of the most powerful supporters of the feminist agenda—Senator Edward Kennedy, for example—have been known for their womanizing.

Women who argue that men who commit adultery show contempt for women are expressing their anger at unfaithful men. The argument is a cry from the heart against adulterous husbands; and as such, but only as such, it should be heard.

THE MEDIA ON THE SUBJECT OF POLITICIANS' SEXUAL BEHAVIOR

One of the problems with the media's concern over a candidate's fidelity are their obvious hypocrisy. If, as many media professionals contend, marital infidelity tells us a great deal about people and their ability to lead, why do media professionals not inquire about the private lives of the heads of all the network news programs, and the editors of our major newspapers and magazines? The media, after all, are no less influential than our political leaders.[1]

Why, for example, did NBC national news anchor Tom Brokaw ask a woman if she ever slept with Virginia governor Charles Robb, yet never ask that sort of question about a single colleague in the media?

This hypocrisy is reinforced by the fact that most people in the media couldn't care less if a presidential candidate has been unfaithful. According to the American Enterprise Institute's journal, *Public Opinion*, 51 percent of major media people *don't even consider adultery wrong.*

Obviously, media people dwell on fidelity for reasons unrelated to leadership ability or morality. Those reasons concern the three things that media professionals really do care about—attention, ratings, and power.

---

[1]As former managing editor and now columnist of the *New York Times* A. M. Rosenthal wrote:

If the press is increasingly insistent on knowing more and more about the private lives of people in public life, does it not have the ethical obligation to tell more and more about itself?

To start easy: Should journalists make their finances public? Not just salaries, but private investments, inheritances and the specific source and amount of extra money from each lecture, television appearance and book. We want to know the last dollar's worth about officials. Many in the press influence public affairs more than most officials.

And is the reader or viewer entitled to know the political votes or inclinations of the correspondents who cover Congress or the White House?

Now, let's get to it. Correspondents and editors, have you ever committed adultery? Are you now? Homosexual experiences, any? Names, please. And surely you will not mind, publisher, if we readers pitch in a few dollars each to put a secret cordon around your house at night, since your reporters extend that attention to others.

Attention

In America, major news people, especially those on television, have become indistinguishable from Hollywood stars. The importance of their appearance in front of the camera, their starlike quality in the public eye, and their salaries are virtually identical to those of Hollywood stars. They also share most actors' deep desire to be the center of attention.

None of this would be true if news people did their jobs properly. Honest news reporting is essential to the functioning of a democracy, but it rarely makes one the center of public attention. Reporting sex and scandals, however, does.

The increasing media attention to candidates' personal lives has reshaped the way many people now examine political life. Rather than asking, "What will the candidates do or say?" the American public increasingly asks, "What will the media do or say about the candidates?" That is attention.

Ratings

Reporters who focus on sex also seem to have an economic motivation for doing so. Far fewer Americans tune in to the network news for serious reporting of a candidate's views and background than to watch Tom Brokaw interview Miss Virginia on her alleged affair with a governor. Sex and scandals therefore mean money to everyone concerned—reporters, anchors, heads of the networks' news divisions, and owners of newspapers and magazines.

Power

Scandals also give the media power. Media professionals know that if they do their job properly, they are only reporters, not power brokers. But if they become the Grand Inquisitors of political leaders, it is they, not politicians, who become society's power brokers.

Given the attention, the money, and the power that reporting about private lives gives to news people, it would take men and women of extraordinary character to ignore this angle.

The real issue in America isn't whether candidates have ever been unfaithful to their spouses, but why the news media have become so unfaithful to their profession.

WHY AMERICANS INCREASINGLY EXAMINE POLITICIANS' LIVES

Why we attach importance to knowing what once was held to be the private lives of political leaders (and still is in many other democracies) needs further explanation.

One factor is the increasing trivialization of public life as a result of widespread reliance on television news. This form of news, which has led to the demise of innumerable newspapers and news magazines, relies on the sensational to keep its audience. Reflection and depth are not the concerns of television news; they are boring in comparison to private revelations.

WHY IT HURTS AMERICA

The media's emphasis on candidates' private lives has already had at least one bad effect on society. A powerful alliance of the media and elements of left-wing feminists and the religious right has ensured that fewer quality people will run for political office. Few great individuals are willing to have their lives dissected in ways that virtually guarantee undeserved personal and family suffering. A person's desire for political office has to overwhelm a desire to protect one's own and one's family's privacy, and such an individual is precisely not the type of person we most want to lead us.

WHAT DOES MATTER ABOUT A POLITICIAN'S SEXUAL LIFE?

If adultery doesn't tell us anything about a person's ability to be a good leader, does *anything* about a candidate's sexual life matter?

When voters choose a political leader, there are two relevant questions concerning sex: Does the person act appropriately *in public*? What values does the person *endorse*?

In choosing public leaders, *public actions and speech* are what most count. Thus, I would reject a married man who appeared in public with a lover. This would reveal a serious moral lapse, since it would involve a public humiliation of his wife, and it would mean that he did not recognize adultery as wrong. And I would reject any man or woman as a potential president who did not publicly hold monogamous marriage to be the ideal. I could not vote for a candidate who said that marital fidelity wasn't important, *even if he him-self were faithful.*

The reason is that what leaders advocate in terms of private behavior is more important than what they do privately. Whether they *condone* infidelity is a matter of public concern. Whether they *are* faithful is a matter between them, their spouses, and their God.

8

■

MEN, WOMEN, THELMA AND LOUISE

For those who didn't see the film *Thelma and Louise*, a brief description is in order. Two women—Thelma, about thirty years old, and Louise, in her late thirties—take a vacation from the men in their lives. Thelma is unhappily married to a football-watching, beer-guzzling male chauvinist, while Louise is unhappy with her nice but unimpressive boyfriend.

Their vacation becomes a tragedy on its first night, when Thelma is almost raped and Louise kills the would-be rapist with a handgun that she had luckily brought with her. (I wonder what antigun people, most of whom probably related to the film's feminist message, thought of the fact that had Louise not been armed, Thelma would have been raped and the rapist would have gotten away with his crime.)

The rapist is typical of the men in *Thelma and Louise*. Except for Louise's boyfriend and the decent detective in charge of capturing the women, almost all the men are "animals." Many reviewers and others took offense at this portrayal of men. I didn't. True, all men aren't like those in *Thelma and Louise*—but the film doesn't claim that they are. It simply depicts what a *part* of the male world looks like to many women.

If you think *Thelma and Louise* grossly exaggerates how women experience men, ask some women you know. When single and dating, I often asked women to describe how men acted on dates. Upon hearing the stories they recounted, I remember cringing. Neither these women nor I ever assumed that all men were like these men, but I had no illusions about the behavior of many men who, in relating to women, act less than fully human.

I also have heard too many men routinely dismiss the very humanity of women, e.g., by referring to those whom they don't consider attractive as "dogs." This is sexist, as proven by the fact that the same individuals never call unattractive men "dogs" or otherwise dismiss their humanity—because men can perceive a reality in other men that goes beyond their physical traits. So, if you want to know what it can feel like to be an attractive woman, see this movie.

I ached to dismiss the film's portrayal of men as exaggerated, not to mention anti-male, which it was, but the film had too much truth. The truck driver who made obscene gestures with his tongue, and who placed his hands on his crotch whenever Thelma and Louise drove by in their car, provided a good example. Just as I was about to dismiss him as a caricature, the movie camera closed in on the truck's mud flaps—those back flaps behind many trucks' tires—which had naked women suggestively outlined on them. It was an eloquent moment: "So you think we're exaggerating," the movie was saying. "Well, haven't you seen thousands of trucks with these? Who do you think is driving these trucks, Billy Graham?"

Many viewers objected to the violence these women committed. In one case, so did I. Their treatment of the police officer who stopped them for speeding was gratuitously cruel (they locked him in the trunk of his car and abandoned him). In general, though, I found the film's violence pathetic, not heroic, and not gratuitous. I certainly was pleased that the near-rapist was shot. While I favor capital punishment only for murderers, the world did become a slightly better place after Thelma's would-be rapist, who had a history of such behavior, departed from it.

The film has been accused of being angry. It is. But the anger was focused where it belonged: on men who treat women awfully. *Thelma and Louise* would have alienated me had it blamed the men's behavior on "sexism in society," "sexist child rearing," or some other politically correct gibberish. But it focused on some bad men, not on some "ism."

The moral is that men need to be raised to respect women as fellow humans, no more—e.g., not "raising them on a pedestal," as some religious groups claim to do, and as feminist groups increasingly do—and no less. I hope that all men who act like the ones portrayed in the film rent it and then look at themselves and other men in the light, or more accurately, the darkness, of *Thelma and Louise*.

But . . .

Now that we have a film depicting the travails of attractive women in a world populated by many boorish men, we need an equally honest one about the travails of not particularly attractive men in a world of female sexual titillation.

If such a film were made, it would show how Not Particularly Attractive Joe—who is also neither wealthy nor famous—fares in the Western world today. Just as *Thelma and Louise* portrayed men leering, engaging in obscene gestures, reducing women to sex objects, this film—let's call it *A Day in the Life of N.P.A. Joe*—would show how many women, wittingly or not, reduce men to sex objects.

It would depict Joe waking alone on a typical morning, turning on the television to be immediately confronted with commercials featuring beautiful scantily dressed women in living color, and with regular programming featuring beautiful woman after beautiful woman in various states of provocative dress.

We would see Joe drive to work in his beat-up old car, from which he keeps noticing attractive women dressed to arouse male desires, none of whom would give Joe the time of day since he is not a "winner," as his appearance and car clearly indicate. He would also pass billboards of bikini-clad women inviting him into their billboard—though nowhere else. He would then arrive at work to experience more stimulation by women "dressed to kill."

Bombarded day after day by sexual stimuli, Joe starts buying pornographic magazines and videos, spends many of his evenings masturbating, and then, lonelier and lonelier, starts calling 900 numbers "to talk to" a woman at $3.99 a minute.

Finally, having spent all his money on porno videos and magazines, 900 numbers, and "escort services," Joe, like Thelma and Louise, resorts to crime and meets the same unhappy end they did.

Such a film isn't likely to be made. For whatever reasons, women's pain is more easily confronted than men's.

Too bad. Men and women need to know the truth about each other's pain—although even when they do, there never will be a full solution to the tensions between the sexes. As long as there are human beings, there will never be full sexual peace. Sex is too powerful, and the needs and desires of the two sexes are often just too incompatible.

But relationships between men and women are often worse than they need be, and they seem to be deteriorating. That is why men must see *Thelma and Louise*, and why some courageous people in Hollywood should make a movie about N.P.A. Joe.

If men could see how many of them relate to women, and if women could begin to empathize with what many men endure daily, there would be hope for a better world. Men and women will begin to realize that when either sex does not control its sexuality in public, members of the other sex truly do become victims—like Thelma and Louise, and Joe.

CHILDREN

9

■

WHEN GOOD HOMES
DON'T PRODUCE GOOD CHILDREN

There is a consensus in America that many homes have not been raising good children. There is little consensus, however, as to why.

People blame, among other factors, television violence, the proliferation of handguns, the absence of fathers, violent music, poor schools, and the prevalence of poverty. And, in varying degrees, these are all factors.

But little attention is paid to assessing what *parents* are doing wrong—especially well-educated parents in intact homes where there are no guns, no violent music, and monitored television viewing.

Here, then, are some reasons that even these parents often fail to instill good values in their children.

GOODNESS IS RARELY PUT FIRST

The problem with regard to parents raising good children is not that most parents don't want their children to be good people. It is that few parents actually make their child's goodness their primary concern. Most parents are more concerned with their child's being a brilliant student or a good athlete or a successful professional.

To test the validity of this thesis, parents might ask themselves these questions:

- Would I rather have a kind child with average intelligence and grades or a brilliant child who wasn't kind?
- What is the ratio of time that I devote to developing my child's ethics relative to developing other achievements?
- Do I reward my child's acts of kindness as much as I reward good grades or making the football team? And do I react less severely to character deficiencies than to scholastic or other deficiencies?
- If my child needed to cheat just ten points on just one exam to get into an elite college, would I be very unhappy if he did? And would my child be certain that I was unhappy over the cheating?
- Do I monitor my child's behavior toward other children and show strong disapproval when she mistreats another child? For example, if my child invites a friend to the house, and is then invited to the home of a friend she would rather be with, would I allow her to cancel the first appointment?
- Do I insist repeatedly that my child thank people?

I have also suggested to parents that they ask their child, whether the child is ten or fifty years old, "What do you think I most want (or "wanted" if the child has left home) you to be: happy, smart, successful, or good?" On my radio show, parents have repeatedly called to tell me how surprised and saddened they were to learn that their child placed "good" low on this list.

As parents, we clearly communicate to our children what we care about most. Unfortunately, even responsible and loving parents often fail to make it clear that they care about their children's honesty and decency more than they care about their grades.

It is difficult to raise a good student, but it is much more difficult to raise a good person. It is a relentless job. In the long run, however, the parents of good children who are moderately successful are far happier than the parents of highly successful children who are moderately good.

THE BELIEF THAT PEOPLE ARE BASICALLY GOOD

One of the reasons that being good is not a high priority is that, in our time, most well-educated parents believe that people are basically good. Thus, there seems to be no need to emphasize what is already present.

As odd as it may sound, no belief is more inimical to making a good society than the belief that people are basically good.

While we are not born basically evil, neither are we innately good; we have tendencies in both directions. Goodness, therefore, needs to be cultivated. It is an art that takes as much time and effort to master as violin playing. Yet far more parents give their children music lessons than goodness lessons.

AN OVEREMPHASIS ON FEELINGS

Many parents have come to value their children's feelings over their behavior. This caring about our children's feelings is a very positive development. Throughout history, children were usually regarded as parental possessions whose feelings were of little more concern than those of slaves or pets.

But many parents have gone to the other extreme, and care about their child's feelings more than about their behavior. Some years ago, when my older son was two, a five-year-old boy ran over to him in a park and pushed him to the ground. The little bully's mother rushed over to him, distraught. "What's troubling you, darling?" she asked. I knew nothing about that woman, but of one thing I have always been certain: She must have attended graduate school. To respond to bullies by asking how they feel is a learned response. And that is what too many parents have learned.

How the child feels should be important to the child, to the parents, and to a handful of others. But to the rest of the world's more than five billion people, the only thing that matters is how the child *acts*.

Our message, given in love, to our children must be: "Your right actions are more important than your feelings. Even if you're upset, you cannot hurt other people." Otherwise we will end up with a society populated by well-understood barbarians.

THE OVEREMPHASIS ON SELF-ESTEEM

Too many contemporary parents overvalue self-esteem. Contrary to the almost religiously held belief among many educators and others that self-esteem is one of the most important ingredients in making responsible individuals, it is not nearly as important as values. In fact, professors Sam and Pearl Oliner, in *The Altruistic Personality*, their widely acclaimed study of rescuers of Jews during the Holocaust, noted that there was no connection between self-esteem and being a rescuer. Some of the world's kindest, most giving people have low self-esteem, and some of the cruelest people, from Mafia leaders to drug kings to Communist and fascist leaders, think very highly of themselves.

Self-esteem is very important in enabling a person to enjoy life, and *when wedded to good behavior*—i.e., when self-esteem is made contingent upon good works—it can be a powerful tool for developing character. But to be a good person, *self-control* is infinitely more important than *self-esteem*. The child-rearing expert John Rosemond has coined the term "Vitamin N " to describe parents saying no at appropriate times. Our children's characters need Vitamin N as much as their bodies need Vitamin C, and as much as their psyches need self-esteem.

PARENTS YEARN TO BE LOVED

Many parents are more interested in being loved than in being responsible parents. But just as it is impossible to be an effective leader if you are afraid of being disliked, you cannot be an effective parent if you need never to be disliked.

This is one reason that many single parents find it so hard to adequately discipline their children. Having no spouse to go to for affection, and not wanting to live alone with someone who is angry with them, many single parents seek uninterrupted love from their children. It is very difficult to discipline someone upon whom you are dependent.

THE ABSENCE OF A HIGHER CODE

Many parents, including perfectly decent ones, provide their children with no higher code of values to which they—the parents and the children—hold themselves accountable.

Yet the people we can most trust are those who believe in a higher code and authority that declares antisocial behavior wrong and who believe that they are ultimately accountable to this code and authority. Many young people are raised with belief in neither a higher code nor a higher authority. And, higher authority knows, we are suffering the consequences of feelings-based behavior.

AN OVEREMPHASIS ON MACRO GOODNESS

Many modern parents, when they think about idealism and compassion, immediately think of broad social concerns, e.g., *government* caring for the poor.

This, too, can be an obstacle to raising good children because there is no necessary connection between commitment to social concerns and personal honesty and kindness. Getting our children to care about society's values certainly is desirable, but they must first, or at least simultaneously, work on their own behavior and values. Otherwise, their social concerns become a cover-up for character deficiencies. Many young people think that being good only requires participating in a charity walk, organizing a petition, or attending a demonstration. As a result, they may feel free to cheat on a test, copy software, and ignore or insult the fat kid in class.

THE BELIEF IN "QUALITY TIME"

The human ability to rationalize is infinite. When well-educated parents choose to have a dual-career marriage and deny that a price in child rearing must be paid, they develop the notion that what children really need from parents is "quality time", not quantity of time.

The reason for this belief's appeal is that "quantity time" means that one parent will have to spend more time with the children than in building a career—and that parent is nearly always the mother. Without discussing whether this is fair or right, it is a fact of life that runs head-on into the feminist fight against gender roles. It has therefore become impossible to advocate the obvious— that children need more time with their parents—without implying that many working women should return to the home. Thus, the well-educated—those who are most likely to be committed to feminism—become the people most committed to the doctrine of "quality time."

Parents should acknowledge that when it comes to time with children, quality cannot be fully separated from quantity. What does "quality time" even mean? That a parent and child who spend little time together will have a very meaningful conversation for an hour? Children open up when *they* want to, which is usually only after much "nonquality" conversation and time have been spent with their parents.

Life consists of constant tradeoffs: When we do X, we can't do Y. Without judging parents who have chosen career over time with their children, we can ask them not to fool themselves and the next generation of parents into believing that no price has been paid.[1]

It is not easy to raise a good person (as opposed to a person who is merely not bad), but we should honor children as individu-

---

[1]There is one other problem in raising good children that does not characterize good homes, yet I still feel needs to be noted—not humiliating children. It is essential to regard a child *from birth* as an autonomous human being whose needs, requests, and feelings are worthy of respectful attention. While this may not guarantee a particularly fine adult, constant humiliation of a child—historically, the most common error in child rearing—almost assures producing a bad adult.

There are innumerable ways to humiliate children. They include ignoring their cries when they are babies and toddlers (clearly conveying the message that they are not important enough to have their pleas responded to); generally ignoring them later in childhood; laughing at their mistakes; not taking their feelings and ideas seriously; administering physical punishments such as spankings; never apologizing to them; and engaging in many other common behaviors. These are "normal" humiliations. Under the heading of serious humiliation are behaviors that are known as "abuse." As any home in which child abuse occurs cannot be considered a good home, abuse is not discussed here.

It is very difficult for parents to avoid all the forms of humiliation mentioned here because nearly every parent was raised in a home that did not take children as seriously as they ought to be. It has been mankind's curse to repeat the sins of our parents on our children. The cycle has to be broken.

Many well-educated parents today are aware of the need not to humiliate their children, and, to their credit, many work hard not to repeat the humiliating actions or inactions of their parents. But these parents often substitute new forms of behavior that treat their child as an owned commodity rather than as an autonomous human being. One example will have to suffice: regarding the child's major purpose in life as being a source of pride to the parent. Long ago, my brother, Dr. Kenneth Prager, coined a term that described the child in such a home—a *"nachas* machine." *Nachas* is a well-known Yiddish word for pride and joy derived from children. Many Jewish, Asian, and other children are raised as if their reason for being is to provide their parents with *nachas*. This, too, is a form of humiliation—you are not an autonomous person, you are my child.

als while following the moral guidelines that have been offered here:

Making goodness our first priority.

Recognizing that human goodness does not come naturally.

Emphasizing behavior over feelings.

Stressing self-control even more than self-esteem.

Parenting children rather than aiming to be always liked by them.

Giving them a higher code to which they feel accountable.

Emphasizing personal ethics over social policy.

Spending more time with them.

By so doing, we will have given the world what it most needs—good people.

10

SHOULD WE PAY KIDS
FOR GRADES?

Several years ago, a wealthy New York City businessman offered money to inner-city students who completed high school.

My initial reaction was, "My God, have we sunk to a new low?" But after thinking a second time about it, I concluded that the idea was terrific. In fact, I now think the businessman's proposal ought to be applied to students from all socioeconomic backgrounds.

I would modify it in one way: Since students from affluent homes do not generally have to be coerced or bribed into staying in school, paying them to do so is pointless. But what is wrong with paying them to *excel* academically, especially when traditional methods of encouraging diligent schoolwork fail?

Ideally, of course, young people would work diligently in school and learn simply out of a desire to expand their minds. But such an ideal is an adult fantasy. Even the minority of young people who do work hard in school rarely do so only because they love learning. Parental and/or communal pressure and rewards are far more likely to be their motivations.

For example, in many homes that produce hardworking students, tremendous emotional and psychological pressures are placed on children to excel in school. The children in these homes often are indeed "paid"—but in manifestations of love, not in dollars. Deliver the grades, children are often made to feel, and you will be shown parental love; if you do not deliver, expect far fewer expressions of this love. Aren't such conditional payments of love far more injurious to young people than payments of cash?

In any case, how many adults do their work out of "pure" motives, with no consideration of monetary rewards? Why, then, is it appropriate for adults, including physicians and clergy, who do humanitarian work, to be paid for doing an excellent job but not for high school students?

It is simply too much to expect schools to cultivate a "love of learning" in most students. Love of learning is the result of the home, societal influences, the rare inspiring teacher, values, psychological factors, the impact of one's friends and one's nature.

Since the age of fourteen, I have had a love affair with books and learning, but this was always despite school. I ignored elementary school, read non–school books under my desk through high school, graduated ninety-second in a class of 110, and skipped most classes in college. I lived Mark Twain's claim to have "never let my schooling interfere with my education."

Because schools recognize their general inability to cultivate love of learning, they bribe students with both monetary and non-monetary rewards: placement on the "dean's list," generous scholarships, and all sorts of academic awards.

Rather than looking to schools to cultivate love of learning, we should ask them to do what they can do best—teach the basics, a task that rarely infuses the student with a "love of learning." It is very difficult for anyone, even the most motivated adult, let alone a hormone-driven, attention-wandering teenager, to love learning algebra or grammar. Therefore, we should not care so much *why* young people learn math, history, foreign languages, and how to write properly. We should be concerned that they *do* learn these things. If their motivation is that they will be paid for excelling, so be it. Is such an attitude mercenary? When physicians are no longer paid for healing patients, but do so only out of love of healing, we'll be justified in condemning students who study for payment and not out of love of learning.

In the meantime, millions of students who will otherwise do little or no schoolwork might begin to do schoolwork, the country will have an educated generation, and young people will have gotten into the habit of working at things they do not necessarily enjoy. In other words, they will be learning to do precisely what most of them will have to do as adults.

Before a parent adopts this policy, however, I suggest six rules:

1: Payments for grades shouldn't be the first resort.

2: The sums of money must not be too high. Obviously, "too high" is a subjective term, but if a generous payment doesn't work for a ninth grader, the parents know that they have the additional problem of a child who doesn't know the value of money.

3: Schools must grade strictly. If teachers award good grades too easily, the entire policy fails and does more harm than good: The children will still not work, and yet will earn rewards as if they did.

4: *The student must be rewarded for excellence (and not necessarily straight A's), not for winning.* Paying a child to graduate among the top ten in the grade is not teaching the child to excel, but to win.

5: I am talking about high school, not elementary school, students.

6: The parent has a say on how the money is to be spent.

If these rules are followed, financially rewarding students for excellence can do wonderful things for young people and for society. A two-thousand-year-old recommendation from the Talmud still remains apt: "People can go from doing something not for its own sake to doing it for its own sake." The student who begins regularly to read books for a reward is more likely to come to read books out of love than the one who awaits inspiration.

The question is not, therefore, "Should we reward kids for grades?" since we already do, but *"How* should we do so?" If you have tried other options and your teenager still refuses to do schoolwork, consider giving him or her what you receive for your work—money.

11

WHEN ADULT CHILDREN DON'T TALK TO THEIR PARENTS

A *Los Angeles Times* article opened my eyes to a frightening phenomenon in modern America. The article spoke of adult children who have decided never to speak to one or both of their parents.

As I read the article—which passed judgment on no one—I had two immediate reactions: First, I wondered how widespread this phenomenon is. Second, though the article implied no such thing, I suspected that in many instances this behavior was wrong.

As a radio talk show host, I am very fortunate in being able to bounce my ideas off many people of every background. I therefore decided to talk about this issue on both my Los Angeles and New York radio shows. In both cities, I was deluged with calls from children and parents from families in which a child had completely stopped speaking to one or both parents.

I rarely devote all three hours of my Los Angeles talk show to one subject. On that day I did—and I could easily have devoted twenty-four more hours to it. As for my New York audience, I received more mail on this program than on any other in the year that I was on WABC. And my office sold more tapes of my three-hour show on the subject than of any other show ever.

My four hours of public discussion of this issue answered my initial question and confirmed my initial suspicion. I have no doubt that this horrifying phenomenon of a child utterly cutting himself or herself off from parents is widespread.

I became aware of something I had long suspected but could only now articulate—in many people, the Therapeutic Mentality has replaced the Moral Mentality.

THE THERAPEUTIC MENTALITY VS. THE MORAL MENTALITY

A personal story will help to illustrate the difference between the Therapeutic Mentality and the Moral Mentality.

My paternal grandmother, may she rest in peace, was a very good woman—she spent most of her time collecting charity for poor neighbors—but she was a very tough woman to her family. Her toughness strongly contributed to neither of her daughters marrying—a particularly rare occurrence in a Jewish family and almost unheard of in an Orthodox Jewish home—and to other problems.

After she was widowed in 1950, my father took it upon himself to see her every week and to call her every day. This was not easy. I was two years old when my grandmother became a widow, but as I grew up, I became increasingly aware of her difficult nature. While she treated my brother and me beautifully, we may have been the only people to whom she showed only tenderness.

I vividly recall a nearly nightly ritual. After dinner, my father would call his mother, only to have her yell at him. My father possesses a particularly strong disposition, yet he found these telephone conversations so disconcerting that he would put the phone down on the kitchen table. I would hear the yelling, and watch my father periodically pick up the phone and say, "Yeah, Ma."

We never spoke about this, but it made a deep impact on me. Despite her verbally abusive behavior, my father called his widowed mother every day. Growing up in a religious home, I instinctively understood my father's behavior: The Ten Commandments say, "Honor your father and mother."

It never would have occurred to my father to stop speaking to his mother, though he certainly would have preferred not to talk to her. Likewise, my mother had many reasons not to prepare a lavish meal for my grandmother every Sunday afternoon. Yet it never would have occurred to my mother to break off all contact with her husband's mother.

My parents had a Moral or Religious Mentality, a mentality governed by "shoulds."

In the 1960s, a sea change took place. The Moral/Religious Mentality was replaced by the Therapeutic Mentality, which holds that "there are no shoulds." "Should" became a dirty word. This was confirmed when nearly every person who spoke to me about a child not speaking to a parent mentioned that the child's therapist encouraged this behavior.

Do some parents deserve no honor or respect from their children? Without question. But let me offer an analogy. The American press corps did not generally respect Ronald Reagan as president of the United States. Yet they all rose when he entered a room. They honored the presidency, not necessarily the man.

So, too, an actual parent may deserve neither respect nor honor nor love. But parenthood needs to be honored. Yes, there are cases of such evil that continued contact is impossible. But those cases are rare.

Indeed, there are cases like that of the twenty-nine-year-old woman from Santa Monica who called my show to tell me that she had not spoken a word to her mother in twelve years *even though she had had a loving and happy childhood.* "But," she explained, "if I would let my mother back into my life, she would try to control me."

When I think of all the pain this woman has caused her mother just because her mother is a domineering woman, I can cry.

Of course, in most cases of adult children not talking to a parent, the parent has been far worse than domineering. On the other hand, in most cases, the parent has not beaten or sexually abused the child, either.

Some of those who don't speak to their parents assert that they will raise their children in such a loving way that they, the parents, will ensure their children's enduring contact. The problem with this attitude is that parents who neglect their own parents may be so afraid of losing their children's love that they will do anything to be loved by their children. This is not a good way to raise a child. A child needs a parent, not just a friend.

A NOTE TO THE ADULT CHILD

If you haven't been horribly abused, I believe that you have an obligation to maintain contact with your parents. The mere fact that you survived childhood is usually a credit to your parents having cared enough to see to it that you ate, were clothed, didn't drown, etc. If you are a parent, you know that this is no mean feat.

By "maintain contact," I do not mean show love, or even have a meaningful conversation, let alone an intimate relationship. Just maintain some formal contact: "Hi, Dad, what do you think of the Dodgers?" or "Hi, Ma, some weather we've been having, isn't it?"

But to cut off all contact with a parent is the most painful thing you can do to that person. It is usually too cruel.

A woman of sixty wrote to me that she had not spoken to her father during the last ten years of his life. Now, years after his death, and with a more mature perspective, she deeply regrets her behavior.

But once parents die, regrets are irrelevant.

If it is absolutely essential to your mental health that you not speak to a parent, consider two other options:

1: *Write* to the parent.

2: Tell your mother or father that for the next six months, or one year, you will not contact him or her while you work out your anger. Place a time limit on what seems to the parent to be a living suicide.

Finally, consider this: When I saw how my father treated his extremely difficult mother, I understood that I would have obligations toward my parents. When your children see you totally ignore your parent, what precedent are you setting for them?

12

___

SHOULD A SINGLE WOMAN
HAVE A CHILD?

___

The following is an edited transcript of dialogue I had on my radio talk show with Susan (name changed), a thirty-eight-year-old woman from Los Angeles.

Susan: Dennis, the *Today* show this morning did a piece on single mothers, and Senator [Daniel Patrick] Moynihan made the comment—he echoed things I've heard you say many times—that the destruction of the family is the root of many of the problems in our society.

    I have a question for you. I'm thirty-eight years old. I'm a professional woman. I make a very good living. I take care of myself. I'm an upstanding citizen. And now, I think, I have the patience and the wisdom to be a parent. I've been fortunate enough not to marry badly, but I'm kind of running out of time to have a child.

    So my question is, if I can't find a husband, or the right husband, to marry—and I'm not saying that a child doesn't need to have a father—do I forgo the right to have a child?

Dennis: If you're asking, "Would I ask you not to have a child?" I would.

Susan: You would?

Dennis: I would say this with great pain and with great conflict, because I know women in my own life who are in your particular situation. And I know one who did, in fact, decide to have a baby on her own.

My answer to you is that we can't have everything we want when there is a price paid by others.

This is what I would hope for you: First, obviously, as you hope, I hope you meet a good man. And remember, you still have a few years to naturally have a child. But let's say you meet the right man and you're past childbearing age. It may still not be too late to adopt a child. And since I see no difference between biological children and adopted children, that is an option for you. It is not like it is all closed off. If we did any educating of women seeking abortions—asking them to give their children to adoptive parents rather than have abortions—we would be able to meet the great desires of innumerable couples to adopt children.

Susan: Well, there's a whole other argument about that. I think you have to put in that scenario "healthy white children" because there are lots of healthy black children that are not adopted. I mean, come on.

Dennis: No. You "come on." I'm glad you raised it because I know this field well. For every newborn child in this country—including children with spina bifida, severely retarded children, armless and legless children, and certainly children of every race—there is a waiting list of couples to adopt that baby. The reason black children are not adopted by whites is because blacks social workers prevent it. They prefer that black children have no family than be raised in a white family. What you just said isn't true, but you didn't know it—I understand that. I used to think what you think. But it's just not true. The only reason every newborn child in this country isn't adopted is because black social workers have prevented it.

Susan: Well, I just find that very difficult to believe. How many black social workers can there be in this country?

Dennis: They have prevailed upon a wimpy white liberal establishment, just like Indian organizations did with the adoption story I told last month [forcing a non-Indian couple to give up their adopted child because the birth father was Native American—even though the man had no desire to raise the child].

Susan: I remember that story.

Dennis: Okay. Well, now you know what goes on in America. Political correctness dominates, not decency.

Susan: If you were to ask most prospective adoptive parents, they want a healthy newborn. They don't want an older child, they don't want a mixed child.

Dennis: Yes, most don't want an older child, but there are people waiting for any newborn baby. There were people applying to adopt the baby who was recently born *without a brain*. You don't know how many good people are on this continent of North America. You just don't know.

Susan: Well, you're right about that. But my question to you really is, why is it that you feel that someone who is not married cannot impart the same values that you believe in and raise a lovely, nontoxic child?

Dennis: I didn't say "cannot."

Susan: Well, should not. Okay.

Dennis: Should not, because children deserve a mother and father. You talk about your rights. But there are children's rights.

Susan: Perhaps.

Dennis: Children have a right to be brought into a world with a mommy and a daddy. If one dies, so be it. If they divorce, and one abandons the child, so be it. But to start them out not having both parents is not fair. It's selfish. It's understandably selfish. I cry for you, but it's selfish.

Susan: So is it better to marry badly so that my child can have a father?

Dennis: No. It is better to understand that we can't have everything.

Susan: Well, see, I don't think that that's asking for everything.

Dennis: It is in this sense: "I'm not meeting the right guy, but it doesn't matter. Until the right guy comes along, I still want to make a baby, and I'll bring it into the world without a father because I want a baby."

Susan: How about because I think that I can be a good mother and I can raise a healthy, nontoxic child?

Dennis: Yes, I think you can, but I think you underestimate the importance of a father.

Susan: No, I don't, and please don't get me wrong. That was the whole point of all of this. I would love to find the right husband, but I haven't.

Dennis: That's a husband for you. I'm talking about a father for the baby.

Susan: Obviously.

Dennis: Do we both agree that ideally a child should have a mommy and a daddy?

Susan: Oh, absolutely.

Dennis: All right. So then you're arguing that nevertheless you still feel it's right to bring a child into the world without a father at the outset because you would be such a good mother? All right. What am I going to say to you—that you are going to be a bad mother? I don't believe you'll be a bad mother. I think you'll be a good mother. But the issue isn't whether you'll be a good mother. The issue is, why start a child out in the world without a father?

Susan: Well, I don't have an answer for that, but I'm not comfortable accepting your answer that because I haven't found a husband, I can't have a child.

Dennis: I know, and I appreciate it, and I'm not comfortable saying it.

Susan: Okay. Well, that's the first time I've ever heard you say that.

Dennis: Okay. Well, that's interesting. Thanks a lot. Goodbye.

Susan, I really appreciate that you allowed me to be totally honest and that you felt you could do the same.

I want to comment, though, on the very last part of that conversation. She said she's not comfortable hearing what I said, and then I said that I wasn't comfortable saying it. To which she said, "Well, that's the first time I've ever heard you say that."

That makes me think about how you never know exactly how you come across. No person can. You don't see yourself as others do. Take looks, for example. I see myself approximately one minute a day, yet everybody around me sees me all day. (By the way, that's the reason to look nice—it's selfish not to, because everybody else has to look at you.)

And it's the same with regard to how you speak. You know what your motives and thoughts are, but others can only know what your words are. They can't know your motives, your thoughts, your feelings. My sense is that it's pretty obvious from all that I say that the biggest concern in my life is that people not hurt each other. And yet I'm convinced that because I'm so strong in a lot of my opinions and about my values, some people may feel that I am just a rock.

But the fact is that it's not easy for me to say to a perfectly decent woman, "Don't have a baby." I *would* have to be a rock, to have a heart of stone, to say that with comfort. But apparently, I don't make that discomfort clear as often as I might. The fact is that it kills me to say that to her. Every ounce of me wants to say to Susan, "I hear you—I hear your pain. I know you wanted to find the right guy, and you just couldn't; and God knows, I know the desire to have a child. It is, for some of us, the deepest desire in life. So go to it."

Every part of me wants to say that. What stops me is not my heart or my feelings. What stops me are values. When I talk to kids around the country about values, I define a value as that which you consider more important than your feelings. My feelings are, "Susan, go to it." My values are, "Kids need daddies." They're in conflict. So, of course, I wasn't comfortable.

I needed to say that because of her surprise when I said that I wasn't comfortable with what I told her. It happens all the time. There is nothing easier than to say, "Oh, yes. I hear your pain. Go to it." Then the person likes you, but it's not right.

13

—

TV AND ME: HOW HAVING A NATIONAL TELEVISION SHOW HELPED ME UNDERSTAND WHAT MATTERS IN LIFE

During 1994–95, my national television show was on 156 stations, covering over 80 percent of America.

Of all the people to have their own television show, I must be the most ironic choice. First, I almost never watch television. Since elementary school, with the exception of animal shows and some sports, I may have watched twenty hours of television a year. Second, I have continually urged people to decrease the hours they devote to watching television.

But since on any given day, about one hundred million Americans will be found in front of their TV sets, and since my primary goal in life is to bring my values and ideas to as many people as possible, how could I turn down the opportunity to have a national TV show?

Moreover, the opportunity was presented to me by Multimedia Entertainment, a major syndicator of television talk shows. And the head of Multimedia, Robert Turner, uttered magic words to me: "I want to do something good on television." The more I learned about him—including the fact that he was a subscriber to my journal, *Ultimate Issues*—the more allayed were any fears I had that I would be asked to be different from who I really am.

As I very quickly realized, however, the question was not whether I would want to do television. It was whether I could do anything good on television and be successful. It is extremely difficult to do anything constructive, let alone deep, on daily commercial television, especially on a talk show. I say this with sadness. But three factors militate powerfully against deep programs appearing on commercial television.

1. The medium is inherently superficial. Television appeals almost only to the most superficial of our receptors, the eye.
2. Programming is solely determined by the bottom line, which is in turn determined only by ratings.
3. There is a lack of serious people watching television, especially daily talk shows.

Everything negative I thought about television has, unfortunately, been reconfirmed by my working in it. What I *have* learned from working in TV is *why* most of it is so bad.

Perhaps nothing summarizes the state of American television and the challenge to anyone wanting to do something worthwhile on television as does this: Of the more than one hundred shows that I recorded, *one* was visually titillating. For about six minutes of one show, models from Frederick's of Hollywood modeled scanty lingerie. *That show, both times it aired, received the highest ratings of all my shows.*

As it happens, the show's topic was a good and serious one: Should a woman wear sexy lingerie for her husband? My guests were a woman psychologist and a woman executive from Frederick's. Both were very intelligent—the Frederick's executive sits on the board of a major orchestra—and the dialogue was on a high level. But the intelligent and important discussion was not the reason so many people watched the show; the scantily clad women were.

T AND A = RATINGS = $

As long as advertising revenue is the sole determinant of what is put on commercial television and as long as advertisers care only about ratings and the bottom line, television will be a medium largely for titillating nonsense.

The reason is one I have known for a long time: Between the eye and the ear—our two primary senses for receiving information—the eye is far more superficial.

The Hebrew Bible was profoundly aware of the eye's superficiality. "Do not go astray following your heart and your eyes," it warned, because they "cause you to prostitute yourselves." This is why graven images were forbidden in the Ten Commandments. The Bible trusts only the ear: "Hear, oh Israel, the Lord is our God, the Lord alone"—*hear*, not see.

That is why radio is far more capable of supporting sustained thought. The ear can be satisfied by thought, but the eye cannot be. Thoughts do not intrigue the eye.

Virtually every term I learned for making good TV, especially the term "good TV," involves something to titillate the eye.

Three terms come to mind: "more action," "eye candy," "good TV."

"More Action"

As anyone in TV can tell you, it is not enough to be very interesting, and certainly not enough to be profound. On TV, you must move around, be "more animated," as I was probably told two hundred times (about twice a show). And my producers were right. When I watched my own show, *I* found myself more interesting when I was physically more animated, e.g., moving my arms, getting up from my seat, making facial expressions.

"Eye Candy"

Just as the palate reacts positively to candy and lusts for more of it, the eye, too, lusts for more tasty input. This is known in television as "eye candy." It is vital to keeping viewers lusting for more of your show. A beautiful woman is the most obvious form of eye candy. That is why even television news almost always features a very good-looking woman. And though not as important, TV also features good-looking men as eye candy.

Obviously, none of this matters on radio. While an overweight Rush Limbaugh is very popular on TV, it is solely a result of his prior popularity on radio. If he had first tried to succeed on television, producers would have laughed at the idea of featuring an overweight man talking.

Further proof of the importance of "eye candy" is that how one looks on television is what many viewers remember from a broadcast. An author told me years ago that after doing a national radio and TV book publicity tour, he found that people who had heard him on radio talked to him about what he said, while people who saw him on television talked to him about how he looked. I received as many comments on how I looked on my TV show as about what I said on it—and I talked about important things! Even people who really did listen to what I said on television commented on my choice of ties. This is not a criticism of these people—I do it, too—it is a statement about the importance of the eye to television programming.

And, during "sweeps," the quarterly ratings periods of about four weeks each, the amount of female skin shown increases dramatically—even on newscasts!

"Good TV"

The aim of television shows is to have as much "good TV" on the show as possible. "Good TV" should not, however, be mistaken for anything analogous to "good book" or "good music" or even "good movie." "Good TV" means either sex or fireworks. On talk TV, "fireworks" refers to people arguing with, preferably shouting at, each other. On other TV shows, it will refer to violence. TV has so much sex and violence because they are the easiest, surest ways to produce "good TV."

New York Times columnist A. M. Rosenthal has written how important it is to CNN, which is widely considered serious television, to have people who hold positions as far as possible from each other on its talk shows. Ideally, the most liberal liberal and the most conservative conservative should confront each other. People who hold a nuanced position, or who sometimes hold a liberal and sometimes a conservative view, or, worst of all, find ambiguity in some issue, do not make for "good TV."

"Good TV" is one of the reasons that TV has so contributed to the coarsening of debate in America. Coarse people with coarse arguments are "good TV."

"Good TV" is one of the reasons that sound bites get shorter and shorter each year. Focusing on one inflammatory sentence, though it may well be wrenched out of context or irrelevant to the rest of a speech, is "good TV."

THE DESTRUCTIVE REMOTE CONTROL

One conclusion that I drew from the lingerie show's high rating is that many people do not actually watch TV shows. Rather, they scan the channels with their remote control unit. They are searching for the sexiest or most violent scene or the most heated argument or the wildest behavior. The remote control unit has probably contributed as much to the low state of television as the primacy of ratings.

There is no other explanation for the uniquely high ratings of my lingerie show. Clearly, the lingerie models drew many people who did not otherwise watch my show.

TO COMPROMISE OR NOT TO COMPROMISE— MEPHISTOPHELES AND ME

That, however, was precisely the argument of my producers. "Dennis," they said with sincerity and goodwill, "we need some sexy shows to draw people to your show. Get them hooked, and then you can do the type of show that you really want to do."

They offered a second powerful argument for me to compromise: "Dennis, if we don't get good ratings early on, you won't have a show later on to do all the good things you want to do on television."

Dear reader, what would you do? If your aim was to do something elevating and worthwhile on TV—thereby possibly touching millions of lives—would you do some shows with sexy eye candy, if such shows could mean the difference between having or not having a show?

This was my very painful dilemma, which was exacerbated by additional factors.

First, my entire ability to influence people rests on my having moral credibility. How much could I compromise—in front of a national audience, no less—before that credibility began to erode?

Second, how could I look into the eye of a reader of one of my books or a subscriber to my journal after I seemed to offer a TV talk show in conflict with my own standards?

On the other hand, how can I ever have an impact on those who know nothing of my work if I don't compromise for some good early ratings? What good are values and ideas that are never encountered?

Those are the questions that went through my mind. And not only regarding sexual titillation. My producers felt that a fair percentage of my early shows had to be on eye-catching subjects—meaning subjects that I couldn't care less about.

For example, would I allow a world championship pool player to hit a billiard ball out of my mouth? I did. Would I do a show on women bodybuilders? I did, although I focused on a question that annoyed my bodybuilder guests: Aren't immense biceps on women a sign of the gender confusion of our time?

In return, I got to do the shows that *I* cared about, shows that are not seen on commercial television. I did entire shows on:

- The validity of the existence of God.
- How parents can raise good children.
- New Year's resolutions about being a better human being, not just losing weight or stopping smoking.
- Whether the Holocaust is the only true genocide, with one of the world's leading scholars of the Holocaust, Professor Steven Katz.
- Why men should get married.
- Why so many Americans are lonely.

And many more shows like these.

Given these high-level subjects, were my compromises then worth making?

Before answering, a word about the problem of compromising. Compromising has a bad name. It suggests the relinquishing of one's integrity for selfish gain.

But what if one compromises for an ideal, not for selfish gain? Then the issue become trickier. If you never compromise, you may never have the opportunity to achieve a much greater good. To cite a major example of this conflict: Were the Allies morally right in allying themselves with the murderous regime of Joseph Stalin to better fight the even more horrific regime of Adolf Hitler? The answer is, of course. People who argue against ever compromising are zealots who will achieve little good.

But once you do decide to compromise, there are other tough questions to answer: How much compromising can you do before you have sold your soul? If I began getting good ratings based on titillating visuals, could I then stop? A fellow Multimedia talk show host, Jerry Springer, lives with this problem daily. He wanted to do something better with his show, but his ratings soared the more he lowered his standards. Now he is stuck. If he raises his standards, he loses the audience that came to him for the lower type of program.

The other issue with compromising is: Are you fooling yourself into believing that you are compromising for an ideal, when in fact you are compromising for personal gain? After all, TV pays well.

These were the issues that preoccupied me. They explain why I compromised when I did. And they explain why I finally chose not to compromise, but to do a show that reflected my values. If I ended up with no show, I would know that I failed on my terms.

As it happened, the compromises that I did make were, in the end, pointless. With the exception of the lingerie show, none of the other compromises, like the billiards show (in which, incidentally, I shot three balls into three different pockets with one shot), rated higher than the shows I wanted to do.

By the fourth month of shooting, we had all decided that I would do shows on the subjects that I most cared about and in the way that I was best suited to presenting these subjects—without guests, interacting with a small, intelligent audience of people who both agreed and disagreed with me. And the ratings began to rise slowly but steadily—too slowly, however, for most local stations.

THE LOCAL TELEVISION STATION

The problem of low television quality lies in part with local stations.

At NATPE (National Association of Television Production Executives), the annual convention of television producers and television stations, station heads would come over to me to tell me how much they personally liked my show. "So why do you put it on at two o'clock in the morning?" I would ask.

"Well, it kills me, Dennis, but it's the Ricki Lake–type shows that get the high ratings." Ricki Lake, Montel Williams, Geraldo Rivera, Jenny Jones, and virtually all other TV talk shows are the shows that feature dysfunctional individuals and families baring their pathetic or titillating stories before live audiences.

I met so many nice people who run TV stations that I was

thinking of titling this chapter "When Good People Do Bad Things." For, make no mistake about it, TV station managers and the heads of TV production companies are doing some bad things.

I am certain that, given time and a decent hour, my show would succeed. There are enough people who would enjoy an entertaining half-hour or hour of television that made them think. But such a show needs time. KABC Radio gave me years to earn my audience for what I call "thought radio." There is no such amount of time on television. Stations give a show a few months, sometimes a year, to garner good ratings. In that short length of time, a mediocre show with a lot of eye candy has an overwhelming advantage over a far better show with little eye candy.

CONCLUSIONS ABOUT TELEVISION

Why, then, is most American television as bad as it is?

1: Because television's appeal is overwhelmingly to the eye—not to the ear, and not to the mind. It is a question whether television is inherently a superficial medium.

2: Because ratings are all that matter to advertisers, and advertising revenue is all that matters to TV stations. And women modeling lingerie will always win over the case for the existence of God or why marriage is good for men.

3: Because a large number of thoughtful Americans watch very little television, especially talk shows. Therefore, the pool of television watchers from which ratings are derived is not of the highest caliber.

These facts should make proponents of the market economy—people such as me—acknowledge that capitalism and its market economy come with serious moral challenges.

HOW CAN WE IMPROVE TELEVISION?

There are a few possible solutions to the dilemma of bad television:

1: We can work on raising the moral, spiritual, and intellectual level of the American people so that they will not watch garbage on television.

This, at best, would take decades. And if we did succeed in elevating the vast majority of people, television would have far fewer viewers, no matter what it televised. Most people, as they deepen their lives, watch less television. An active and interesting life is far richer and more exciting than almost any television.

2: We can hope that television producers and station heads will decide that they are willing to go with good television over "good TV" even though it will mean lower ratings for a period of time.

3: If advertisers sponsored programs based on their quality, or at least if they didn't sponsor garbage, ratings would cease to be the only decisive concern. This is one way that companies, often professing to hold traditional values, can put their money where their rhetoric is.

The problem, however, is that today so many advertisers, both national and local, sponsor any given television show that no one company is associated with the awful shows. As my friend Dr. Stephen Marmer pointed out, when the names of companies were associated with television shows, the level of those shows was quite high. Recall "GE Theater," "Texaco Star Theater," "Colgate Comedy Hour," "Kraft Television Theater," and "Hallmark Hall of Fame."

What company would want to be associated with Geraldo? Can you imagine "The General Electric Geraldo Show" or "Ford Motors Presents Jenny Jones"?

For producers, local stations, and companies to decide to put values before ratings and profits, all the people involved need to ask themselves questions such as those I had to ask myself when I had a television show.

I discovered one question, however, that really did it for me: Can I return home each day and tell my children, with pride, what their dad did that day at work?

If every TV producer, station manager, and advertiser asked this question, television could become a real asset to a floundering society. As it now stands, television contributes to that floundering.

Like everything else in life, television reflects the values of its creators. And when the rewards for not living according to higher values are as enormous as they are in television—vast amounts of money, fame beyond one's wildest imagination, and endless glamour and excitement—choosing values over all of that takes a special type of person. Given its power, television needs producers, talent, sponsors, and station managers who are all special people. That is unlikely to happen. And even if it did, we still have the problem of a coarsened viewing public.

POSTSCRIPT: WHAT I LEARNED

Compromise

My experience in Television Land has been a wonderful education for me.

First, I return to the issue of compromise. Compromise, while at times morally necessary or at least justifiable, is more often only the first permission for a person (or society) to begin a long downhill descent.

The problem is simple: When do you stop? Very rarely do people make big compromises with their integrity. Almost every compromise is a small one that is easily justified. The downhill slide is usually a result of many little compromises. In the case of people working in Hollywood, the loss of one's soul begins with giving in to something like this: "Just do this one scene or this one movie or this one show, and then you can call your own shots."

But as my friend Jerry Zucker, director of *Ghost*, said to me, for most people in Hollywood, the perks stemming from the original compromise become too good to give up. As he and I have seen, the benefits become literally addictive. People can become addicted to fame, money, and attention as deeply as they become addicted to drugs. When a compromise is rewarded, it is as difficult to stop further compromising as it is to stop taking heroin after the first pleasurable experience.

If I learned nothing else other than the nature of compromise and the ubiquity of addiction, my sojourn in television has been amply rewarded.

What TV Can Accomplish

As I assumed when I agreed to do a TV show, when you talk daily to more than a million people, you can make quite a positive impact. Permit me just a few examples.

A Hertz Rent-a-Car bus driver in San Francisco told me that he was looking into his responsibilities as a man because of my show on masculinity. I received a letter from a young woman in Lincoln, Nebraska, telling me that, as a result of becoming acquainted with me and my ideas through my TV show, she and her husband had decided to study Judaism and were in the process of converting to it. Many Christians thanked me for producing a Christmas show that actually honored Christmas as a meaningful religious holiday. They added that they were particularly moved that it was a committed Jew who had made the show. One small step in helping Christian-Jewish relations.

Thinking about all the good that television can do and how much more bad than good it does is quite angering.

What's Really Important?

Virtually every minister, priest, and rabbi tells the same story: They never met a man in his dying days who lamented, "I wish I spent more time at the office."

As people get old, they usually better understand what is truly important in life. Since I was a kid, I always wanted to know what old people knew, so that I could apply that knowledge to my life while it was still possible to do so.

My experience in TV confirmed and further taught me the relative emptiness of so much of what we tend to value. In the case of television, it is fame, money, and glamour. In politics, it is primarily power. In other professions, it is any of them.

I understand why so many people wondered whether TV would change me. I don't think it did, and I give credit to these factors: I have a strong value system; my wife and children are central to my life and are therefore strong stabilizing factors; my religion is more important than success; I have friends whom I love and who love me, and who also provide a brake on career worship and self-preoccupation; and most important, I went into TV to touch people's lives, not to achieve great success and fame.

Most people in the medium are in it for the success, fame, money, and attention, not for an opportunity to elevate an audience; many have no marriage and children to ground them; and few are deeply committed to a religion.

Whatever one does for a living, three questions need to be confronted before it is too late: What really matters to me? What price do my spouse and kids pay for my career success? What price does my soul pay?

Whatever happens with my TV career, I will always be grateful to Multimedia Entertainment for having given me the opportunity to have a national television show. Aside from the wonderful, challenging, and educational experience, it forced me, at age forty-six, to answer some big questions.

14

THE FALSE WORLD OF TELEVISION NEWS

Like millions of other Americans, I was overjoyed several years ago at the successful conclusion to the drama of little Jessica McClure, who had fallen into a dry well.

Still, the extensive attention and nationwide anxiety over one girl's fate prompted me to ask: Why, with all the horrible suffering in the world, was so much attention devoted to the suffering of one family in Midland, Texas?

One answer, of course, was the inherent drama of the rescue. Another was the joy of seeing many people working heroically to save a little girl. It does us good to see goodness in action.

There is an additional answer, however, that does not speak as well about human nature and conduct. Most people do not empathize with other people's suffering unless they actually *see* it.

Between visible and invisible anguish, the visible nearly always wins, *even when the invisible suffering is far greater*. Whenever I see a crowd of candle-holders standing vigil outside a prison where a murderer is about to be executed, I wonder why these people never do the same at the home of the murdered person's family. And then I realize that one reason is that the murder victim is invisible—as was the murder itself—while the murderer and his execution are visible.

Abortion provides another example. I believe that, alongside public efforts at discouraging them, first-trimester abortions should remain legal—despite my belief that the great majority of abortions are not morally right. In other words, while I support its legality, I am ambivalent about abortion. There seems to be, however, no moral ambivalence on the part of "pro-choice" activists; and I am convinced that a major reason for this lack of ambivalence is that the pregnant woman is visible, while the fetus is not. That is why the anti-abortion film *The Silent Scream*, which shows a fetus being killed, so angered pro-choice advocates. For once, the fetus, too, was rendered visible.

In international affairs and history, the same rule holds. Take, for example, the utterly differing responses to the Nazi Holocaust and to the Soviet Union's mass murders during the Stalin era. As a Jew, I am pleased that the Western world has not forgotten the Holocaust. But why has there been almost a total lack of sympathy or even interest in the more than forty million Russians, Ukrainians, and others murdered by the Soviet Communists?

Again, the answer leads us back to the question of visibility. We have many photos and films of Auschwitz and other Nazi death camps, some of them taken by Allied soldiers liberating the camps. (During the war, when no such visible images existed, there was little concern in the West for the Nazis' victims.) Yet, because the Soviets were on the victorious side in World War II, there were no photographs or films of the Soviet labor and death camps (the Gulag Archipelago) shot by liberating troops. We also can meet and speak with Holocaust survivors, while few of us have ever seen or met any of the survivors of the terror-famine in Ukraine.

More recently, nearly all the world cared about the mistreatment of South African blacks as depicted on television. Yet relatively few people cared about the Afghan people who, during the Soviet invasion of the 1980s, suffered a fate far worse than apartheid—the death or exile of over a third of their population. The Afghans were rarely seen on television. Out of sight, out of mind. It was as simple as that, and the Soviets knew it, which is why they announced that they would kill any Western journalists found in Afghanistan. The same has held true for the Tibetans whose suffering under the Chinese Communists has been horrible and relentless for almost half a century—there has been no television coverage of the Tibetans' suffering.

To regain some balance in the sympathy we apportion to those who suffer, we must become conscious of our natural tendency to care more about the suffering of those whom we see, and consciously sensitize ourselves to concern ourselves with the suffering of those whom we cannot see. One way to begin achieving this is by not relying on television news, especially of international events. The more one relies on television for one's perceptions of the world and its evils, the more skewed one's perceptions of human suffering will be.

TELEVISION AND INTERNATIONAL NEWS

Television coverage of Palestinian protests during the *intifada* provided a good example of the false world of television news. To any television viewer who, night after night, watched Israeli troops battling with rioting Arabs, the situation appeared morally clear—an occupier was suppressing the occupied. Without denying the misery inherent in any occupation, however benign, the situation as seen on television distorted reality more than it illuminated it.

Television news has no memory; it wants pictures, not perspective; drama, not understanding. In the words of ABC TV's Ted Koppel, "We have substituted facts for knowledge."

Thus, the reasons Israel occupied Gaza and the West Bank were of no importance to the nightly network news. That the war which brought about the occupation was thrust upon Israel was simply irrelevant to television news. Whatever one's perspective on the Israeli occupation, the historical record is that Israel was forced into the Six-Day War of 1967 by Egypt, Syria, and Jordan; Israel never sought to occupy either the West Bank or Gaza. All this is readily available in books, newspapers, and magazines. But it is not viewable, and almost never conveyed, on television news.

What about television news reporting on the occupation itself? No occupied people find their situation tolerable, but the Israeli occupation must rank as among the most benign in history. Was this ever communicated on the network news? Of course not—not because TV is anti-Israel, but because it is antiperspective.

An Arab living under Israeli occupation has had more civil rights than Arabs living in almost any Arab state. The Arab press in the West Bank has been among the liveliest and freest in the Arab world, and it routinely attacked its occupier. Was any of this publicized on television news? No, because it is hard to videotape freedom. On the other hand, video is perfect for riots; they have action, color, and violence, and can easily fit into the half-minute of film allotted to major news stories.

While most TV viewers of the rioting came away feeling how terrible the occupation must be, the coverage repeatedly conveyed to me a different message: how little fear Arabs experience under Israeli occupation. Otherwise, how can one explain away the utter lack of hesitation of so many West Bank and Gaza Arabs to appear on Western television vehemently denouncing Israel? When was the last time a Syrian, Iraqi, or Libyan publicly attacked one of his or her leaders?

But television news cannot, or at least does not, report what people do *not* do. One can videotape riots, but not people who are afraid to speak out.

TELEVISION AND WESTERN FLAWS

Another extremely important lesson to learn from television coverage of Israel and the Palestinians: While TV may *report* some of the flaws in police states, it can only *show* the flaws of democratic and near-democratic countries.

The greatest evils in the world occur in countries that do not allow Western cameras to report such events. Therefore, almost all the violence that one sees as news on American and Western television takes place in free or relatively free countries. Thus, the violence shown on TV news nearly always takes place in those nations that have the least political violence and repression. Riots in Israel are covered, as are murders in the United States, and political violence in South Korea.

But the political violence in these countries is dwarfed by that of totalitarian states such as North Korea and China, and police states such as Syria or Libya. The nation of Tibet has been under a decades-long effort by the Chinese to annihilate its culture. But while small numbers of Palestinian rioters were often the first item of news on Western television, the same programs have never featured the killing of a single one of the countless Tibetans murdered by the Chinese.

When it comes to international—and now, with its reliance on sound bites, even domestic—events, television news can be worse than worthless: Those who rely on it to understand the world will have distorted perceptions, news-wise and morally.

THE POWER OF TELEVISION NEWS

During an East Coast lecture tour, I became even more aware of the overwhelming influence of TV news, and to a lesser extent, of radio. I realized that they shape viewers' perceptions not only of events happening far away, but even of those occurring literally in their own backyards.

Awakening one morning in New York City, I looked out my window and saw snow falling. Television and radio newscasts led to me to believe that I was in the middle of a terrible snowstorm that was virtually paralyzing America's largest city. They repeatedly warned of an "emergency" situation in the city, and told the public to avoid driving unless absolutely necessary. Since I intended to drive all the way to a Philadelphia suburb to deliver a lecture, I feared for my safety.

When I walked outside, I found a light snow falling and about two to three inches of snow on the ground.

Although I worried greatly about driving all the way through New Jersey, which, reports warned, was even worse off than New York, I decided to brave the roads. I left three hours ahead of time, not knowing what havoc the emergency situation might be causing on the New Jersey Turnpike.

Much to my surprise, getting out of Manhattan was effortless, so I could only imagine that it was New Jersey that had been "really hit." But in New Jersey, I found identically safe, utterly unremarkable conditions of light snow and clear roads. Apparently, most everybody else had believed the mass media reports, rather than his or her own eyes, and stayed home. The New Jersey Turnpike was virtually empty—on a Friday afternoon!—and I drove at a constant sixty miles per hour, arriving three hours early.

When I arrived in the Philadelphia suburb of Cherry Hill, New Jersey, I found a city that had reacted to a few inches of snow as if it were next door to the Chernobyl reactor. Many stores were closed, and the open ones had few customers. When another person and I purchased books at a bookstore, the cashier noted that it was the first time that day that two customers had been in the store at the same time.

"Television and radio scared everybody into staying home," the woman behind the counter explained. "Isn't it incredible? Look at how powerful the media are; people are influenced by them even when they can see for themselves that the situation isn't that bad."

Although I had long realized that television's national news gave people distorted impressions of world events, I had assumed that local news was less distorted. This experience disabused me of that belief.

From the media reports of the "snowstorm" I drew some conclusions.

First, the impact of television news, and to a lesser extent radio news, is awesome, even frightening. What became apparent in this situation was the medium's ability to influence people's perceptions and conduct *more than reality itself*. People were more affected by what television told them than by what they could see happening right outside their windows.

Over the years, I have come to understand that, for many Americans, unless an event is reported on television or radio, it has not really happened. I get a sense of this at baseball games when I see fans listening to the game on the radio. Merely seeing the game without hearing it on the radio is not enough. This also explains why so many Americans have a deep need to appear on television, even if in a degrading manner, as a guest on the many TV talk shows that specialize in humiliating their guests: Life untelevised is life unlived.

The need for media hype likewise reflects a deep boredom that many Americans evidently feel in their lives. I do not know whether this need for constant excitement has nourished media excitement, or whether the diet of constant media excitement, news reports that hype reality, larger-than-life advertisements, and violent horror movies has produced an addiction to it. Whichever the cause, for many Americans actual life is not exciting enough, and thus they need media excitement—even concerning the weather.

Americans are drowning in hype. Wanting drama and excitement in their own lives, many people lead what may be called "television lives." And since addictions lead to greater dependency, and since television is only interested in greater profits–which come about through the creation of more addicts—the problem of TV hype won't solve itself. The best solution is for millions of Americans to tear themselves away from television, particularly from television news. Unfortunately, for most people that is as difficult as it is for an alcoholic to stop drinking.

There is a simple way to test the validity of my thesis that television distorts people's understanding of the world. For three months, watch and listen to all the news talk shows, news analyses, documentaries, and interview shows you wish; some are excellent. But stop watching TV news during this time, and see if your understanding of the world declines or, as I suspect, improves.

While I watch almost no television, I have nothing against those programs that are most frequently attacked—sitcoms, quiz shows, soap operas, and the like. Many may be vapid, but they do not take themselves seriously. Their task is not to transmit reality, but to provide entertainment. Hence, they do little harm. Television news provides entertainment but claims to transmit reality.

Hence, it often does real harm.

HEADLINES I WOULD LIKE TO SEE AND OTHER SHORT TAKES ON LIFE

15

—

HEADLINES I WOULD LIKE TO SEE

Jerry Falwell Declares That All Good People Can Attain Salvation

Lynchburg, Va.—The Reverend Jerry Falwell announced here yesterday that the Lord had communicated with him, telling him that the Fundamentalist Protestant belief that salvation is attainable only by those who affirm a specific belief in Jesus Christ is mistaken.

Just as many Fundamentalists once believed in racial segregation and the Lord showed us the error of our ways, so, again, God has made His will clear to us. Of course, we continue to believe in the Father, the Son, and the Holy Spirit, and continue to affirm that Jesus Christ was God in the flesh, died for the sins of humanity, and thereby made salvation possible. But we now understand that God, in His infinite wisdom and compassion, has not closed off the possibility of salvation to a person only because that person does not personally know Jesus Christ. We will continue to preach the Good News of the coming of Christ, but we will no longer assert that we can know for certain who is not saved. God has reiterated what he first told the Hebrew Prophets: that He cares more about people's ethics than about their theology. Our Father in heaven made it clear to me that His primary desire is that His children on earth act toward each other morally and lovingly.

Reactions to the Reverend Falwell's announcement were immediate and mixed. Some Protestant ministers declared Falwell a "heretic," while others said that prayerful consideration should be given the reverend's communication from above. Catholic bishops welcomed the call, as they have been preaching for some time that salvation is open to all individuals who follow their consciences in obedience to God's will. And Jews were especially delighted. "Just a few years ago, the Pope visited a synagogue, and now we have this statement by one of the leading figures among American Evangelicals. We are living in a blessed age," declared Rabbi Isaac Rosengarten of the Rabbinical Council of America.

Mysterious "Disease" Afflicts
American TV Transmitters

New York and Los Angeles—As tens of millions of people were about to sit down for another evening of television watching last night, television sets across America went blank.

Engineers, physicists, and other scientists have provided no explanation for what can only be described as an incredible mystery.

Cries of excruciating boredom have been heard emanating from homes throughout America.

As tens of millions of Americans enter their second day without television, the president and the White House staff are debating whether to declare a national state of emergency.

Going without TV has particularly affected Washington. "For some people in this town, this is worse than losing the ability to read," said one member of the White House staff who asked to remain nameless. "Where will they now get their news from? Newspapers?"

Throughout America, scenes long thought to have disappeared from the American landscape were becoming almost commonplace. Some people were seen reading books. Others were seen having long discussions with family members and friends. And, it is widely rumored, many couples were rediscovering physical intimacy.

ACLU, Declaring Civil Liberties in America "Quite Secure," Disbands

New York—Ira Glasser, head of the American Civil Liberties Union, made the following announcement before a national press conference:

The ACLU does not want to repeat the problem confronted by the March of Dimes when polio was conquered. We are big enough to recognize that the raison d'être of the ACLU, ensuring civil liberties in America, has in fact been achieved. No country in history has ever had such protection for all its citizens'— including mass murderers'— basic civil rights. We therefore see no justification for spending tens of millions of dollars annually when that money could be better spent on the poor and homeless. Intellectual honesty demands that we acknowledge that in order to stay in business, the ACLU has taken on more and more cases that have little to do with civil liberties, such as our defense of students wearing obscene T-shirts, or our opposition to school uniforms. Former board members such as Nat Hentoff are right—we have essentially become another left-wing interest group. And that is not what I hoped the ACLU would be. Since there are a number of fine organizations with a left-wing political agenda already in existence, we see no need to continue with our present work.

16

LITTLE EVENTS THAT CHANGED MY THINKING

We tend to remember the events that have shaped us emotionally and psychologically since they are often major events in our lives. But what about the events that shape us intellectually? Frequently, they are "small" happenings.

Having always been interested in the life of the mind, I recall three "minor" events that had a big impact on my thinking.

THE VEGETARIAN ON THE AIRPLANE

It was mealtime on a flight somewhere over the United States: I noticed that both the middle-aged woman seated next to me and I had ordered special meals. I had a kosher meal, she a vegetarian one.

"Are you a vegetarian?" I asked the woman.

"Yes," she responded.

"Why?"

"Because we have no right to kill animals. After all, who are we to claim that we are more valuable than animals?"

I vividly recall my thoughts. When she said that we have no right to kill animals, I felt a certain sympathy for her and her position. After all, I thought, here I am eating a kosher meal, and I have always understood kashrut to be Judaism's compromise with vegetarianism.

But when she delivered the second part of her explanation, I couldn't believe what I was hearing. In fact, I was so certain that she was engaging in hyperbole that I said, "I certainly understand your opposition to killing animals, but you can't really mean what you said about people not being more valuable than animals. After all, if an animal and a person were both drowning, which would you save first?"

I was sure I had posed a rhetorical question. So, when I received no response from the woman, I asked her if she had heard me. "Yes," she responded, "I'm thinking."

That was a bombshell. I recall my reaction as if it had happened last week: She's "thinking"? What on earth was there to think about?

Finally, she responded, "I don't know."

I was stunned. This was no young radical, just a perfectly normal-looking middle-aged woman.

Musing over her reaction for a while, I drew the obvious conclusion that either she was an aberration or she wasn't. And if she wasn't, she was symptomatic of an increasing confusion in our society over the relative worth of human and animal life.

Soon after this encounter, and based on other similar experiences, I concluded that the latter was the case. All of a sudden, a significant aspect of modern life became clear: With the breakdown of religion, the belief that human beings are created in the image of God is no longer taught. From where, then, does the belief in human sanctity derive? What nonreligious reason could be offered for regarding people as more valuable than animals?

As a result of that encounter, I understood why I had never liked the famous antiwar button of the Vietnam War generation, "War Isn't Healthy for Children and Other Living Things"— it was a subtle identification of children with all other living things.

Shortly thereafter, I began asking high school students throughout America: "If your dog and a person you didn't know were drowning, which would you first try to save?" In fifteen years of posing that question before students in secular schools, no more than a third of the group has ever voted to save the person.

As a result of this encounter, I have come to understand that part of the environmentalist movement is a protest against the Judeo-Christian elevation of the human species above other species. That explains the head of Earth First! declaring that human beings are a "cancer on the earth," and the head of People for the Ethical Treatment of Animals (PETA) comparing the barbecuing of six billion chickens with the killing of six million Jews. And it explains the movement against any use of animals for medical research.

The woman with the vegetarian meal first opened my eyes to

the fact that, without religion, man is no more worthy of life than "other living things."

FRIDAY NIGHT IN HELSINKI

I was raised in an Orthodox Jewish home, which meant that I grew up observing a traditional Shabbat (Sabbath) that lasted from Friday at sunset to Saturday at dark. To those Jews who experience the Shabbat each week, Friday night takes on a completely different meaning from the other nights of the week.

I spent my junior year of college in Europe, during which time I traveled from the Arctic to Morocco. I decided to experience life that year without the religious practices with which I was raised. I didn't want to practice anything out of habit or without having at least "tested" nonobservance.

To be honest, I didn't long for many of the observances that I dropped. I hardly missed keeping kosher; being able to order and eat anything on a menu was almost a euphoric experience. Feeling free to do anything I wanted on Friday nights and Saturdays—go out, eat in restaurants, travel, shop—also seemed exhilarating and liberating.

But something transformative happened inside me on Friday night, August 1, 1969.

I had spent the day on a train traveling from Lapland in northern Finland south to Helsinki, arriving in the Finnish capital at around 11:00 P.M. As I disembarked from the train, it occurred to me that it was a Friday night.

But no—it didn't just "occur" to me; it hit me with great force. Exactly what hit me isn't easy to convey, but I knew precisely what I felt. It wasn't guilt or a feeling of having sinned. Rather, I felt as though I was losing the rhythm of life that I once had—a rhythm that gave time structure and meaning. The thought hit me that I had allowed Friday night to become exactly like Thursday, Wednesday, Tuesday, Monday, Sunday, and Saturday nights. I traveled and traveled, and shopped and shopped, and ate out and ate out. Life was becoming biological; the holy and the distinct, and the day that let the other days have meaning and rhythm, were disappearing. I decided that I did not want to lose that distinctive day or that life rhythm.

The next Shabbat, I went to synagogue. And with few exceptions, I have not missed a Shabbat since my twenty-first birthday, Saturday, August 2, 1969.

COCKFIGHTS IN BALI

In my late twenties, I visited Bali, Indonesia. I recall the beauty of that fabled island, but I also recall seeing men gathered in various parts of the island, cheering and betting money on what I first thought were sporting events.

Upon closer inspection, I saw that these "sporting events" were in fact cockfights. Men were cheering on animals that were trying to scratch out each other's eyes, and wagering on which one would die first.

Two powerful realizations came to me.

One was how bestial human nature is. The Holocaust is what first made me aware of humanity's enormous potential for doing evil. But it was this visit to human ugliness amid natural beauty that confronted me in a less threatening way than the Holocaust with what lurks in people beneath the veneer of civilization.

The other, even more powerful realization was what a tremendous moral revolution ethical monotheism had wrought. I imagined what sort of a world it was over three thousand years ago, when the first Jews introduced a universal invisible God who demanded goodness. It was far more than cockfighting that had to be fought: Human sacrifice was commonplace.

As I stood watching the men laughing at the suffering animals, I thought about how, millennia ago, the Hebrew Bible had already demanded humane behavior to animals. Indeed, one of the seven laws that Judaism expected all people to observe is not to eat the limb of a living animal. And the Bible included an obligation to animals in the Ten Commandments (the Sabbath Commandment demands that we give beasts of burden a weekly rest).

I imagined how difficult, if not dangerous, it would be for me to begin yelling that the cockfight was immoral, and assumed that, in effect, that is what it meant to be a Jew for much of Jewish history. That belief eventually took shape as the underlying thesis for the book I wrote with Joseph Telushkin, *Why the Jews? The Reason for Antisemitism*—how natural man, the child-sacrificing, cockfight-loving man, has reacted to a few people telling him in the name of God that he is wrong.

17

ASTROLOGY ISN'T HALF
AS BAD AS WHAT
MANY INTELLECTUALS BELIEVE

When it was revealed that the first lady of the United States, Nancy Reagan, believed in astrology, I found the reaction far more interesting than the revelation itself. The snickering at the former first lady struck me as a remarkable display of intellectual snobbery.

Belief that the planets' locations in the constellations influence human affairs is generally associated with nonintellectuals. Elitists often enjoy mocking what they perceive as the nonintellectual thinking of lower classes—whether it be astrology or the glorification of motherhood and apple pie.

I would submit, however, that some beliefs commonly held by intellectuals have been considerably more irrational and deserve far more ridicule. Indeed, I wouldn't have minded the snickering at Mrs. Reagan if the equally irrational—but far more dangerous—beliefs held, for example, by left-wing intellectuals had been subjected to an equivalent amount of snickering.

Take the belief in Marxism. The notion that a planet's location determines events is hardly more absurd than the belief that history is determined by "scientific laws" of dialectical materialism. *Every* major prediction of Karl Marx has failed to materialize. In fact, the very opposite of what he predicted came about. Yet, despite its lack of rational basis, its unparalleled series of failures, and capitalism's ability to thrive and improve the lot of its working class, many intellectuals continue to believe in Marxism.

Why aren't these intellectuals laughed at? Why is astrology more laughable than Marxism? Because the educated elite helps dictate what merits ridicule. Few of its members have believed in Marxism, but nearly all of them have respected those who do believe in it. But, as with all of us, those doing the laughing only recognize irrationalities in others.

As one who believes neither in astrology nor in Marxism (though I would rather have a dinner conversation with a serious astrologer than a serious Marxist), I wish that more people believed in the former than the latter. While belief in astrology is, at worst, a foolish way to make decisive life choices, it hasn't led to cruelty; belief in Marxism, however, has led to more cruelty than any other conviction except racism.

Apparently, the desire to believe that our fate is predetermined is an almost universal one. Life is hard, and many people would prefer to believe that something outside them is responsible for what happens to them. There is a certain peace in believing that one's fate is not in one's hands. Whereas astrologers see our fate constrained by the planets, Calvinists see it determined by divine predestination, Marxists see it in dialectical materialism, many Western intellectuals believe that crime is caused by poverty, and others see our lives as the result of karma, the effects of our actions in past lives.

Nor are such beliefs the only silliness believed in by some of those who laughed the most at Mrs. Reagan's astrological beliefs.

What about the belief—again, overwhelmingly held by intellectuals—that men and women are basically the same? Is there any belief about Jupiter and Sagittarius that is as irrational as that? Anyone with male and female children can tell you how different boys and girls are, irrespective of societal influences. Yet to have stated on most campuses during the heyday of feminism that men and women are basically different was to have been declared sexist and foolish.

Consider, too, the belief that the Third World ("the South") is poor because of the First World (the industrialized democracies, or "the North"). There is as much verifiable truth to this widely held intellectual belief as there is to a belief in Neptune's effects on one's love life.

So, just as it might be provocative to ask future presidential candidates and their spouses if they believe in astrology, it would be interesting to ask them and their advisers whether they believe that Third World poverty is a result of Western policies, or that poverty causes crime, or that men and women really are the same.

When these questions are posed, those of us who doubt these beliefs as much as we doubt astrology can choose which superstitions we most fear being represented in the White House.

18

─

THE VIRTUE OF HYPOCRISY

I don't like hypocrisy, but I fear a world without it. As long as it continues to exist, it means that standards continue to exist. You can only have hypocrisy when you have standards. The end of hypocrisy won't mean that everyone is always living up to moral standards. It will mean that there are no longer moral standards against which people's behavior can be judged hypocritical. That is why only people who at least pay lip service to a standard of behavior can be hypocrites.

This explains a fascinating phenomenon in our society. We often hear about religious hypocrites. For example, the televangelist Jim Bakker was labeled as such for his sexual encounter with a young devotee. Yet we never hear talk of secular hypocrites. Hugh Hefner, for example, who slept with thousands of young women devotees over the course of a lifetime, was never labeled a hypocrite.

The reason is not antireligious bias. There is a good reason that Hefner wasn't called a hypocrite; *he wasn't one.* He lived consistent with his standards. *His* standards—which is the entire point. Those who don't claim to be religious are rarely judgeable by external standards. Irreligious people therefore can almost never be deemed hypocrites. How can we ever judge them hypocritical when there is no higher standard by which to judge them? Moreover, since they are responsible only to their own standards, they can change these standards at a moment's notice, and thereby never be deemed hypocrites. On the other hand, a religious Christian or Jew can easily be judged hypocritical. Since we know Christianity's and Judaism's standards, we can judge religious people accordingly.

This may be one reason that many people don't affiliate with an organized religion. The refrain, "I don't need organized religion—I can pray on my own," states a truth, but it is an irrelevant one. Of course people can pray on their own, but prayer is not religion's major goal. Prayer is a consequence, not the purpose, of religion. Its primary purpose is (or should be) ethical: to provide a standard to which people are held accountable.

Many people want to do whatever they want and not be judged. Religion doesn't allow for that. It provides an external standard by which we can assess our and others' behavior.

The death of religion usually means the death of external standards, and therefore the death of stigma. An article in the *New York Times* attributed the 89 percent out-of-wedlock birthrate in Harlem in part to the absence of any stigma attached to having a baby without a husband. As much as we might call these young girls and their inseminators irresponsible, immature, or destructive, we cannot call them hypocrites. They violated no standards that they preach.

Our use of "hypocrite," therefore, needs to be rethought. It is almost never applied to the irreligious, no matter what they do; and it is too readily applied to the religious. The moment a religious person does something wrong, many people are ready to dismiss him or her as a hypocrite. Yet human inconsistency, even moral failure, is not necessarily evidence of hypocrisy.

This labeling of people with religious standards is not only often unfair to those people, it is also destructive to society and its values; and it is disheartening to individuals trying to lead lives in accordance with high values. I often speak on the biblical law of tithing, giving a tenth of one's income to charity. If I did not give that much, would I be a hypocrite for teaching, even advocating this law? Should I cease telling people about tithing to maintain consistency between my ideals and my practice? Would that be constructive?

The next time you hear about, or call someone, a religious hypocrite, remember that subjecting themselves to such labeling is a price the religious pay for being identified with standards higher than themselves. And remember, too, that some of the worst people aren't hypocrites. Hitler acted consistent with his values.

PART TWO

LIBERALISM: WHAT HAPPENED TO A GREAT IDEOLOGY?

19

WHAT HAPPENED TO A GREAT IDEOLOGY?

I do not like attacking liberalism for a number of reasons, chief among them being that I long considered myself liberal.

I was raised in a liberal Jewish (almost a redundancy) home in which Adlai Stevenson ranked just under religious heroes, in which "Democrat," "labor," and "liberal" meant looking out for the little guy, and in which "Republican," "business," and "conservative" meant selfishness and occasionally even anti-Semitism. These were powerful influences on a child growing up in a middle-class home in Brooklyn, New York, in the 1950s.

I believe in the separation of church and state, pluralism, openmindedness, tolerance, personal freedom, fighting for the downtrodden, a higher minimum wage, women's equality, a color-blind society, legal (though discouraged) abortion, legalized prostitution, and free trade, to cite but a few "liberal" positions that I hold. Until the late 1960s, this list would have qualified me beyond question as a liberal. Since then, however, liberalism has become identified with positions that were always regarded as left or even radical, but not liberal, and sometimes not even moral.

Is the liberal position on abortion liberal or anarchic? It is one thing to argue on behalf of legalized abortions; it is quite another to argue that abortion is nothing more than "a woman controlling her own body" or labeling abortion "reproductive rights."

Was the post-Vietnam liberal position on fighting Communism liberal or leftist? Communism has been, with the exception of Nazism, the greatest organized evil in history. Until the late 1960s, liberals were proud to be identified with this view and to be counted as anti-Communist. Yet liberalism moved so far left that liberals who continued to call themselves and act anti-Communist were labeled right-wingers. Indeed, it was the liberal opposition to anti-Communism that shocked me into reassessing liberalism.

Is the current liberal position on church-state separation liberal or antireligious? It is one thing to insist that the government not foster a state religion. It is quite another to seek a secular *society* in which religion is relegated to an increasingly small private sphere. The knee-jerk and passionate opposition of liberals to a moment of silence or even a clergyman invoking God's blessings on a graduating class, while at the same time they passionately support a years-long immersion in sex education, tells me that liberalism has gone awry.

Is the liberal position on looking at America through race-based eyes liberal or racist? The liberalism I learned held that the skin color of a person is no more important than his or her eye color, that the American ideal is integration, and that liberals must oppose segregation, yet today liberalism supports racial quotas, race norming (grading an exam differently for members of different races), and segregating students in college dorms by race and ethnicity. I loathe racism more than I loathe any other ideology. My life is devoted to minimizing the significance of blood and race, and affirming the greater significance of love, values, and personhood. This defines me as a "conservative" today.

In large part due to liberal policies of the past twenty-five years, great numbers of Americans have become welfare addicts; the American university has declined as it replaced the search for truth with the pursuit of an ideological agenda; public school standards have been eroded; many criminals receive more compassion than do their unprecedentedly large number of victims; the rate of out-of-wedlock births has risen beyond what anyone could have imagined a generation ago; countless blacks, Hispanics, and women have been infantilized; and the Balkanization of one of the few countries in the world not to have a Balkan-like problem has begun.

My critiques of liberalism are not arguments on behalf of conservatism. The only "ism" I care about is ethical monotheism (see Part Three).

20

IS LIBERALISM JEWISH?

The United States is facing a struggle for its soul. And if we can characterize this struggle as essentially liberal/left/secular vs. conservative/right/religious, most Jews have allied themselves with the liberal/left/secular forces. They believe that liberal positions are morally superior, and that these positions are essentially Jewish.

I respectfully disagree. Though the liberal impulse is a moral one, and liberalism has played a profoundly positive role in American political life, in the last thirty years, it has changed in fundamental ways. These changes are so fundamental that an honest inquiry into Judaism would reveal that many contemporary liberal positions are neither moral nor Jewish.

It is with great sadness, therefore, that I have concluded that in the struggle for America's soul, many American Jews have too often taken positions that hurt America.

The problem is this: Most American Jews do not derive their values from Judaism. They derive their values from the dominant secular liberal culture, and these values are no longer congruent with Judaism, even a nonfundamentalist Judaism.[1]

Most Jews believe that all they need to do to formulate a Jewish position is:

---

[1]To test this thesis, I often ask Jewish liberals to cite where Judaism and liberalism actually differ. I have almost never encountered one who could cite a single difference. It is no wonder that the children of Jewish liberals so frequently abandon any commitment to Judaism. Why be a Jew when one can embrace all its values by being a liberal?

1. Note that "Judaism teaches compassion."
2. Take the liberal position, usually the one that seems to be the most compassionate.
3. Label that position "Jewish."

To cite one example, when the most liberal of Judaism's denominations, the Reconstructionist movement, voted to marry men to men, and women to women, three thousand years of Jewish teaching that sexuality, that infinitely elastic drive, should be channeled into heterosexual marriage was discarded. The reason? Compassion for the individual homosexual. When there is tension between a social value and compassion for the individual, the liberal inclination is to discard the value. My heart, too, goes out to a homosexual who wishes to marry his or her lover. It is axiomatic to me that a gay person has the same desire to lead a happy and fulfilled life that I do. But I am not prepared to forsake the heterosexual marital ideal. Nor should we enable same-sex couples (gay or straight) to adopt children as readily as we do married husband-wife couples; a child has the right to begin life with a mother and father.[2]

Abortion provides another example. Judaism does not consider the fetus fully human, and it allows abortion for the sake of the mother's health, but otherwise opposes it. The Jewish position is, therefore, neither that of the secular left nor that of the Christian right. Yet Jewish liberals have sided entirely with the secular left—in large part because, again, they have elevated compassion (for the pregnant woman) over a value (of nascent human life).

It is a Jewish and American tragedy that Jewish organizations have only served as liberal mouthpieces on an issue where the Jewish position would have been so healing to Americans. "Permit but discourage" is what the great majority of Americans feel about abortion—and what Jews should have been articulating. Because so many Jews believe in liberalism rather than in Judaism, they missed a great opportunity to bring an important Jewish value into American life.

---

[2]It should be noted here that as a non-Orthodox Jew, I am open to reforming Jewish law. But the Torah's ban on homosexuality is not only a Jewish law, it is one of the seven laws that Judaism demands that all mankind observe. Judaism transformed history by directing that the sexual drive be confined to heterosexual marriage. Acceptance of homosexuality is not new; it pervaded nearly every society prior to Judaism and outside Christianity's influence. For an in-depth discussion, please see my essay, "Judaism, Homosexuality and Civilization" in my quarterly journal *Ultimate Issues*, Spring 1991, or the somewhat abridged version in *The Public Interest*, Summer 1993.

I would characterize the essential differences between Judaism and contemporary liberalism in the following ways:

THE ISSUE	LIBERAL	JEWISH
Primary role of government	Compassion	Justice
Human nature	Basically good	Not basically good (or bad)
Primary source of evil	Forces outside the individual	The individual
Primary cause of:		
Criminal violence	Poverty	Lack of values
Riots	Racism	Lack of values
Murder	Guns	Lack of values
Unwed teenage mothers and irresponsible fathers	Lack of condoms and sex education	Lack of values
Greatest fear	Christian right	Moral dissolution of society
Heterosexual behavior	Genetic predisposition	Value to be inculcated
Abortion	Allow with no restrictions and no discouragement	Allow with restrictions and try to discourage
Morality	1. Relative to the individual 2. Relative to race and class	Universal

COMPASSION VS. JUSTICE

Jews who note Judaism's love of compassion are entirely right. The Jewish self-perception has always been of a people wanting to be compassionate. The ancient rabbinic description of the Jews is "compassionate ones, the children of compassionate ones." We are not surprised (unfortunately) when we read of a Jew convicted for an economic crime, but we would be shocked to read of a Jew convicted of mass murder or some other violent and cruel crime.

Liberal Jews, however, have done to compassion what many Christians have done to faith: elevated it over all other values.

Yes, *we* are to be compassionate. But the *state* must first be just. "Zion will be redeemed through justice," said the prophet Isaiah, *not through compassion*. Compassion, by definition, is selective. Thus, when the state is compassionate to blacks because of past racism, it enacts laws that are often unjust to individuals who are not black. When the state enacts budgets to be compassionate on behalf of the poor souls suffering with AIDS, the far greater number of poor souls who die of cancer and heart disease lose out. In the name of compassion, the American government unfairly spends many more dollars per AIDS patient than per cancer patient.

SECULAR VS. RELIGIOUS SOCIETY

Contemporary liberals seem to believe that the Judeo-Christian tradition upon which America was founded is no longer needed. That is why they work passionately to keep mention of God out of public schools, why they sue the Boy Scouts and Girl Scouts for insisting that scouts take the Scouting Oath, which includes God's name.

Of course, all this is done under the banner of concern for "separation of church and state." But the result—and for some, the agenda—is the removal of religion and God from as much of American life as possible.

Unlike secular liberal Jews (and their organizations), this Jew fears a post-Christian America. We have seen post-Christianity in Nazism and Communism; and I saw what religion-free America might be like a few blocks from my home during the riots in Los Angeles. Those were not Christians who destroyed thousands of innocent people's businesses and who beat people to death or near-death for not being black. While American Jews see in Christian resurgence a potential pogrom, something quite similar to a pogrom did take place in Crown Heights, Brooklyn—and it wasn't carried out by Christians. Had it been, incidentally, Jewish life would have mobilized mass demonstrations that would have shaken American society.

Many Jews refuse to acknowledge how profoundly Christians, especially in America, have changed for the good—particularly in their attitudes toward Jews—since the days of Christian-inspired anti-Semitism. This has paralyzed organized Jewish life from an accurate assessment of where threats to their well-being come from. This is not unique to Jews; many blacks, too, do not acknowledge the sea change that has taken place in most white people's views of blacks. It is difficult to think a second time, and it is difficult to stop hating people who once did earn your animosity.

Insofar as the welfare of the American republic and its Jewish population is concerned, the people I most fear are not Christians; they are white and black racists and, to a lesser degree, the well-intentioned members of radically secular organizations like the ACLU when they work to remove the Ten Commandments from public school walls, the oath affirming faith in God from the Boy and Girl Scouts, and chaplains from the armed forces.

I am as desirous of keeping American government secular as the most activist secularist is. That is why, though I am a religious

Jew, I actively support secular government in Israel. But while a secular government is a blessing, a secular population isn't. The people who brought God into the world shouldn't be among the most active in eliminating Him from it.

But, liberal Jews argue, "Religions have caused nearly all of the world's evils."

This is an enormously destructive myth. I write elsewhere in this book about religious evil, and I fear it. But more evil has been committed, i.e., more innocent people have been slaughtered, tortured, and enslaved, by secular ideologies in this century—Nazism and Communism—than by all religions in the history of the world combined.

In addition, it has been the societies influenced by Judaism and Christianity that first outlawed human sacrifice and slavery, raised the status of women to its present unprecedentedly high level, and created democracy. And in these societies, literature and the arts thrived as nowhere else.

Of course, belief in God and religion does not assure goodness. But their deaths assure moral collapse. Nazism and Communism provide two extreme examples of what happens when God-based religion is supplanted by man-based ideology.

The contemporary American campus provides another example of what happens in a wholly secular atmosphere. With its political correctness and speech codes, the secular liberal university has become, as the late Professor Allan Bloom noted, one of the most closed-minded institutions in America today. Having attended an Ivy League graduate school and having been a member of a Rotary Club, I found more diversity of thought in the latter than in the former. The liberal university is also home to the only anti-Semitic and racist organizations to be found outside white supremacist fringe groups; more than a few black student organizations invite Jew- and white-hating speakers and publish race-hate literature.

One reason for the moral and intellectual decline of the university is to be found in the Psalms (111:10): "Wisdom begins with awe of God." When God is removed from society, within a generation or two, moral foolishness prevails. Marxism, for example, had devotees almost only among Western secular intellectuals. Only secular intellectuals believed that the United States and the Soviet Union were moral equivalents, equally responsible for the Cold War.

And Jews, the most highly (secularly) educated group in America, have therefore absorbed more of such secular foolishness than other groups.

SOURCES OF EVIL: PEOPLE OR FORCES?

One of Judaism's greatest teachings is that the human being knows good from evil and therefore has freedom of moral choice. One of the most dangerous teachings of the left since Marx is that people are not morally free: They do bad things because of outside forces, especially economic ones. Thus, the belief that poverty causes violent crime has become a credo of liberals.

- When poor people or people of color rape, maim, and murder, liberals cite economics and racism as the reasons. Jews should cite the miserable values of the rapist, mugger, and murderer.
- When boys or men impregnate and then abandon young girls, liberals attribute this behavior to lack of condoms and sex education. Jews should attribute it to a lack of self-restraint and moral education.
- When criminals use guns to murder, liberals blame the object more than the person. They call for more handgun control as if there were a relationship between handgun control and reduced crime (I wish there were—I support firearm registration); Israeli Jews are highly armed, and they commit virtually no murders. Jews should call for punishing murderers and for the teaching of values.

People do bad things to other people because they do not have good values. That is Judaism's greatness—preoccupation with teaching goodness: "And you will teach these things to your children when you sit in your house, when you go on the road, when you lie down and when you arise" (Deuteronomy 6:7).

The Jewish task is to bring the world to ethical monotheism, not to liberalism and not to conservatism. That is the only reason for our being here as Jews. We have a mission—to teach that God without universal ethical demands leads to a Khomeini or a Crusader; and to teach that ethics without God leads to Nazism and Communism and the moral anarchy we are creating in America.

If liberal Jews devoted their abilities, efforts, and passions to Judaism and ethical monotheism as they now do to liberalism, Jews would change America and the world. Indeed, only then would Jews help produce the very type of beautiful world that liberals want.

21

A GUIDE TO THE LIBERAL USE OF LANGUAGE: HOW MEANINGS OF WORDS HAVE BEEN CHANGED BY LEADING INSTITUTIONS IN THE MEDIA AND ACADEMIA

In abandoning many of its traditional values, contemporary liberalism has redefined many terms. I offer a listing of some of them and their new definitions.

CONSERVATIVE A person with selfish motives.

LIBERAL A person with altruistic motives.

> During more than ten years of doing talk radio, I have never spoken to a liberal who believed that a person who voted for Ronald Reagan or George Bush could be motivated by altruism. Republicans, by definition, "vote with their pocketbooks."

ULTRA-CONSERVATIVE A person who is too conservative.

ULTRA-LIBERAL Term not used; one presumably cannot be too liberal.

> I read six newspapers and countless journals. I have almost never encountered the term "ultra-liberal" or "arch-liberal," yet often read about "ultra-conservatives" and "arch-conservatives."

CHRISTIAN RIGHT Contemptible people who always try to impose their values on other Americans.

LIBERALS Idealistic people who never try to impose their values on other Americans.

When Christians try to put their values into law (e.g., preventing government funds from going to what even many liberals would consider obscene art), they are attacked for trying to impose their values on others. However, when liberals pass laws reflecting their values (e.g., allowing same-sex couples the same right to adopt children as married couples), that is regarded not as imposing values, but simply as the right thing to do.

WOMEN'S RIGHTS Supporting the right to destroy a fetus for any reason, including personal convenience.

ANIMAL RIGHTS Opposing the right to destroy a rabbit for cancer research.

In our liberal age, the intellectual and moral norm is to regard a baby seal as of more worth than a human fetus.

FETUS An unborn child that is to be aborted.

BABY An unborn child that is not to be aborted.

When a woman who wants to give birth is pregnant, no one asks her, no matter how early in the pregnancy, "How's the fetus doing?" We only use the term "fetus" when we plan to destroy it. Otherwise, we speak of the "baby" from the first day of pregnancy.

WOMAN, AUTHENTIC A woman who holds liberal views.

WOMAN, INAUTHENTIC A woman who does not hold liberal views.

Thus, Gloria Steinem called conservative Texas Senator Kay Bailey Hutchison, a "female impersonator" (*USA Today*, June 11, 1993).

CENSORSHIP The refusal of the government to fund an artist liked by the radical wing of the arts establishment.

Censorship was always understood as governmental prohibition of expression. According to the arts community and its supporters, however, censorship now means *governmental refusal to fund* a work of art.

CENSORS Christians who boycott violent television shows.

SOCIAL ACTIVISTS Hollywood actors who boycott Colorado because its voters rejected a gay rights amendment.

FASCISTS People who drown out liberal speakers with whom they disagree and destroy liberal newspapers with which they disagree.

PROGRESSIVE STUDENTS People who drown out conservative speakers with whom they disagree and destroy conservative newspapers with which they disagree.

Thus, the "progressive" students who stole all copies of the conservative newspaper at the University of Pennsylvania were exonerated, while the guards who tried to stop them were chastised for interfering in student protest.

SOVIET UNION (BEFORE ITS FALL) An alternative system of government, which should not be condemned with such Cold War labels as "evil empire."

SOVIET UNION (SINCE ITS FALL) An evil empire.

Since the fall of the USSR, almost everyone speaks of Communism in the same terms we "Cold Warriors" once used.

MILITARISM The use of force by a democracy against a Third World tyranny.

The National Council of Churches has condemned every use of force by the Western democracies against Communism, anti-Western terrorism, and Saddam Hussein, but supported "revolutionary" violence such as that of the African National Congress and the PLO.

RELIGIOUS EXTREMIST A person who is too religious (usually meaning that the person holds religious beliefs and applies them to politics).

SECULAR EXTREMIST A term not used; one presumably cannot be too secular.

Those who call for the right to mention God's name at high school graduation exercises are "religious extremists," while those who litigate against schools that post the Ten Commandments on their walls, like the ACLU, are never described as "secular extremists."

SEXIST A man who disagrees with women who hold liberal views. (For the term for a *woman* who disagrees with women who hold liberal views, *see* Woman, inauthentic.)

Thus, Senator Edward M. Kennedy, well-known for "womanizing," was never called sexist because he supported liberal women's groups. On the other hand, men who treat women beautifully and respect them as equals, but do not agree with the National Organization for Women, are likely to be called sexist.

VICTIMS Nearly all blacks and women, but essentially members of every group, except heterosexual males and ethnic groups that tend to hold conservative views. Thus, Korean-Americans, although they were the primary victims of the Los Angeles riots, are never referred to as victims; they hold conservative views.

PROGRESSIVE VIEW OF HUMANITY Dividing people by their race, gender, and class.

REACTIONARY VIEW OF HUMANITY Dividing people by their values and behavior.

GAY RIGHTS Society publicly announcing that homosexuality is as desirable as heterosexuality.

> Most heterosexuals abhor gay-bashing and the treating of a homosexual as anything but fully human. But this is irrelevant to gay rights activists whose real aim is to have society regard homosexuality, heterosexuality, and bisexuality as equally desirable.

HOMOPHOBE A person who believes that man-woman love and marriage ought to be society's ideal.

BLACKS, AUTHENTIC Blacks who hold liberal views—in particular, that America is racist and that racism is the greatest problem confronting blacks.

BLACKS, INAUTHENTIC Blacks who do not hold liberal views—especially that racism is not the greatest black problem. Such blacks also are known as "Uncle Toms."

RACIST A white who does not agree with positions held by the civil rights leadership.

> To cite one example, a number of black leaders have labeled support for school vouchers as racist, although they tend to be supported more by inner-city blacks than by suburban whites. But, since the liberal black leadership is opposed to vouchers, support for it is deemed racist.

WHITE SUPREMACIST VIEW OF BLACKS People who are not to be judged by the same criteria by which all other people are judged.

LIBERAL VIEW OF BLACKS People who are not to be judged by the same criteria by which all other people are judged.

POVERTY The reason for murder, rape, and carjackings.

GREED The reason for embezzlement, insider trading, and other white-collar crimes.

MINORITIES Groups whose spokespeople are angry at America. Thus, Cuban, Japanese, Korean, and Jewish Americans are rarely referred to as minorities.

COMMUNITY A term for groups whose members hold liberal views.

> "Community" is rarely used to describe a group that holds conservative views (e.g., you seldom hear about the "Mormon community," or "the gun owners community"). You do hear about the "AIDS community" (liberal views) but not a "cancer community" (all sorts of views).

CIVIL RIGHTS ORGANIZATIONS Organizations that hold white people responsible for the majority of black people's problems.

FEMINIST ORGANIZATIONS Organizations that hold men responsible for the majority of women's problems.

BLAMING THE VICTIM Making moral demands of any members of a victimized minority (*see* Victims).

POGROM An attack by a mob of Christians in Eastern Europe against innocent Jews, leading to the beating and murder of Jews.

ETHNIC TENSION An attack by a mob of blacks in Crown Heights, Brooklyn, against innocent Jews, leading to the beating and murder of Jews.

22

BLACKS, LIBERALS, AND THE LOS ANGELES RIOTS

To see the midday sky over your city turn black with smoke from fire is frightening. To see this outside your home, and to know that the fires were not acts of nature but were set by people intent on burning your city is more than frightening. It is traumatizing.

On Thursday, April 27, 1992, I watched my city burn. And I saw thousands of people, most of whom live within ten miles, some within blocks, of my home laugh as they broke into stores and stole whatever they wanted. I watched the police of my city watch along with me, and I watched my city's and country's media deny that what was happening was evil. I watched all this and I was traumatized.

Traumatized, but not surprised. For the Los Angeles riots only reconfirmed my most deeply held beliefs about what is happening in America in large part because of what happened to liberalism.

For generations a moral beacon, one that regarded America as mankind's greatest hope for freedom and democracy, liberalism began in the mid-1960s to view America as an enemy of those precepts. A well-known historian of the sixties, himself a liberal spokesman, Professor Todd Gitlin of the University of California–Berkeley, described the transformation this way:

Little by little, alienation from American life—contempt even for the conventions of flag, home, religion, suburbs, shopping, plain homely Norman Rockwell order—had become a rock-bottom prerequisite for membership in the movement core.[1]

Though this alienation from mainstream America began on the left, the left soon became largely indistinguishable from liberalism. That is why, for example, to this day, the *New York Times* refers to the leftist Institute for Policy Studies as a "liberal" think tank.

Many liberals came to reject values they had long cherished, and sometimes embraced their opposites. Were a liberal who went to sleep in 1960 to awaken in the 1990s, he would not believe how profoundly people and institutions calling themselves liberals had changed, particularly with regard to racial issues:

- Liberalism in 1960 pushed for a color-blind society; afterward it advocated a color-based society and color-based governmental regulations.
- Liberalism in 1960 opposed racial quotas; afterward it supported them.
- Liberalism in 1960 regarded society's battle as one between right and wrong; afterward it began to see the battle as between blacks and whites, between men and women, and between the rich and the poor (race, gender, class).

In thus reconstituting itself, this new liberalism has played a major role in the moral and spiritual decline of America, especially black America.

I do not write about liberalism's contribution to the Los Angeles riots, and to increasing the probability of future riots, to advance a political agenda. I am well aware that it was conservatives who opposed the landmark civil rights legislation of the 1960s, and that the Republican Party has largely ignored blacks since that time.

I also know that many individuals who identify themselves as liberal do not hold every position cited here. But the *influential* liberal segments of American society *do*: the media, academia, the civil rights establishment, and the dominant wing of the Demo-

---

[1]Todd, Gitlin, *The Sixties: Years of Hope, Days of Rage* (Bantam, 1987), p. 271.

cratic Party.[2] In this attack on the moral credibility of American society; this lowering of moral, intellectual, and professional standards for blacks; and this cultivation of black rage against America, they contributed significantly to the burning of Los Angeles.

LOWER MORAL EXPECTATIONS OF BLACKS

During the riots, I heard a local NBC TV reporter say, "Here at the corner of [two L.A. streets] I see five black gentlemen throwing stones at cars." Can anyone imagine a reporter saying, "I see five *white* gentlemen throwing stones at cars"? Liberalism has so stifled moral honesty in relation to blacks that a reporter instinctively felt it necessary to call black thugs "gentlemen."

This refusal to call a black thug a thug is the result of the last quarter-century of liberal thinking on race. As William Julius Wilson, the highly respected black sociologist, has noted, "Sociologists, like other liberal social scientists, tended to avoid describing any behavior that could be construed as unflattering or stigmatizing to racial minorities."[3]

This has become the most pernicious form of racism in America. No Ku Klux Klansman in the past twenty-five years has done as much to hurt blacks as those liberals—white and black—who have lowered moral expectations of blacks by condemning white evil but *explaining* black evil:

---

[2]These are often referred to as the "elite." The media "elite" is here defined as journalists working for the *New York Times, Washington Post, Wall Street Journal, Newsweek, Time, U.S. News and World Report*, and the ABC, CBS, NBC, and PBS television networks.

The most authoritative analysis of their views was undertaken by Robert and Linda Richter and Stanley Rothman, who randomly interviewed 238 members of the news staffs and upper echelons of these media. Their views were almost universally liberal:

... the proportion ... who supported the Democratic candidate in presidential elections never drops below 80% In 1972 ... over 80% among the media voted for McGovern.

Though they would tend to call themselves liberal (rather than leftist) *they rated Fidel Castro above Ronald Reagan*. Among graduates of the prestigious Columbia School of Journalism, 71 percent regard America as an alienating society and 75 percent held the United States responsible for Third World poverty. The elite in the motion picture industry held similar views, while in book publishing, they were so overwhelmingly liberal and radical that *"fewer than 20% regarded themselves as moderates ..."* [Emphasis added.]

[3]*U.S. News and World Report*, May 25, 1992.

Blacks are economically deprived and systematically discriminated against.

Blacks are therefore victims.

Thus, blacks, understandably, have uncontrollable rage.

Blacks Are Enraged

Liberal reactions to the riots often emphasized the need to "understand the rage" of that minority of blacks who terrorized innocent people and torched nearly a thousand Los Angeles businesses. For most reporters, academics, and politicians, and for the civil rights establishment, blacks who burned and rioted were not criminals, but people enraged by injustice.

One prominent black liberal, Michigan representative John Conyers, announced, "Those weren't criminals, those were outraged citizens."

Senator Bill Bradley, identified as a moderate liberal, described the riots as "desperation and anger that boiled over into sickening violence."[4]

And Jesse Jackson explained the riots this way: "Desperate people do desperate things." While this is an unassailable truth, it is the kind of reasoning that could also explain mass murderers and white racists, who, after all, are also quite desperate. But it is unimaginable to think of a white leader saying such a thing about white murderers.

In the aftermath of the Los Angeles riots, "black rage" dominated media analyses of the riots. For five consecutive days after the riots ended, the *Los Angeles Times* published special supplements on "the roots of the riots." One day, the entire supplement was titled, "Witness to Rage." And the cover of an issue of *U.S. News and World Report* featured but three words: "Race and Rage."

I wonder if in 1938, after Kristallnacht, when German racists burned Jewish establishments and murdered Jews, there were those who said, "We have to understand the rage of these people— they've had to endure the humiliating Versailles Treaty, authoritarian upbringings, and awful economic problems." Did Nazis not have rage? Do Ku Klux Klansmen not have great rage? In fact, is not all evil accompanied by rage?

---

[4]Stated in his speech before the Democratic National Convention, July 13, 1992.

Indeed, we do not have to look only at criminals to find rage. We are psychologically sophisticated enough to recognize that rage is present in all of us. What, after all, is one of the most common emotions people express in their therapists' offices if not rage—at a parent, a sibling, a boss, a spouse, or life itself? The difference between moral people and immoral people is not that moral people don't have rage; it is that *moral people control their rage, and immoral people don't.*

Moral people channel their rage inward (and become depressed) or in moral directions, but not against innocent people. When a person says, "I am enraged, so I'll beat an innocent person or burn down his livelihood," the rage in which we ought to show interest is the victim's. Yet the rage of the Koreans and blacks whose livelihoods were destroyed in Los Angeles was a nonissue to liberal media and politicians.

Nearly two thousand Korean businesses were burned or looted. But through the type of moral inversion that has characterized some contemporary liberal thought, the rage of the burners, not the burned, was the focus of attention.

Blacks Are Poor

Other liberals invoked the more traditional explanation for "minority" crime: poverty.[5]

As the then Democratic presidential nominee, Bill Clinton, said, "Oh, to be sure, it was heart-breaking to see some little children going into the stores in Los Angeles and stealing from their neighbors, but they live in a country where the top one percent of Americans have more wealth than the bottom ninety percent."

For contemporary liberals, income disparity, not the moral disparity between criminals and honest people, explains looters.

But if this is so, why did the great majority of poor people refrain from looting? And if income disparity explains looting, how

---

[5]I place quotation marks around "minority" because it is a politically loaded term. To liberals, to qualify as a "minority," a group must ideally be distinguished by four characteristics: victim status, rage against America, demands for support for large government programs, and many votes. Thus Asian-Americans and Jews, for example, smaller minorities than either blacks or Hispanics, are never defined as a "minority." And Cuban-Americans are rarely considered a "minority" though they are both Hispanic and a minority. Why not? Because they possess few of these four characteristics. They do not consider themselves victims (at least of American society); rather than feeling enraged at America, they love it and appreciate it; and they demand no large governmental programs for themselves.

do liberals explain the multimillionaires who looted the savings and loans associations? It would seem that liberal doctrines hold that when whites loot, *they* are responsible, but when nonwhites loot, *society* is responsible. Couldn't it be that looters suffered from value deprivation more than from material deprivation? After all, very few of the looters stole food. Unfortunately, the future president's economic argument was just another instance of the way in which liberals excuse blacks and other selected minorities from normative moral demands.[6]

I do not wish to single out Mr. Clinton for condemnation. On the contrary, he alone among 1992 Democratic candidates actually confronted racism among blacks—at a symposium organized by Jesse Jackson, no less—by courageously condemning the racist language of black rapper Sister Souljah, who had argued that instead of blacks murdering blacks, it would be preferable if they murdered whites.[7] I cite his reaction because he became president of the United States and to show how instinctive it became for liberal leaders to add a "but" when discussing crimes committed by "minorities."[8]

We never heard a moral condemnation of the rioters by a liberal without the person's qualifying it with denunciations of American racism, economic inequality, and Republican policies. We did not hear black civil rights leaders call black thugs by their proper name or publicly apologize to Korean-Americans. Indeed, at least

---

[6]In an article on this topic, I wrote, "Blacks and white liberals make fewer moral demands of blacks than they do of other human beings." Nationally syndicated columnist Walter Williams quoted these words, and wrote: "Prager is right; it's part of a long-standing pattern." Williams is black.

[7]The *Washington Post*, May 13, 1992, had quoted her as saying, among other things, "Maybe we should have a week of killing whites. Just give back what whites have done to us."

[8]Many liberals don't add a "but," they simply blame society for all violent crimes committed by "minorities." As one distinguished liberal, Kenneth R. Clark, professor of psychology emeritus of the City University of New York, wrote:

How do so many young people become mindlessly anti-social? . . . mugged communities, mugged neighborhoods and probably most important, mugged schools spawn urban muggers.

Not able to express their frustration in words, their indignation takes the form of more crime. Having been robbed of the minimum self-esteem essential to their humanity, they have nothing to lose. [*New York Times*, January 14, 1985]

In these few lines, Professor Clark expresses a number of classical liberal themes on the criminals who have so devastated American life:

1. The mugger is the victim, not society.
2. Muggings must not be regarded as vicious crimes, but as the muggers' expression of rage against their mistreatment by society.
3. People beat up innocent people because they have been robbed of self-esteem.

some liberal black leaders (nonliberal blacks are not allowed to become black leaders) have not only defended the rioters but also threatened society with future burning, as when Congresswoman Maxine Waters repeatedly declared, "No justice, no peace."

Blacks Are Victims

Another method of excusing evil committed by blacks has been to depict them as victims. This has a terrible moral upshot: *Victims are not morally accountable for their actions.*

Since, by definition, victims are "oppressed," almost anything they do is a justified response to oppression. And because they see riots as a justified response to a racist society, some liberals actually rejected the term "riots." Since that term has moral implications, "events," "explosion," and even "uprising" and "rebellion" are used.

Meanwhile, those who hold members of minorities morally accountable for their behavior are accused of "blaming the victim."

Rage, poverty, and victimhood—the three liberal excuses for black people who do bad things to good people.

LIBERALISM AND THE FOMENTING OF BLACK RAGE

Many black Americans are enraged. But far from absolving liberalism, this leads to the greatest indictment of it—the relentless fomenting of rage against American society among many blacks.

It is not surprising that many blacks who have been told all their lives that white America is racist, that whites have it in for them, and that no matter how hard they try, whites will trample on them (see next section), will have some rage.

It would be as if I, a Jewish parent, raised my children saying, "America is an anti-Semitic country; scratch a gentile, and you'll find a Jew-hater. Sure, you can make it in some professions, but this is a relatively new development. Don't think a Jew can ever be elected president, don't forget those country clubs that still don't allow Jews, and remember all the swastikas that are painted on various synagogues. The *goyim* hate you, my Jewish child." What would happen if, in addition, most other Jews, and much of the non-Jewish world, said such things to Jewish children? They, too, would become angry.

Granted, even without such relentless attacks, some blacks would be angry at America. Ironically, however, it is not the oldest blacks—who suffered the longest under racist laws—who are particularly angry. There must, therefore, be an additional reason for the most intense black rage. That reason, the absence of fathers, is discussed below.

Depict America as Racist

Liberals have cultivated black anger by (1) constantly depicting America as a racist society, (2) rewarding blacks who have rage at America, and (3) punishing blacks who defend American society against charges of racism.

Though they certainly don't believe it in their hearts, the words of many leading liberals have stated in essence that America deserves to be burned. For example, a chief liberal spokesman on the issue of race has been Professor Andrew Hacker, whose book *Two Nations Black and White: Separate, Hostile and Equal* received lavish praise from the mainstream press. Immediately after the riots, the *Los Angeles Times* published long excerpts from Hacker's book on its opinion page, including the following:

> At times, the conclusion seems all but self-evident that white America has no desire for your presence or any need for your people. Can this nation have an unstated strategy for annihilating your people? How else, you ask yourself, can one explain the incidence of death and debilitation from drugs and disease, the incarceration of a whole generation of your men, the consignment of millions of women and children to half-lives of poverty and dependence? . . .
>
> Just as your people were once made to serve silently as slaves, could it be that if white America begins to conclude that you are becoming too much trouble, it will find itself contemplating more lasting solutions?[9]

Thus, one of the leading white liberal scholars on race relations tells blacks that America might soon conclude that they should be exterminated (notice the use of the words "lasting solutions"—a parallel to the Nazis' term for the genocide of the Jews, "Final Solution")—and the major newspaper in the city in which the riots occurred published this a week after the riots.

[9]*Los Angeles Times*, May 12, 1992.

Here are the words of a black liberal author, Walter Mosely, published by the *Los Angeles Times* on its opinion page less than a week after the riots:

> America is a brutal land. Its language is violence and bloodshed. That is why [Rodney] King was beaten; that is why another King was assassinated.[10]

To Mosely, as to other liberal spokespeople, it was not one vile racist who murdered Dr. Martin Luther King; it was brutal America. Blame America, not an American. To put this into perspective, can anyone imagine that the *Los Angeles Times* would publish an article blaming black America for the rape and beating of the Central Park jogger? Of course not, because such an article would be correctly considered racist, and therefore not worthy of publication. But liberal racial attacks are published and honored.

On the same opinion page, the same day, the *Los Angeles Times* published this America-is-racist accusation by Leon Litwack, Morrison Professor of American History at U.C. Berkeley:

> The lawlessness began with the clubbing of black America, the conscious and criminal neglect and fashionable racism characteristic of the Age of Greed, over which Ronald Reagan and George Bush have presided.[11]

Again a liberal indicts America for the acts of *individuals* in it. One policeman—Officer Laurence Powell delivered nearly all the blows to Rodney King—beats a black criminal, and a distinguished professor of history at Berkeley depicts the act as "the clubbing of black America" by white America.

Writing about the riots, the Jewish liberal writer Leonard Fein made this charge against America:

> We have, as a nation, decided to bequeath to our children the rotten fruit of racism and bigotry, decided that it will be for them to choke on it . . .
>
> [We must] stop now the persistent looting of human life, end the stealing of hopes and the torching of health.[12]

Note the moral inversion—Americans in general, not the rioters and arsonists, are the real looters and torchers.

[10]*Los Angeles Times*, May 5, 1992.
[11]Ibid.
[12]Leonard Fein, "The Rotten Fruit of Racism," *Forward*, May 15, 1992.

This attitude was not generated by the riots alone. Paul Conrad of the *Los Angeles Times*, one of the nation's best-known liberal cartoonists, drew George Bush in a Ku Klux Klan outfit when Mr. Bush opposed the 1991 Civil Rights Law because he understood it as establishing racial quotas.[13] The point was clear: If you don't agree with liberals on race, you are in effect a Ku Klux Klansman. Isn't a country that elects such an evil man as its president worthy of some burning?

Adding fuel to the fires was another angry black liberal spokesman, the Reverend James Lawson of Los Angeles, who said on his own national television show:

> The rioters and looters were doing exactly what the United States had done to the men, women and children of Central American countries and in the Persian Gulf War.[14]

At America's leading universities, the pervasiveness of American racism is taken for granted and taught as fact. In 1989, Harvard University sponsored a week-long program against racism called AWARE (Actively Working Against Racism and Ethnocentrism), at which students learned from the keynote speaker, Professor John Dovidio of Colgate, that 85 percent of white Americans harbor some form of racism and that the other 15 percent are outright racists. They also heard a Dartmouth dean say that major American universities are "genocidal in nature."[15]

The president of Occidental College said in 1990 that blacks on predominantly white campuses "face a level of hatred, prejudice,

---

[13]The reason for opposing the liberal Kennedy-Hawkins "civil rights" bill was that it betrayed the civil rights principles for which liberals originally fought. That is why two famed early civil rights fighters came out against the bill.

One was Morris Abrams, *the man who argued the one-man, one-vote case before the Supreme Court*. He wrote that the bill "is not a civil rights bill but a quota bill because it will achieve precisely what the landmark 1964 Civil Rights Act stood against." [*Wall Street Journal*, July 20, 1990]

The other was Ed Koch, former mayor of New York, who wrote in a letter to Congress:

> You might ask, how can it be that I, your former colleague who voted for every civil-rights bill when in Congress, and as a young lawyer in 1964 went to Mississippi to defend black and white civil-rights workers who were registering voters, could take such a position? The answer is simple. [This] is not a civil-rights bill. It is a bill which will encourage quotas based on race, ethnicity, religion and gender.

Koch added that his former Democratic colleagues in Congress "got out of touch because they are so frightened by the militant black and white leadership in the civil-rights groups." [*Wall Street Journal*, May 22, 1991]

[14]"Lawson Live," VISN Network, May 30, 1992.

[15]Robert R. Detlefsen, "White Like Me," *New Republic*, April 10, 1989.

and ignorance comparable to that of the days of Bull Connor, Lester Maddox and Orval Faubus."[16]

Liberal depictions of America as racist, oppressive, callous, and greedy could fill volumes. I don't doubt that many liberals have good motives. But good motives cause at least as much evil as bad ones.

The burning has happened, and is likely to happen again, in large part because of the reaction of the American media and liberal politicians: "Arsonists, we understand your rage."

That certainly was the message of Representative Maxine Waters when she screamed, "No justice, no peace." In other words, "Meet our demands (i.e., give us the verdicts we demand) or we'll torch your cities again." It is truly extraordinary that a member of the House of Representatives would threaten her own country with violence at a rally in Washington, D.C. But to the best of my knowledge, not one member of the Democratic Party publicly repudiated her views.

Reward Angry Blacks, Punish Those Who Aren't

For some twenty-five years, since the day that the late Leonard Bernstein threw a party at his Manhattan penthouse to raise money for the Black Panthers, the liberal elite often has glorified blacks who hate American society and scorned those who love it. The message to blacks who are enraged at America has been clear: The elite of America will honor you, you will appear on the cover of *Time*, you will get the support of major liberal foundations, and you will get exposure on national television. For you blacks who say that America has earned your love and is not racist (without denying that racism certainly exists), there is usually contempt: We will ignore you; if you somehow rise to positions of influence, we will dismiss you as an inauthentic black and try to destroy you.

Thus, when Dartmouth College celebrated its fifteenth anniversary of coeducational studies, Angela Davis, a black who twice ran for vice-president on the Communist Party ticket (and a woman who denied that the Soviet Union incarcerated any political prisoners), was the woman it chose to honor.

Similarly, in 1989, New York State appointed Professor Leonard Jeffries to its curriculum board for multiculturalism—*after* he had been teaching racism and anti-Semitism, i.e., that blacks are the superior "sun race" and whites are the inferior "ice race," and singled

[16]*U.S. News and World Report*, January 8, 1990.

out Jews as enemies of black people. He has said that "If I had my way, I'd wipe them [whites] from the face of the earth."[17] New York's liberal educators rewarded Jeffries for his racism and anti-Semitism.

Conversely, it is inconceivable that liberal educators would appoint a black who said, "Color doesn't mean much to me; I think that how human beings act morally is much more important than their color." The academic elite would dismiss such a black as a reactionary. For it has become a tenet of the contemporary university that it is reactionary to believe that an individual's moral behavior is more important than his or her color.

A black who says, "Sure, America has racists, but it's a wonderful country, so if a black really tries, he has real opportunities," is scorned. Clarence Thomas provided the classic example. Liberal leaders found intolerable a black man who affirmed Judeo-Christian values, self-sufficiency, the primacy of family, and the belief that America is a land of opportunity. Liberals, therefore, made every effort to block his appointment to the Supreme Court.

Yet ABC News named Maxine Waters as its "Person of the Week" after she made her threats against America.

BLACK HATRED FOR WHITES

The writings of liberals like Andrew Hacker have helped to reinforce black rage at America.[18] About 25 percent of blacks believe that whites started the AIDS epidemic to perpetrate genocide against blacks. As least as many are persuaded that whites are using drugs to commit genocide against blacks.

As the *Los Angeles Times* reported:

> . . . a significant number of blacks believe that the white establishment has intentionally allowed narcotics to devastate their communities, even encouraged drug abuse as a form of genocide.

---

[17]Eric Breindel, "Leonard Jeffries and White Guilt," *New York Post*, August 15, 1991.

[18]According to many liberal writers, interest groups, media, and academics, America is worse than merely racist. They routinely accuse America of subjugating its women to a patriarchal sexist society, in which one out of every two women will be a victim of rape or attempted rape twice in her lifetime; causing three million of its citizens to become homeless; being dominated by a military-industrial complex that was at least as responsible for the Cold War as the Soviet Union; and callously neglecting the health of its infants, resulting in one of the highest infant mortality rates in the industrialized world.

"It's almost an accepted fact," said Andrew Cooper, publisher of the *City Sun*, a Brooklyn-based black weekly, "It is a deep-seated suspicion. *I believe it . . .* "

. . . the Rev. Lawrence Lucas, a Harlem priest known for his acerbic criticism of the white Establishment [said], "You're killing them with drugs. You're killing them with the crimes connected to drugs. You send them to jail and eliminate African-American males as fathers."[19]

Dr. Frances Welsing, a noted black psychiatrist, has "charged [that] racism was behind the crack epidemic."[20]

Arsenio Hall, on his national television show, "paid respectful attention last month when rap singer Kool Moe Dee charged that AIDS is a genocidal plot."[21]

Other black leaders attribute any criticism, even legal prosecution, of black public figures, no matter how deserved, to white racism. To cite one example, Washington, D.C., mayor Marion Barry was convicted of narcotics use during a trial in which he was seen acquiring narcotics on a videotape. Nonetheless, the Reverend Jesse Jackson and Benjamin Hooks, then head of the NAACP, among others, blamed Barry's legal problems on white racism. As one black commentator, Carl Rowan, wrote:

> Despite the incredible array of evidence that Barry bought, used, and dispensed cocaine, crack, opium and more; that he traded jobs for dope, and that he was a flagrant adulterer, Hooks opened the NAACP convention talking about the "Nazi-like" tactics used against Barry.[22]

THE RODNEY KING VERDICT

Liberals believe that the immediate reason for the rage that led to the rioting in Los Angeles was obvious—a jury's acquittal of

[19]*Los Angeles Times*, January 2, 1990. Emphasis added.
[20]*U.S. News and World Report*, March 12, 1990. Dr. Welsing and I were participants on a national television talk show. The subject was white supremacy, which Dr. Welsing holds responsible for all evil in the world. Midway in the show, I asked her if she held white supremacy responsible for Idi Amin's slaughter of hundreds of thousands of fellow black Africans. "Yes," she replied. And that was that.
[21]Ibid.
[22]Cited in *National Review*, August 20, 1990.

three of the four white police officers who beat Rodney King.

This belief, shared by most of the world, needs to be analyzed.

The Media and the Video

For over a year, Americans were shown again and again a frightening videotape of white police officers beating a black man. Indeed, the sight was so shocking that the president of the United States remarked on national television that he was surprised by the not-guilty verdict.

No one who saw the few seconds of the video that were repeatedly shown could imagine an acquittal of any of the officers involved.

But those who saw what the news media *refused* to show, or watched the entire trial, or understood that overly harsh charges were brought against the policemen, had a far fuller understanding of what happened, and why the jury reached its verdict. They saw a 230-pound, six-foot-three-inch man, with a .19 blood alcohol level (.08 is legal intoxication), acting wildly and lunging at policemen, four of whom he actually threw off.

Those who saw this, or learned of it from the *prosecution's* eyewitnesses, understood that the policemen suspected that King was under the influence of the hallucinogenic drug PCP. Like other PCP suspects, he could not be subdued by "tazing," the shooting of powerful electric shocks. Even after being shot *twice* with the Taser gun, King still resisted being handcuffed. He also put his hands on his buttocks and made obscene gestures at a female officer who had ordered him to stay still.

Only after their verbal orders had been ignored and "tazing" and other techniques had failed to subdue him, did the police use their batons to beat King. And all this was after an eight-mile car chase at speeds of up to one hundred miles an hour on a freeway, and eighty miles an hour through city streets.

It is almost impossible to overstate how responsible the media were for the rage over the Rodney King verdict. Los Angeles and national news programs deliberately and repeatedly showed only the most brutal seconds of the tape, thus never providing viewers with a context. It was as if all that Americans ever saw of the riots were pictures of Korean-Americans armed and shooting.

Yet, when confronted with this prejudiced, inflammatory use of the Rodney King tape, Stephen Weiswasser, the executive vice-president of ABC News, dismissed the issue, saying, "The part of the tape not regularly shown does not shed light on the jury's action, one way or the other."[23]

Fair-minded people of all political persuasions who have seen the full tape know that statement is false. Indeed, Roger Parloff, a Democratic attorney and senior journalist for *American Lawyer*, concluded after viewing the entire tape that he "might have done the same thing the jury did." He ended his article with these words:

> I can't remember a time when I have ever felt so hesitant to say what I believe . . . And I am terrified at the prospect of quotation out of context. After all, imagine if the media were to summarize [my] article the way it summarized the trial.[24]

Yet the *New York Times* and other leading newspapers, whenever discussing the incident, *always* referred to King as "the black motorist Rodney King," as if white police were looking for an innocent black motorist to beat up.

Rodney King was anything but an innocent "black motorist." In 1989, he was arrested for armed robbery and served nine months in state prison. He was a felon on parole when the chase occurred. He knew that, had he been caught, he would have been reincarcerated, which is why he drove at life-threatening speeds.

Had King been described even half the time as "the paroled armed robber who had just eluded police in a hundred-mile-per-hour car chase," passions might not have been nearly as stirred up. Certainly, had news programs shown more of the tape, the incident would never have engendered as much rage as it did.

---

[23]*New York Magazine*, July 6, 1992.

[24]*American Lawyer*, June 1992. It is not possible to read Parloff's article and still believe that the jurors acted out of racism. It is also not possible to read Parloff and conclude that the leading American media figures do *not* deserve contempt for their agenda-filled reporting. Here is Parloff on the *New York Times*, for example:

> . . . was there really not space in its 3,250 word coverage for the *Times* to mention that the officers said they believed King was on PCP, or that King was, in fact, heavily intoxicated? No space to mention that officers had tried unsuccessfully to handcuff King forcibly; that they then had to subdue him by shooting two electrified Taser darts into him, to no effect; and that King had then jumped to his feet and charged the lead defendant?

The Police

None of this is to say that the police did no wrong. It seems obvious that excessive force was used. Indeed, the jury did *not* acquit Officer Laurence Powell, who administered nearly all the blows that struck Rodney King. Nevertheless, since the prosecution sought conviction on much more serious charges than excessive force, the jury was not prepared to render a guilty verdict that would have necessitated severe punishment.

In any event, the officers *were* punished. In addition to their legal fees, public humiliation, and personal and family tensions, the rookie officer involved was summarily dismissed from the police force, two of the three veterans were relieved of duty without pay and after a second trial were sent to jail. Compare their punishment with Rodney King's nine months in prison for armed robbery.

Nor do I deny for a moment that there is police brutality in America, or that there are racist police officers. But anyone who has seen tapes of brutal police treatment of, for example, antiabortion demonstrators, nearly all of whom are white (and conservative), would find it difficult to believe that police brutality is exclusively a racial issue.

On this question, crime expert James Q. Wilson of UCLA has written:

> The average big-city cop is much less prejudiced today than he was three decades ago, but he (and now she) is more fearful. When police stop a young black male, they expect defiance rather than submission; when they enter a housing project, they expect taunts, not thanks; when they encounter a gang, they fear a fusillade of bullets instead of just sullen complaints.[25]

Arch Puddington, a former aide to the black civil rights leader Bayard Rustin, has noted that:

> . . . fatal shootings of blacks by the police have undergone a steady *decline* in recent years, and amount to 40 percent less than two decades ago. . . .
>
> True, blacks are still three times more likely than whites to be killed by a policeman's bullet . . . [but] blacks are also three-to-five times more likely than whites to be arrested for crimes of violence. . . .

[25]*Wall Street Journal*, May 6, 1992.

Those blacks who die at the hands of police are disproportionately the victims of black policemen.[26]

The charge of racism made in the Rodney King incident may be true in some instances, but it was probably a smear in the case of at least one of the officers involved, Stacey Koon. A few months prior to the King beating, Officer Koon, to the amazement of onlookers, applied mouth-to-mouth resuscitation to a dying black transvestite prostitute who had open sores on his mouth.[27] Why didn't we hear about this on local and national newscasts?

Moreover, if racism, rather than Rodney King's violent behavior, caused the police officers' beating of him, why did the officers do virtually nothing to King's two black companions who obeyed police instructions?

In a country with a vast number of highly armed violent criminals, the nature of police work is terribly difficult. I am, therefore, amazed that many people who caution against passing moral judgments on criminals—insisting that we understand their socioeconomic background, etc.—reach sweeping conclusions about police. Perhaps we should require all students attending a school of journalism to spend time walking the streets with their local police.

I am well aware from the experiences of black friends that police sometimes stop blacks for no other reason than that they are black. In general, however, the facts of life conflict with what we might want them to be. When black males are disproportionately involved in violent crime, it is as inevitable as it is tragic that innocent black men will be disproportionately suspect. That is not always racism; it is always a tragedy. What must be demanded of a policeman is civil behavior when he stops a black person for questioning, and sincere apologies and explanations when he realizes that he has questioned an innocent person.

Liberals and the Verdict

Given both how little the public was shown of the videotape and the small number of people who watched the entire trial, most people drew one of two possible conclusions:

[26]Arch Puddington, "Is White Racism the Problem?" *Commentary,* July 1992.
[27]Reported by Charles Oliver in "You Had to Be There: What the Networks Didn't Show the World," *Reason,* August-September, 1992.

1. The jury was composed of twelve racists and/or fools.
2. In the course of half a year, the jury saw and learned far more than we did from a few seconds of carefully chosen video.

Liberal media, politicians, and organizations, without an exception of which I am aware, all espoused conclusion number one.

The most obvious reason is that liberals, like all decent people, were repulsed by the few seconds of the video that they saw. But that cannot be the only reason. Liberals, like the rest of us, are horrified by crimes of violence far worse than that committed by the four officers against King, crimes that leave innocent people maimed or dead. Yet when the perpetrators of those acts of violence are given light sentences that defy common sense and elementary justice, it is overwhelmingly conservatives who speak out against a criminal justice system that does not sufficiently punish violent criminals.

Why, then, the liberal outrage at *this* verdict? Why the extraordinary rage over a verdict that involved police hitting a convicted felon who was driving intoxicated and speeding from police at one hundred miles per hour, and who wasn't maimed, let alone killed?

The answer is obvious: Rodney King is black and the police officers are white. For liberals, the Rodney King verdict was, or could be depicted as, further proof that most white Americans are racist. Take any twelve whites, the argument went, and look at the results: racists who acquitted cops for mercilessly beating an innocent black man. The liberal agenda seems to have been, once more, to depict white America as racist, and thereby turn a complex case into a simple racial one. Some liberals were even willing to distort the truth by constantly repeating that it was an "all-white jury," when in fact two members of the jury were not white. One was a Hispanic woman, another was a Filipino woman.

The Consequences of Liberal Condemnation of the Jury

America will suffer from the widespread liberal condemnation of the "white racist jury."

First, it is difficult to imagine that many people will willingly sit in judgment in politically sensitive criminal cases—or that if they do, they will render verdicts that black activists and liberals do not want. This was affirmed by the extraordinary light sentences meted out to the blacks who beat white truck driver Reginald Denny nearly to death.

Second, liberals made it respectable to try people via ten-second TV sound bites.

Third, by unleashing torrents of outrage at the verdict while "explaining the rage" of the rioters, liberals have assured future riots at unpopular verdicts, even at verdicts with which most liberals might concur. About six weeks after the Los Angeles riots, a Mafia leader was convicted in New York, and supporters who opposed the verdict expressed themselves by overturning cars outside the courthouse. In the words of New York's police inspector Michael Julian:

> Ever since L.A., people seem to think that violence is a natural part of these things. Look at the Gotti verdict. When did you ever see cars turned over in the street because someone didn't like a verdict?[28]

Rage at the Verdict

It is demeaning to blacks, hence racist, to hold that it is understandable that they would burn and loot out of rage over a verdict that strongly offended them. (It is important to note that more Latinos than blacks were arrested for looting, further proof that the motive of the looters was thievery, not rage.)

The number of trials in America in which violent criminals are acquitted or given absurdly light sentences is mind-boggling. Many of us are enraged at America's criminal justice system for its lenient treatment of evil people. Moreover, given that black men in their twenties are four times overrepresented among violent criminals, and that a white person is far more likely to be murdered or mugged by a black person than vice versa, there are at least as many verdicts in this country that unfairly favor black defendants who have hurt whites as favor white defendants who have hurt blacks.[29] According to those who justify rage over bad verdicts, whites ought to have as much justification for rioting.

Here is one of many examples:

---

[28]*New York Times*, July 5, 1992.

[29]Professor William Wilbanks, a criminologist, found that of the 629,000 interracial crimes in 1985, where victims survived to identify attackers, nine out of ten crimes were by blacks against whites.

In February 1991, a nineteen-year-old white Yale student, Christian Prince, was robbed and murdered while walking back to his campus. The accused perpetrator, James Fleming Jr., was black. One of Fleming's companions gave thirty-one pages of taped testimony describing the robbery and murder. In a verdict that confounds plausibility, the New Haven jury found Fleming guilty of robbery, but innocent of the murder charge.

Discussing this episode, Dartmouth professor Jeffrey Hart, a well-known conservative thinker, posed the essential question:

> Yale has a real problem on its hands because of its environment. . . . The streets [are] crawling with thugs. . . . Yale University needs a heavily armed private army of security police. Its quadrangles squat behind heavy iron gates, looking like fortresses— because they are fortresses. . . . If Yale students had rioted and killed in the wake of this absurd jury verdict, would the media have announced that this was an expression of their "rage" and "despair"?

Over the past several years, there have been a number of instances in which Israelis have rioted after Palestinian terrorists had murdered Israelis. If these Israelis had burned hundreds of Arab stores and killed innocent Arabs, would any liberals in the media or academia speak of the need to "understand Israeli rage"? I doubt it. *And neither would I.* Although I am a Jew—indeed especially because I am one—I would condemn the rioters. In fact, I have condemned them on those occasions when they chanted, "Death to Arabs!" although they have neither set fire to Arab stores nor killed Arabs. Like others, I have moral expectations of Jews. Those who don't condemn black rioters, but rather "understand" them, do so because they have lower moral expectations of blacks. This is racism, the liberal form of it.

Every liberal whose reaction to the Los Angeles riots was to "understand" the "rage" of black rioters, rather than to condemn the rioting, has sent two messages to the vast majority of blacks who, enraged or not, hurt no one:

1. We expect little from blacks.
2. We understand why blacks would torch buildings and beat whites, and we don't understand why you didn't; perhaps you weren't enraged enough.

When the King verdict was first announced I, too, found it

unbelievable. However, unlike most liberals, I found something else equally implausible; that twelve American men and women randomly picked to serve on a jury were all racists.

THE ROOTS OF BLACK RAGE

Ask enraged blacks or liberals why many blacks are angry, and they will tell you that it is because of endemic white racism and the legacy of slavery and segregation.

I would like to offer two additional reasons that I have learned from nonenraged blacks: the lack of fathers, and the patronizing attitude implied by racial quotas.

According to my friend Jesse Peterson, the founder of the Brotherhood Organization of a New Destiny (BOND), a Los Angeles–based group dedicated to helping black males deal with their anger at their absent fathers and their often overworked and angry mothers, black males are angry primarily because they were abandoned by their fathers, not because of white racism.

Given that 60 to 70 percent of black boys grow up without fathers present as moral models and disciplinarians, rage and violence are not surprising. Damian Williams, one of the young black men who hit Reginald Denny in the head with a brick, told police shortly after being arrested: "I never seen my daddy. I bet if I had a father, I wouldn't be in this predicament that I'm in right now." According to the *Los Angeles Times*, Williams said this with "his voice cracking with sobs."[30]

But instead of focusing on the absence of black men to serve as fathers and role models, white and black liberals have focused on white racism.

They have labeled "racist" those whites who, as Senator Daniel Patrick Moynihan did in 1964, described the breakdown of the black family as the greatest problem facing black America. (Indeed, at the time Moynihan wrote that, the rate of illegitimate births among blacks was 30 percent. The attacks on Moynihan were so intense, however, that the subject of black illegitimate births became taboo for more than twenty years. As of 1994, rates of illegitimate births among blacks were about 60 percent.) And they have vented their greatest fury on those blacks who have pointed to

[30]*Los Angeles Times*, August 8, 1992.

the same problem. This is how Benjamin Hooks, former executive director of the NAACP, described such blacks:

> . . . these black conservatives are some of the biggest liars that the world ever saw. . . . They have no following. . . . They're just a new breed of Uncle Toms as far as I'm concerned, maybe with a Ph.D. or something of that sort. . . . One wrote an article that black leaders ought to tell the public what they tell their children: study hard, learn good English, etc. etc. Don't use dope or crack. And I sat there in amazement as he lets himself be used by the white Establishment. . . . [31]

Liberals have contributed to a second source of anger—a diminished sense of self-worth—through affirmative action and racial quotas. The sense of inferiority that this instills in many blacks has been eloquently described by Professor Shelby Steele, the black author of *The Content of Our Character*:

> One of the most troubling effects of racial preferences for blacks is a kind of demoralization. Under affirmative action, the quality that earns us preferential treatment is an implied inferiority. However this inferiority is explained—and it is easily enough explained by the myriad deprivations that grew out of our oppression—it is still inferiority.[32]

No wonder so many black college students are seething with rage. So would I, if I thought that nearly everyone around me saw me as inferior—which, as Steele points out, is an implication of affirmative action and quotas.

RACE MATTERS MORE THAN VALUES

The lowering of moral expectations of blacks is an outgrowth of other liberal attitudes. One is moral relativism, the other is the belief that society is composed not of individuals, but of racial, sexual, and economic groups. These two dangerous ideas are closely related.

Judeo-Christian civilization has been dominated by trinities. In Christianity, it is the Father, the Son, and the Holy Ghost. In Judaism,

[31]*Los Angeles Times*, July 8, 1990.
[32]"A Negative Note on Affirmative Action," *New York Times Magazine*, May 3, 1990.

it is God, Torah, and Israel. For the left and many liberal intellectuals today, it is race, gender, and class.

This reductionist way of perceiving human distinctions is at the heart of the culture war that is engulfing America: Will America continue to believe, as Judaism and Christianity have taught, that there is one universal morality for all people, emanating from a source higher than human beings? Or will it adopt the view that moral rules emanate from race, gender, and economic class?

The idea that race, gender, and class, rather than one's behavior and values, are what divide people provides the intellectual justification for not holding blacks accountable to the same moral standards as whites. That is why a leading liberal such as Professor Derrick Bell, formerly of Harvard Law School, could have claimed that Justice Clarence Thomas "doesn't think like a black."[33]

THE SECULARIZATION OF SOCIETY

Liberalism also contributed to the Los Angeles riots because of its relentless attempts, both philosophical and political, to secularize society. It was coincidental but fitting that two days after the rioting ended, the California Supreme Court handed down a ruling that to be a member of the Boy Scouts of America one need not be required to mention God in the Boy Scout oath. It was another victorious liberal attempt to remove God from everywhere but the church or synagogue.

The riots and this radical secularization of America are related. To the best of my knowledge, no churchgoing black torched any buildings or beat anyone in the Los Angeles riots, and the centers of black resistance to rioting were the churches in South Central Los Angeles. Moreover, three of the four black heroes who rescued Reginald Denny identified themselves as Christians.

For years on my radio show, I have posed one question to those who dismiss religion in America as morally irrelevant: "Imagine it's midnight, and you are walking in a very bad area of the city. You're alone in a dark alley, and all of a sudden you notice that ten men are walking toward you. Would you or would you not be relieved to know that they had just attended a Bible class?"

Even as a Jew, let alone as an American, I greatly fear a post-

[33]*Wall Street Journal*, July 17, 1991.

Christian America. It is symbolized in American youths' lives by the difference between the Boy Scouts and Kurt Cobain. In black life, it is symbolized by the difference between Martin Luther King and Leonard Jeffries.

Liberal activists yearn for a post-Christian America, but this Jew believes that in the Los Angeles riots we saw a preview of what such an America would look like.

WHAT IS TO BE DONE?

As already noted, this indictment of liberalism's role in the Los Angeles riots and in the deterioration of black life is not meant as a partisan defense of Republicans or conservatives. Neither Republicans nor Democrats can be proud of their record vis-à-vis blacks. Republicans ignore blacks and Democrats infantilize them. In recent years, the Republican attitude has been less harmful, but still not praiseworthy.

We need solutions without partisanship. Here are some brief suggestions.

Honesty

At the time of the riots, the Los Angeles NAACP described the Los Angeles City Council, which has left-leaning liberals on it, as a white racist group because it failed to appoint a black activist to the board of directors of Water and Power. It may be a good omen that one of the most liberal members of the council, Ruth Galanter, attacked the NAACP for its libel. Only when liberals of all races begin to exhibit courage and confront the blacks and whites who racialize all issues and ascribe nearly all black problems to white racism will progress be made.

The greatest problems in black life, as in Jewish life, white life, and American life in general, are internal. In the case of blacks, this is so self-evident that it takes no insight, only courage, to acknowledge it.

Every day that a black or white liberal leader focuses on white racism is another day lost in the battle to rescue the large number of dysfunctional black males.

The obstacles are formidable, and often set up by liberals. For example, recent attempts by blacks to address the unique problems of black males by establishing all-male black schools were stopped by the ACLU and the National Organization for Women, who sued the schools for sexual discrimination.

End Racial Quotas

Legally binding affirmative action, racial quotas, and race norming must end. They demean every black accomplishment.

At the same time, white employers must make major efforts to recruit and train blacks, especially young black males, and laws prohibiting discrimination on the basis of race should be rigorously enforced.

Universal Draft

The United States should institute a universal draft of young men. This will:

- Give society a chance to inculcate social and ethical values in every young black and white male.
- Lessen drug and other criminal activities that involve so many young males.
- Force young blacks and whites to work together.
- Teach trades to those without employable skills.

Draftees can choose among a number of possible services—military or civilian.

ETHICAL MONOTHEISM INSTEAD OF ETHICAL RELATIVISM

One morning, a week after the riots, I did a broadcast at an outdoor shopping center in South Central Los Angeles. While giving a brief talk, which revolved around the thesis that "If you can't call a black thug a thug, you're a racist," I noticed a young black man wearing a Malcolm X T-shirt. He appeared to be very angry with me, and a colleague who had spoken to him verified my suspicion.

After my broadcast, I walked over to the young man and asked what bothered him. "You whites," he responded, "have no right to judge black behavior." Amplifying on this thesis, he stated almost word for word that "whites have their morality and we have ours."

This is part of the harvest we are reaping from multiculturalism. In theory, multiculturalism is something we should all celebrate; unfortunately, in practice, multiculturalism means multimorality. To cite some examples:

- Danny Goldberg, a top officer at Time-Warner and chairman of the Southern California ACLU, said, "What is vile to a Mormon family in Utah is not vile to a black family in South Central Los Angeles."[34] In other words, a Mormon cannot judge any black rap music lyrics as vile, since a black family may not find them vile.

- A liberal feminist, Ellen Snorklen, wrote in the *Los Angeles Times* opinion page in 1992: "Traditional family values is a right-wing euphemism for a white family where Daddy is the boss."[35] In other words, it is "white" to object to out-of-wedlock births and it is sexist to condemn the absence of fathers in black homes.

- A front-page article in the *Los Angeles Times* on black attitudes toward the four black men who beat and almost murdered white truck driver Reginald Denny was headlined: "Denny Suspects Are Thugs to Some, Heroes to Others." The article begins, "Depending on who you ask, they are either vicious gang members who deserve to spend the rest of their lives behind bars, revolutionary soldiers who sounded the first shots of a racial insurrection, or decent young men who are falsely accused."[36] The article implied that it is entirely a matter of opinion: Some people deem it heroic to beat an innocent human being unconscious, and others deem it wrong.[37]

The only antidote to such nihilistic thinking is ethical monotheism, the belief in one universal code of ethics. Differing cultures glorify humanity, but differing moralities destroy it. We must teach what Professor Viktor Frankl concluded after surviving Auschwitz: There are only two races of human beings, the decent and the indecent. That is how the world is divided: not between rich and poor, men and women, North and South, black and white, the powerful and the powerless, or any other nonmoral division that too many contemporary liberals have been advocating.

[34]*Time*, May 7, 1990.
[35]*Los Angeles Times*, May 22, 1992.
[36]*Los Angeles Times*, May 25, 1992.
[37]It is important to recall that Denny's life was saved by four heroic blacks. But far more press attention was paid to the four black thugs than to the four black saints.

"Dinners with a Difference"

A white man once called my radio show to tell me that as a result of being mugged by a black man, he was experiencing racist feelings against blacks.

I asked him one question: "Do you have any black friends?"

"No," he replied.

"I knew it," I told him, "because if you had any black friends, you wouldn't be able to generalize about blacks, any more than you would condemn all whites if a white had robbed you."

The best way to combat racism is to have blacks and whites relate to one another as individuals, rather than as racial abstractions.

To combat racism, I have begun a program of "Dinners with a Difference." In this program, people of every different race, ethnicity, and religion will have reciprocal dinners at one another's homes. This is no panacea, but if it catches on nationally, it can make a significant impact on how members of different races and religions view one another. It becomes much harder to make a nasty generalization about another group after you have spent time in the home of one of its members.

EPILOGUE: BODY BLOWS TO AMERICA

There has been, I believe, a profound naïveté on the part of liberals with regard to civilization. As a Jew, I am particularly aware of the fragility of civilization. I know that the people who gave us Bach, Beethoven, and Schiller also gave us Auschwitz. No matter how highly developed a civilization may be, there is always a thin line dividing it from the possibilities of an Auschwitz or a Gulag Archipelago.

Those who do not recognize this fragility think that they can constantly attack the moral credibility of a decent society without weakening it. They think that they can ceaselessly attack its character-building institutions—such as the Boy Scouts, organized religion, and the nuclear family—without weakening society, but they are wrong.

Whenever I hear denunciations of "oppressive sexist, racist America," I recall the sobering warning of the eminent historian Walter Laqueur. Responding to the excesses of 1960s radicals,

Laqueur wrote an article he called, "The Tucholsky Complaint." During the Weimar Republic (1918–33), Kurt Tucholsky was "the leading spirit" of German left-wing intellectual circles. Tucholsky and the German leftists constantly railed against the Weimar democracy, which they denounced as "a facade and a lie."

Laqueur continued:

> In some American circles the Tucholsky Syndrome has been rapidly spreading . . . A radical force has come into being even more emphatic in its rejection of America, its way of life and the aspirations of most of its citizens. . . . Its more extreme members are firmly convinced that fascism has already prevailed . . . that American policemen are more vicious than the *Gestapo*. . . .

And he concluded:

> Tucholsky and his friends thought that the German Judge of their day was the most evil person imaginable and that the German prisons were the most inhumane; later they got [Nazi judge] Freisler and Auschwitz. . . . They sincerely believed that fascism was already ruling Germany, until the horrors of the Third Reich overtook them. . . . [38]

Of course most liberals do not think this way about America, and of course the Weimar democracy was far weaker than the American democracy. But there is just so much beating that American society and institutions can take. There are just so many times that the elite of a society can declare that it is racist, sexist, and oppressive, and that it wishes to commit genocide against one of its races. And it can survive just so many excuses for the evil behavior of the barbarians within it.

America has taken a body blow. The smoke rising near my home made me aware of that. For the first time in my life, I feared for this country. The tragedy, and the irony, is that many of the people delivering these blows to the greatest, most liberal, democracy in history are often called liberals.

[38]Walter Laqueur, "The Tucholsky Complaint," in *Out of the Ruins of Europe* (Library Press, 1971).

THE STRUGGLE
FOR AMERICA'S SOUL

23

THOUGHTS ON
CALLING AMERICA RACIST

It may not be a great film, but all Americans should see *Gettysburg*. It tells the story of the battle at Gettysburg, Pennsylvania, the battle that cost the most lives in the Civil War.

When I returned home, I looked up how many Union soldiers were killed in the Civil War, not because the Confederacy's losses were not tragic, but because I agree with the values for which the Union was fighting, specifically the abolition of slavery. The number killed on the Union side was 360,000. Three hundred and sixty thousand Americans died to free four million slaves. This is an impressive figure.

I cite this figure because there is a need for Americans of all races to be aware of a fact that it is not politically correct to note: Many white Americans were killed or maimed to end slavery.

It is fashionable to call America racist, and to label it as always having been racist. At its founding, the country certainly was racist, as was every other society in the world. But, if there is an afterlife, those who blanketly label the country racist since its founding should be prepared to make this charge when they meet those young Americans who were slaughtered to end slavery. I would like them to also be prepared to look at these men's orphans and say, "Your dad got his limbs blown off to end slavery, but it doesn't mean a damn thing to me because white Americans have always been racist, and are so today."

I am increasingly impatient with the libel that America is racist. Yes, there are racists in America—of all colors, I might add—and racism is the most despicable belief a human being can hold.

But knowledge of history should restrain one from making unfair generalizations.

Some of *Gettysburg's* powerful monologues—which I checked in the *Oxford History of the Civil War*—were historically quite accurate.

Many of these soldiers volunteered, and were prepared to die for the Union, because they believed first and foremost that slavery was wrong. Of course, they also believed in the indivisibility of the United States of America. But, as one of the film's monologues points out, these men also believed that America had fashioned an entirely new view of humanity: namely, that who you are is more important than who your father was. This was an utterly novel idea in a world in which family background and ethnicity had always been more important than the individual. This has been the Great American Challenge: to consider the individual, not the group, as primary.

But it would seem that this American ideal hasn't been passed on successfully to many in our generation. During the last few decades Americans have done a poor job of transmitting to the next generation what it is that renders America distinctive. Unlike other countries, the United States is more an idea than a place, ethnicity, or race. Unfortunately, most American young people today cannot answer, "What is America for? What is it about? Why was it founded? Why is it different?"

They can't answer these questions because they haven't been taught an answer.

Our public schools no longer teach what makes America distinctive. They have a Gay Pride Month in the Los Angeles Unified School District, but they don't have an American Pride Month. My point has nothing to do with gays and everything to do with the fact that we celebrate just about every group except Americans. It's well and good that we all have pride in our particular group (symbolized by St. Patrick's Day, Salute to Israel Day, and Black Pride Month), but if we're only a collection of diverse groups, then America is no longer an idea but only a geographical entity.

That is what "multiculturalism" has become—a denial of Americanness and the American idea. This frightens me because the older I get, the more I appreciate how unique America and the American idea are.

These were some of my thoughts on seeing a film that reminded me how many white Americans died to liberate black Americans.

POSTSCRIPT

My friend Joseph Telushkin makes the telling point that when you are angry at a friend, even if your anger is justified, it is foolish to go on and on making the person feeling guilty. At a certain point, the friend, who might well have atoned for his error, will stop feeling guilty and start feeling fury at you.

Now, if it is angering to provoke guilt in friends who really have done something wrong, imagine how much more angering it is to invoke guilt in people who are neither your personal friends nor guilty.

I am referring specifically to the constant labeling of white Americans as "racist."

The blacks who call my radio show and tell me that I cannot fully appreciate what it is to be black are absolutely correct. Of course I can't. My God, I can't fully appreciate what it is to be the closest person in the world to me, my wife. One can't fully appreciate what it means to be any other person. Clearly, groups have different experiences and memories that shape their members' consciousness.

But now let me turn the tables and say to black listeners that you cannot understand what it is like, for one who is an essentially good person, to be told, often, how bad you are. You don't realize the demoralizing and infuriating effect that the daily volume of criticism, "You're a racist, you're an oppressor," has had over the course of a generation. Do not believe those whites who say to you, "We know you're right. We are oppressors, we are racists." They only speak for themselves and their own racism; and they patronize you.

If a black correctly resents being lumped together with criminals, why would a white not resent being lumped together with racists? Could somebody please explain why it has become acceptable for black leaders to lump all whites with white racists while it has remained unacceptable to lump all blacks with black criminals?

24

PSYCHOLOGY AND
THE DENIAL OF EVIL

If asked what aspect of reality most people deny, most of us probably would respond "death," as did Ernest Becker in his classic *The
Denial of Death*. Our mortality, we believe, is the toughest of all
realities to confront.

Yet I am convinced that there is a reality as significant as death
that is even more widely denied: evil, particularly the realization
that evil emanates from *within* human beings. People want to
believe that evil comes from an external source.

Attempts to ascribe evil to sources outside human beings can
be found in almost every culture. In the Western world, Christians
have often blamed evil on the devil (thus the expression, "The devil
made me do it") or on the "original sin" of Adam and Eve. But
rooted as Christianity is in Judaism, which ascribes evil overwhelmingly to human nature, Western civilization has generally
accepted that there are evil people and that they are responsible for
their evil behavior. The Western world has long adopted the view
that Genesis attributes to God, "The tendency of man's heart is evil
from his youth" (8:21). This verse does not mean that the Bible
believes that man is essentially evil, just that human beings have a
strong innate attraction to evil.

However, in the eighteenth century, when religion began to lose
its influence, the belief that people were responsible for the evil
they commit evil also began to wane. To this day, virtually every

worldview rooted in a secular outlook denies that evil emanates from human nature.

What until recently was the most influential secular idea, Marxism, is based upon the rejection of man as the source of evil. This was an essential component of Marxism's appeal. Evil, Marx and Engels taught, is caused by socioeconomic forces, not by human nature.

The common thread running through most secular ideologies has been the focus on forces outside man as the sources of evil. The list of external forces held responsible for human evil is nearly endless—nationalism, religion, money, television, weapons, corruption in government.

The only good thing to be said about these attitudes is that at least they acknowledge evil's existence. In our time, there has been a two-pronged attack on the belief in evil's very existence.

The first was moral relativism. As historian Paul Johnson has noted, the West has applied Einstein's theory of relativity in physics to good and evil, creating moral relativism: "Everything is relative" has come to encompass morality, a particularly sad irony given that Einstein himself strongly affirmed universal standards of morality.

The second attack often emanates from the world of psychology. Although psychology has invaluable insights and is capable of massively helping humanity, it is now commonly used to deny evil. Good has been replaced by "healthy" and evil by "sick."

Psychological terms that deny evil are even applied to national behavior. When the Soviet Union shot down a Korean civilian airplane in 1983, an editorial in *Psychology Today* opposed describing the Soviet action as evil or aggressive. Rather, the author, a professor of psychology, wrote, it must be understood in psychological terms as an "act of paranoia."

Both California and Los Angeles have official task forces on developing self-esteem as a way to prevent antisocial behavior (I was a member of the Los Angeles task force). The underlying assumption behind the establishment of these groups is that psychopathology explains violent behavior.

This is wrong.

First, acts of violence can sometimes be moral and psychologically healthy. The Allied soldiers who killed German soldiers to liberate Nazi death camps were engaged in morally virtuous acts, and their desire to inflict violence on Nazis strikes me as quite healthy. So, too, a woman who uses necessary violence to stop an abusive husband is engaged in a considerably healthier response than a woman who submits to repeated violence.

Second, violence that is immoral is not necessarily psychopathological. Society may take it for granted that a person who rapes, mugs, or murders is sick. But why? As incredible as it may sound, *it is quite possible to murder or rape and not be sick*. It is time to announce loudly, clearly, and repeatedly that such acts may be normal—but evil. In *The Politics of Experience*, psychiatrist R. D. Laing made this point very effectively: "Normal men have killed perhaps 100,000,000 of their fellow normal men in the last fifty years."

Why should we think that murder is necessarily sick? Is it sick for a criminal to murder a witness to the crime or is it simply evil?

And why is rape necessarily sick? Polls of male college students have revealed that about half of them could see themselves forcing a woman on a date to have sex if they were certain that they would not be punished. Is the implication, then, that about half of America's college men are sick? I'm more inclined to think that they suffer from pitifully weak moral values rather than mental illness.

Of course, in some cases, such as the rape of little girls and elderly women, rape is far more than an expression of an uncontrolled sexual urge; it is also pathological. But what about date-rape? What about all the soldiers who rape because they hunger for a woman's body and know that they won't be punished? Aren't these examples of men who let their libidos dominate their consciences, rather than expressions of psychopathology?

Finally, why is good behavior necessarily psychologically normal? Was a non-Jew who risked his life to save a Jew during the Holocaust acting "normally"? Such an action was noble, but by what criterion was this behavior "normal"?

Evil behavior, in sum, is not necessarily sick. Until we face the uncomfortable reality that evil stems far more from within our nature than from forces outside us or from psychopathology, there is no hope for making a better world.

25

CAPITAL PUNISHMENT:
A RORSCHACH TEST

In America today, I believe that opposition to the death penalty reveals more about people than do their views on almost any other contentious issue.

When two individuals differ about abortion, their positions do not necessarily reflect anything more than their differing understanding of when life begins. So, too, opinions, about welfare, gay rights, national health insurance, and a host of other controversial issues may reveal little more than individual views on those particular issues.

But I believe that opposition to capital punishment is revealing. With regard to almost every other controversial issue, I am able to understand and even empathize with people with whom I disagree. Although I agree fully with neither the pro-life nor the pro-choice movements, I appreciate the motivations of both. While I often disagree with feminist groups, I strongly support the goal of sexual equality. Although I believe that society should promote heterosexual marital sex as its sexual ideal, I certainly can understand why homosexuals would feel otherwise.

But a person who believes that putting Adolf Eichmann or Charles Manson to death is an immoral act thinks so differently from those of us who support the death penalty for murderers that the philosophical gulf between us may be unbridgeable. The belief that every person who premeditatedly murders another deserves to live seems to me so unjust, so cruel to the victim and to those who loved the victim, and such a denial of the decent human instinct of just retribution, that this position needs to be analyzed as much as it needs to be refuted.

I am convinced, nevertheless, that when the case for capital punishment is articulately made, its appeal to logic, morality, and our highest emotions will be convincing to most people, including some who now oppose the death penalty. In this belief, I offer arguments on behalf of the death penalty, and responses to arguments against it. I conclude by explaining why I believe that opposition to capital punishment is often a Rorschach test revealing a person's other values and attitudes.

ARGUMENTS FOR CAPITAL PUNISHMENT

It Is the Only Just Response to Murder

I assume that nearly all people would deem it terribly unfair if I were to steal my neighbor's car and be allowed to go on using my car while he is deprived of his. Why does this fundamental tenet of fairness not hold true concerning life? On grounds of justice and fairness alone, why should I be allowed to keep my life after I have deliberately taken someone else's away?

Does it at all disturb opponents of capital punishment that while a little girl or a Robert F. Kennedy lies dead, their murderers eat, laugh, hope, make friends, play, and even search for love (yes, search for love; some murderers marry while in prison).

For a moment, disregard the issue of capital punishment and consider only the issue of what is *deserved*. Do opponents of capital punishment believe that all murderers *deserve* to go on living? Do they really feel that Adolf Eichmann, Idi Amin, and the Hillside Strangler *deserve* to live out their days?

Opponents of capital punishment might respond that many such murderers truly do not deserve to continue living, but capital punishment is still wrong for a host of other reasons. I will address each of those reasons. For now, all I ask is that opponents of capital punishment acknowledge the injustice of allowing those who rob others of life to retain their own.

It Is the Only Compassionate Response to Murder

In the large majority of instances, relatives and friends of murder victims suffer enduring and terrible pain knowing that the murderer of their loved one continues to live.

Were a family member or friend murdered, the thought that the killer would be allowed to live out his or her days—in prison, or even worse, free on parole—would cause me terrible, and permanent, pain. And if I were the victim and could speak from my premature grave, I would cry out for my killer's death. As I write these words, I am filled with anger at the thought that although I could never again see my children, be with my wife, see a sunrise, read a book, or talk with my friends, *my murderer could do every one of those things*.

Compassion, as much as justice, dictates the death penalty for murder.

It Is the Only Way to Declare Murder Evil

Society expresses its attitude toward any crime *solely* by the punishment it metes out. A society such as ours that generally punishes murder with a few years in prison does not deem murder particularly terrible. *Imprisonment for murder declares murder a lesser evil than does the death penalty.*

It May Deter Other Murders

Most of us who support the death penalty do so for reasons having little or nothing to do with its deterrent value. If it were proven that capital punishment didn't deter a single murder, I would still be passionately pro–capital punishment.

But of course such proof is impossible. I am well aware of the famous old argument that in Britain, at the very moment of a public hanging of a pickpocket, pickpockets would be busy plying their trade. This, however, only proves that some people are not deterred by the death penalty, not that nobody is. Of course some people will murder even when there is a death penalty, but this in no way answers the question of whether the death penalty deters *anyone*; it only demonstrates that it doesn't deter *everyone*.

Since, by definition, deterrence is not perfectly measurable (it is impossible to precisely measure what people *would* do), we have to use common sense—just as we do with regard to prison terms. Whether or not there are data to prove that long prison terms deter more than short prison terms, no one assumes that long prison terms are useless in terms of deterrence. Doesn't common sense suggest therefore that if the death penalty were given to most murderers, this might deter some people from murdering? Isn't it absurd to assume that long prison sentences deter some criminals, but that the death penalty does not?

THE BIBLE UNAMBIGUOUSLY DEMANDS IT

That the Bible unambiguously demands the death penalty for murder may be irrelevant to secular opponents of capital punishment. But to those who claim to hold the Bible sacred, its passion on this subject ought to be relevant. It is therefore surprising that many religious people oppose the death penalty—often in the name of religion.

Religious Jews or Christians who oppose capital punishment should be able to say forthrightly, "While the Bible demands the execution of premeditated murderers, I believe that this position is no longer valid." What that person should not do is claim that a position that is diametrically opposed to the Bible is rooted in it.

Very few commandments in the Torah are demanded of all people, not only of Jews. One of these is the death penalty for murderers. The commandment to put murderers to death is listed in Genesis, *prior* to the existence of the Jews: "*Whoever* sheds the blood of man, by man shall his blood be shed, for in His image did God make humankind" (Genesis 9:6).

Indeed, the Hebrew Bible considers capital punishment so essential to creating civilized society that it is *the second commandment God gives to mankind* (the first is to be fruitful and multiply).

Capital punishment for murder is understood as necessary for preserving the sanctity of human life. Precisely because the human being is created in God's image, anyone who intentionally takes the life of a human being loses the right to life. Any lesser penalty means that the taking of life is not considered the horrible offense that it is.

Genesis adds another critical element: It is human beings, not God, who are to execute murderers. It is as if Genesis had foreseen the argument that "only God can take life." It makes it as clear as possible that such a view must be rejected: "By *man* shall his [the murderer's] blood be shed."

So important is capital punishment for murder that it is listed in all five books of the Torah. *It is the only law in the Torah repeated in each of its books.*

Exodus 21:12: "He who fatally strikes a man shall be put to death."

Leviticus 24:17: "If anyone slays a human being, he shall be put to death."

Numbers 35:31: "And you shall not take reparation for the soul of a murderer who deserves to die, but he shall be put to death." This verse makes it clear that "a life for a life," unlike "eye for an eye" and "tooth for a tooth," is meant literally. All other crimes are compensable by monetary payments.

Deuteronomy 19:20 adds the commonsensical notion that the death penalty is necessary "so that people shall hear and be afraid." Twice (19:19, and 24:7) it appends, "And you shall burn out the evil from your midst," to its demands for capital punishment. As the quintessential doer of evil, the murderer cannot be allowed to continue to live in your midst.

The Bible feels so strongly about capital punishment that it decrees that "You shall take a murderer from my very altar to die" (Exodus 21:14). Murderers cannot claim sanctuary, because it desecrates God to have a murderer seeking to live by invoking God's sanctuary.

In Judaism, the Bible is not the only source of law: The Talmud carries almost equal weight, and Jewish opponents of the death penalty frequently cite the famous Talmudic statement that any Jewish court that sentenced one man to death every seven years— one rabbi said, even every seventy years—was known as a killer court (Makkot 1:10).

Yet on the very same page of the Talmud, another rabbi dismisses this view, noting that had the Jews lived by such sentiments, bloodshed would have increased in Israel. In other words, there was rabbinic doubt on this issue.

Moreover, at the time this was written, Jews had neither a state nor the political power to put these views into practice. But, as the authoritative *Encyclopedia Judaica* notes, when "the Sanhedrin [the Jewish High Court] had power to inflict the death sentence . . . they exercised it." The rabbis' tendency was to make it exceedingly difficult to administer capital punishment, but the Talmud notes that in times of great violence, capital punishment should be restored to wide use. It would appear, therefore, that the rabbis who made capital punishment difficult to administer were thinking in terms of a state in which murder was extremely rare. Their thinking, however, was not intended to apply to a state in which murder was common, as is the case in America today.

ARGUMENTS AGAINST CAPITAL PUNISHMENT

An Innocent Person May Be Executed

That an innocent person may be executed is the one moral argument against capital punishment. Nonetheless, the remote possibility of an innocent person's execution does not invalidate the death penalty. For one thing, judicial and technological safeguards (e.g., DNA testing) could be erected so as to make this all but impossible. Some safeguards may not now be strong enough. For example, in instances in which conviction is based on a single witness with no other corroborating evidence such as fingerprints, hair samples, etc., a person should not be sentenced to death. But even with the best of safeguards, an innocent person might still be executed, and that is a horror.

Still, *far more innocent people will be murdered if there is no death penalty than if there is*. Murderers who are not executed will murder other prisoners and prison guards, or they will escape or be released on parole and murder civilians outside prison.

Our choice is clear—either the remote *possibility* of an innocent person being executed if there is a death penalty, or the *certainty* of many more innocents murdered without a death penalty. Nothing is risk-free—from driving an automobile (in which some forty thousand Americans die each year) to the death penalty. The issue is: Can we minimize the risk so it becomes almost nonexistent?

The argument that an innocent person may be executed is the argument opponents most often offer, because it is the one moral argument against capital punishment, and because of that it appeals to people who are otherwise for executing murderers. Yet opponents of the death penalty are opposed to executing a murderer even when his guilt is indisputable, such as a Charles Manson or an Adolf Eichmann. They use the argument that an innocent might be executed because of its debating value; in fact, opponents oppose capital punishment because they think it is wrong to kill murderers, period.

The Death Penalty Doesn't Accomplish Anything:
The Dead Person Cannot Be Brought Back to Life

The first part of this argument isn't true, and the second mocks the intent of capital punishment. No one believes that capital punishment brings the dead back to life, although even if it did, I wonder how many abolitionists would come to favor the death penalty.

But while it cannot revive the dead, capital punishment does revive the spirit of the dead person's loved ones. I have followed news reports of executions for ten years, and in *the large majority of instances*, the murdered person's loved ones express immense relief after the murderer is executed—"Finally, we can rest." As long as a murderer lives, there can be no closure; and until there is closure, healing cannot begin. Every day that a murderer is allowed to live, not to mention allowed his freedom, compounds the suffering of the victims' loved ones.

Capital Punishment Is State Murder

As William F. Buckley Jr. has argued, if capital punishment is state murder, then imprisonment is state kidnapping.

Many opponents of capital punishment claim not to grasp the moral distinction between the murder of an innocent person and the execution of a murderer. This reductionist mode of thinking (moral equivalence) has come to dominate opposition to capital punishment. Thus, the head of Amnesty International-USA has called the United States "a serial killer" because it executes murderers.

To put it succinctly, this claim that the murder of an innocent and the execution of the murderer are morally equivalent because they both involve taking a life is as morally perverse as a claim that rape and lovemaking are morally equivalent because both involve sexual intercourse. (That some prominent radical feminists, such as Andrea Dworkin, make such a claim doesn't diminish its moral perversity, it only illustrates the prevalence of moral equivalence and moral illiteracy in our time.)

Capital Punishment Doesn't Deter

This is probably not true. Statistics are inconclusive, and only if there were a prolonged, fair, speedy, and widespread use of capital punishment would we be in a position to assess whether it does deter. In the meantime, we have to use common sense, which strongly suggests that the death penalty does deter. Since other punishments deter other crimes, why wouldn't capital punishment deter murder?

Moreover, before one accepts the claim that capital punishment does not deter, consider the experiment proposed by Ernest van den Haag: Let society mandate the death sentence for murders committed on Mondays, Wednesdays, and Fridays, and life imprisonment for murders committed on the other days of the week. In a short while we could see if murders continue to be committed equally on all days of the week.

Capital Punishment Is Simply Societal Revenge

The oft-repeated labeling of capital punishment as "revenge" is an emotional appeal to all those who consider "revenge" a dirty word.

But the argument is only that—emotional. All punishments have an element of revenge. What is life imprisonment for murder if not partially revenge? Are we really "protecting society" when we keep in prison a seventy-year-old man who committed a murder forty-five years earlier? Isn't this "revenge"?

There are two types of revenge, just and unjust. Just revenge is punishment; unjust revenge (e.g., the death penalty for robbery) is what is usually meant when we speak of revenge.

The human predilection for unjust revenge must not be allowed to express itself; that is evil. But the human desire to see that the hurt a person has deliberately inflicted upon another person be returned to him or her only reflects a good and healthy desire for justice.

Nor does the oft-cited citation from the New Testament (Romans 12:19, based on Deuteronomy 32:35), "'Vengeance is Mine, I will repay,' says the Lord," apply to capital punishment. Indeed, in the very next chapter of Romans, Paul writes, "The ruler bears not the sword in vain: for he is the minister of God, a revenger to execute wrath upon him that doeth evil."

Blacks Are Disproportionately Executed

This argument is not true. Murderers who are *poor* are disproportionately executed, because expensive lawyers are better at manipulating the judicial process. But while we would want wealthy murderers also executed, the argument that poor murderers are disproportionately executed is irrelevant to the question of whether capital punishment should be retained.

If a punishment is unequally meted out, the solution is to mete out the punishment equally, not to drop it. Murderers from all racial, ethnic, and economic backgrounds should be equally liable to capital punishment. Nonetheless, as Ernest van den Haag, America's most eloquent defender of the death sentence, writes, "Unequal justice is preferable to equal injustice."

If We Executed Most Murderers, There Would Be a Bloodbath

There already is a bloodbath in America, except that almost all the blood is that of innocent people.

Other Western Societies Do Not Have Capital Punishment

Other Western democracies do not have capital punishment because the death penalty is less necessary where there are very few murders. But in the United States, to cite just one example, more black Americans are murdered in any two-year period than died during the ten years of the Vietnam War. There is a war taking place in American society (which is not the case in the other Western democracies), but only the evil side is allowed to kill. If there were murder on a scale such as America's in other Western countries, they, too, would have capital punishment. Problems unique to a specific society call for unique approaches. Because of terrorism in Northern Ireland, Britain enforced certain laws there that other democracies do not allow.

CONCLUSION

The Death Penalty as Rorschach Test

I began this chapter by calling one's attitude toward capital punishment a Rorschach test: the stronger one's opposition to the death penalty, the more that says about a person's stances on some of life's most fundamental questions. I do not mean this as an ad hominem attack on all opponents of capital punishment. Some very fine people oppose capital punishment. Yet, if all I know about a person is that he or she actively opposes the death penalty, I am hesitant to trust the person's judgment on other moral issues because the person's real reasons for opposition to capital punishment rarely are the ones offered. This can be easily shown.

The argument that an innocent person may be executed is not the reason most people who oppose capital punishment do so; even when there is no doubt about a person's guilt, they oppose it.

Likewise, the argument that poor murderers and murderers of white people are disproportionately executed is not the reason for opposition. Were capital punishment dispensed utterly equitably, opponents would still oppose the death penalty.

Nor is the argument that the death penalty does not deter the primary reason for opposition. Were it shown beyond reasonable doubt that capital punishment did deter, few opponents would change their minds.

Ernest van den Haag notes that in debate with America's leading opponents of the death penalty—former attorney general Ramsey Clark; Henry Schwarzchild, director of the anti–capital punishment project for the ACLU; Professor Charles Black of Yale; and others—all of them "admitted that if they had the choice, *they would rather see 500 innocents murdered than execute one convict found guilty of murder.*" This incredible admission further proves that the arguments offered by most opponents of capital punishment are rarely the real reasons for their opposition. What, then, are those reasons?

I believe that they have to do with one's ability to recognize evil and to be willing to confront it. That is why I suspect that the more vociferous a person is in opposing capital punishment, the more vociferous that person probably was in opposing Ronald Reagan's characterization of the Soviet Union as an "evil empire." The denial that people are the primary cause of evil, that some people are evil, and that they must be fought might be the strongest denial mechanism operating in the world today.

This denial of evil accounts for another major belief of most opponents of capital punishment—the moral equation of capital punishment with murder. As John P. Conrad, the eloquent opponent of the death penalty chosen to debate Ernest van den Haag

(*The Death Penalty: A Debate*, Plenum, 1983) wrote: "To kill the offender is to respond to his wrong by doing the same wrong to him."

This doctrine of moral equivalence, whether of the United States and the Soviet Union, Western values and all other value systems, or of murder and capital punishment, is the contemporary expression of the denial of evil. Nothing is morally better or worse; no one is morally better or worse (except those who believe that some people are morally worse).

Whatever people's reasons for not fighting the greatest evils, one terrible consequence is that these people often end up fighting those who do fight evil. The Midrash, a compilation of ancient rabbinic reflections, summed up the problem very concisely: "Those who are merciful when they must be cruel, will, in the end, be cruel to those who deserve mercy." Whether they intend it or not, activists against capital punishment direct their compassion toward those who commit the greatest evil man can commit. And that misdirected compassion inevitably expresses itself in misdirected cruelty—toward society at large and, especially, toward the bereaved who yearn to see justice done.

26

—

THE CASE FOR SCHOOL CHOICE

On Election Day, 1993, California voters had an opportunity to improve American life by enabling poor and middle-class parents to enjoy an option that wealthy parents already have: send their children to a private school. An initiative would have given California parents a $2,600 voucher that the parents could then give to any school that accepted their child.

The measure was defeated largely because of organized liberal opposition to vouchers.

For three reasons, I find this opposition unbecoming of liberals.

First, analyses showed that poor people across the country tended to support the voucher initiative more strongly than did the affluent; in fact, its leading proponent nationally was an inner-city black woman, Polly Williams of Milwaukee. Inner-city and other lower- and middle-class support for vouchers should make liberals at least question their instinctive opposition to vouchers. It won't, however, because, in the area of education, liberalism has identified with teachers unions more than with personal choice and effective education.

Second, it is remarkable that the people who are most pro-choice when it comes to extinguishing nascent human life—and support the use of public funds to enable that choice—are usually the same people who are most anti-choice when it comes to providing poor people with the ability to send their children to a private school. The liberal position is that society should give people money to have an abortion because the vast majority of people will make a wise and moral decision, but we should not give people money to enable them to choose a school for their children because many people will not make a wise decision.

The question is: Why do liberals believe that people are far wiser in deciding whether to have an abortion than in deciding whether to send their child to public school? Isn't the first a more morally complex issue?

Third, when affluent people who send their children to private schools oppose giving that opportunity to poorer people, it probably connotes a disdain for people of lower economic class—we are smarter than they are. As for the many urban public school teachers who oppose vouchers, yet send *their* children to private schools—*40 percent of them*, according to the president of the National Education Association (NEA)—the only fair description of this behavior is hypocrisy.

THE ANTIVOUCHER CAMPAIGN

Non-Californians did not see or hear the advertised arguments against vouchers. These ads, to put it gently, reflected poorly on the ethical state of educators, whose associations sponsored most of the antivoucher advertisements. Californians were repeatedly warned that witches and David Koresh–types of religious fanatics would start schools as a result of people having school vouchers. Of course, witches and David Koresh–types can start schools even without vouchers, but they haven't because almost no American parents would send their children to such schools.

The contempt that these ads displayed toward American parents—implying that if parents only had a little more money, many would send their children to schools sponsored by fanatics—was remarkable. But what the educators really feared was not that parents with vouchers would choose witches' private schools, but that they would choose good private schools.

The opposition to vouchers was largely about power and money. The NEA and California Teachers Association (CTA) spent fifteen million dollars to prevent giving vouchers to the middle class and poor because they would reduce the power of the NEA, one of America's wealthiest and most powerful interest groups. It is also the largest donor to the Democratic Party; one out of every eight delegates to the last Democratic National Convention was a teacher; and teachers represented 40 percent of the delegates needed for the Democratic nomination (*Wall Street Journal*, October 6, 1993).

WILL CHOICE DESTROY PUBLIC SCHOOLS?

The major argument against school choice is that it will "destroy the public schools."

It is not true.

First, good public schools will continue to prosper. Parents will not remove their children from good public schools—and many parents are quite satisfied with their local public schools—and put them in schools that have no equivalent track record for excellence.

Second, while school choice will mean that some public schools will close, it will also mean that many public schools will become better. There is a simple rule in life: *Excellence is almost impossible without competition.* Years ago, Detroit auto makers fought the same battle the NEA is now waging—they tried to "protect" people from choice among cars, by not letting the Japanese have equal access to the American market. But thanks to Japanese competition, American auto makers now make better cars than ever.

Third, to the extent that the NEA and CTA really believe that choice will "destroy the public schools," this only reveals what these organizations really think of public schools—that the moment American parents actually have a choice, they will flee the public schools. This is an admission of failure that, if true, is the single best argument for vouchers. Think about what the NEA argument would sound like if it were actually presented with its implications spelled out: "Don't empower poorer Americans to choose because if they have this power, they won't choose *our* product."

The same holds true for the argument that public schools will be left with only the problem students. If all the "non–problem" students leave the public schools, it means that there is something better for them, and that is good for both these students and society. While we have a moral obligation to educate the least capable student, we also owe it to society and its future to give the best possible education to the most capable young people.

The argument that all the best students will flee public schools is, in sum, not true; and if true, then the public schools will be able to devote all their resources to the special students who remain in the public schools. Maybe it is not best for anyone that one school try to be all things to all students.

IS MONEY THE PROBLEM?

The Economist, one of the world's most respected news journals, has reported what many of us have long suspected: *There is no relationship between extensive government spending on education and excellence in public education.*

The most telling instance reported in *The Economist* occurred in Kansas City.

> In 1986, district judge [Russell] Clark suggested a radically different remedy [to cure the poor performance of Kansas City public schools]. Instead of forcing the middle classes to send their children to the public schools, Kansas City, Missouri, should bribe them to do so, using heaps of taxpayer money.
>
> To this end, he ordered the city to scrap its existing school system and replace it with the best school system money could buy. So far, the price tag for the experiment has come to $1.3 billion over and above the normal school budget. That is an extra $36,111 for each of the system's 36,000 students.
>
> Both in scope of their programs and in the quality of their physical facilities, Kansas City's schools now match any in the world. An "agribusiness" high school has two greenhouses and laboratories galore; there also is an engineering and an advanced-technology high school.
>
> The range of courses and the variety of teaching methods is mind-boggling. Two elementary schools use Montessori methods. Eleven schools concentrate on international studies, and teach foreign languages through "total immersion." Eight schools concentrate on math and science, six on the visual and performing arts, four on Latin.
>
> The Central High School even boasts a $5 million swimming pool, a six-lane indoor track, a weight-training room, a lavishly equipped gymnasium, and fencing courses taught by the former head of the Soviet Olympic fencing team.

The results?

... the money has done nothing to improve the educational performance of the people it is supposed to benefit: the local black population. The past six years have seen no improvement whatsoever in children's scores in standardized tests of reading and math.

Moreover, the drop-out rate [at the high school level] has risen every year and now stands at a disgraceful 60%.

When public education in America fails, it is rarely due to lack of money, but to many other factors, from the failure of schools to inspire to the failure of homes to motivate.

In light of the Kansas City experiment, consider this front-page *New York Times* report (October 5, 1993) on what happened when civic leaders in Baltimore, tired of the miserable results in its public schools, gave over inner-city schools to a *private, for-profit* educational corporation:

> Baltimore: A year ago, the Harlem Park Community School here seemed to represent the worst of what was wrong in public schools: graffiti covered the halls, crack vials littered the grounds, students did not have enough textbooks and, because the toilets did not work, the children sometimes defecated or urinated in stairwells.
>
> Today, the building is clean, attendance has improved and there are early indications that students are learning faster than expected, and with more enthusiasm. One mother, Pamela Brown, said last week: "A lot of parents say their kids come home singing. Kids are excited about going to school."
>
> The difference: Harlem Park and eight other Baltimore public schools have been taken over by a private company that runs them for profit.

The results are so impressive that even the Baltimore politicians who initially opposed the plan have come to support the privatization program. According to the *Times* article, schools that had feces and urine in their halls now produce children who come home singing about their schoolwork. Accountability works.

WHAT ABOUT RELIGIOUS SCHOOLS?

Ah, but many opponents of school vouchers will respond, what about public funding for religious schools?

This objection would have more credibility if such people had opposed the GI Bill and other public assistance that gave American students the funds with which to attend *any private, including religious*, college. Why is choice with public funds okay for college, but not for high school and elementary school?

Yes, some parents will use the funds to send their children to Catholic, Protestant, or Jewish schools. The prospect delights me. Many of us yearn to see more American kids attending schools that are permitted to post the Ten Commandments in their halls (public schools are forbidden to). That the prospect of more American children attending Christian and Jewish schools frightens many secular liberals is only an example of how deep the fear of religion remains among these people.

Those who voted for vouchers voted for the empowerment of poor parents, the resumption of value-based education, and competition as the best way to improve public education. When I grew up, these were all liberal values.

27

THE TWO GREAT LIES
OF THE TWENTIETH CENTURY

Why has there been so much mass murder and torture in the twentieth century, more than in any previous century?

Most attempts to analyze this phenomenon focus on two factors. One is the rise of the all-powerful state. While strong, centralized governments arose primarily to protect their citizens against domestic and foreign attackers, in the twentieth century, the all-powerful state itself became the attacker.

The second factor is the rise of technology. Modern innovations such as mass transportation, communications, and powerful weapons have made possible the apparatus of mass murder.

More than anything else, however, it is *bad ideas*, specifically two Big Lies, that have made the horrors of the twentieth century possible. Most of the twentieth century's slaughter was caused by two ideologies, Nazism and Communism, each of which was founded on a great lie.

Nazi mass murder was the result of the Lie of the Right.

Communist mass murder was the result of the Lie of the Left.

The Lie of the Right is that race is the most important determinant of human behavior.

The Lie of the Left is that economics is the most important determinant of human behavior.

Each lie denies the one, indeed the *only*, belief that can prevent evil: that *moral* values matter more than anything else and are what most determine an individual's and a society's behavior.

The Lie of the Right enabled the Nazis to view "Aryans," no matter what their behavior, as inherently superior, and Jews, no matter what their behavior, as innately "subhuman." The Lie of the Right has also enabled Nazis and other racists to regard blacks as innately inferior.

The Lie of the Left enabled Communists to hold that an economic class, the proletariat, is innately superior to other classes.

Thus, the Nazis used their lie as justification for murdering Jews, and the Communists used their lie to justify the murder of millions of capitalists and landowning peasants.

The problem today is that while few people—e.g., white supremacists and black Afro-centrists—still believe in the Lie of the Right, vast numbers of people, particularly those who dominate the political and intellectual life of American and other Western societies, still believe in the Lie of the Left.

ECONOMICS AS FAITH

Many of these people believe with a religiouslike fervor in the determinative power of economics. Followers of the Lie of the Left are as fundamentalist in their belief in the saving power of economics as religious fundamentalists are about the saving power of their faiths.

Like all other religious believers, these believers have a credo that encapsulates their faith: "Poverty causes crime." And like other religious credos, this is rooted in faith rather than in empirical facts. They believe that "Poverty causes crime" despite these facts:

- The vast majority of poor people do not engage in criminal behavior.
- Rich individuals are as likely to break the law as poor ones (it is their means that differ—poor people of minimal conscience express their criminality violently; richer people of minimal conscience do it less violently). *If poverty causes crime, affluence causes honesty.* Yet this is obviously preposterous, and the very same people who most argue that poverty causes crime usually believe that the affluent are particularly greedy and corrupt.
- Crime was extremely low during the Great Depression, when

a far larger percentage of Americans was unemployed and experiencing great poverty.

- Few robberies, let alone rapes or murders, are committed to obtain subsistence items such as food or clothing.

None of these facts matters to those who believe the Lie of the Left, any more than the achievements of Jews or blacks matter to believers in the Lie of the Right.

Until "Poverty causes crime" is regarded as foolish and dangerous as the belief that "Race causes crime," there is no hope for the regeneration of American society. As long as prominent politicians, intellectuals, and media leaders continue to believe that economics determines whether people act decently, society will continue to ignore what most determines whether people will hurt other people: values.

It will take a long time for the Lie of the Left to be rejected because the human desire to reject the primacy of values is deep. The reason? As soon as we hold values responsible for human conduct, we must hold people, ourselves included, responsible for the bad that we do.

Only when we blame criminals rather than poverty, and seek answers to society's problems through the inculcation of moral values more than through increased social spending, will we give up the Lie of the Left. But for those who truly believe that poverty causes crime, to reject that belief and come to blame people for their criminal behavior is tantamount to a Christian rejecting belief in Christ.

IDEALISTS CAN BE
VERY DANGEROUS

28

WHY PEOPLE BECOME EXTREMISTS

Everyone knows that "extremism" is a terrible problem. But when people try to define the term, "extremist" often turns out to be little more than a euphemism for "I don't like them," or "They're just too much for my taste." Obviously, that won't do. If extremism really exists, it cannot merely be a subjective dismissal of people who are politically or religiously to the right or left of us.

Therefore, in the belief that extremism need not just be a subjective term of dislike, let me suggest eight characteristics that I believe define extremism and explain why it is so appealing.

1. EXTREMISTS USUALLY BELIEVE IN A GOOD VALUE

A great deal of evil emanates not from selfish or cruel motives, but from *good* motives. This is particularly true regarding extremism. The most important thing to appreciate about extremism is that it is usually based on a good value. One reason it is so difficult to fight extremists successfully is that those of us who oppose them often hold the same decent value that the extremist holds—only more moderately.

2. EXTREMISTS THINK YOU CAN NEVER HAVE TOO MUCH OF THIS GOOD VALUE

What distinguishes extremists from those moderates who share their good value is that *extremists believe that it is impossible to have too much* of that value. Extremists start by affirming a fine value, then draw the understandable, but completely erroneous, conclusion, that there can never be enough of it. The extremist's motto is "More, more."

3. EXTREMISTS DO NOT ACKNOWLEDGE COMPETING GOOD VALUES

Extremists believe that the value they affirm is supreme, and thus higher than even goodness. Extremists do not acknowledge that life has many good values, and that theirs is *only one* of them. Moreover, good values are often in competition with one another. *All* good values need to have the opportunity to be expressed in our lives. When you hold that you cannot have too much of *one* of them, you push other values out of your life.

4. EXTREMISTS IGNORE CONSEQUENCES

To extremists, the values they affirm are so important that they ignore any adverse consequences of their commitment to them.

5. EXTREMISTS CANNOT COMPROMISE

On the rare occasions when extremists do acknowledge that some bad has come from their position, they still won't consider changing course. To change, they believe, is to compromise, and to the extremist, compromise is the road to hell.

6. EXTREMISTS HAVE THE ADVANTAGE OF "PURITY"

Extremists see themselves as purer than the rest of us. Thus, even when we also affirm the importance of their value, but without the same intensity, we are perceived as less pure than they in our commitment. Thus, *we*, not the extremists, are nearly always on the defensive. Compared to them, we are "compromisers," less devoted to the ideal, and therefore less pure.

7. EXTREMISM IS OFTEN A RESPONSE TO EXTREMISM

People who are repulsed by extremists often become extremists themselves because they conclude that the value that fanatics affirm is unworthy. But the denial of any legitimacy to extremists' values is itself usually extremist.

8. EXTREMISM IS MORE COMFORTABLE THAN MODERATION

Nonextreme idealists frequently are plagued by the realization that competing good values almost always exist, and are always assessing the consequences of their commitments to any given value. Extremists have no such problem. They latch on to one good value, feel pure in their unswerving commitment to it, and have little anxiety over the consequences of their position.

Life is filled with moral ambiguities, which the extremist hates. Extremism is a way of leading a simpler life, free from the tensions of competing values and truths.

Take any good value, apply these characteristics, and, presto, you have an extremist.

EXAMPLES OF HOW GOOD VALUES ARE CORRUPTED BY EXTREMISM

Love of Country

Love of one's country is a wonderful value. However, taken to an extreme, it leads to right-wing fanaticism and fascism.

When people hold that there can never be too much patriotism, patriotism displaces other values, most importantly right and wrong. The nationalist zealot does not ask whether and when devotion to country can become immoral because that would imply that something (morality) is above patriotism.

Among its other negative effects, uncritical patriotism often engenders an equally uncritical dismissal of patriotism. Many people are uncomfortable with passionate patriotism because it is the soil in which fascism grew. Instead of creating a morally accountable patriotism, they have dismissed all patriotic sentiments as right-wing buffoonery.

Secular Government: Separation of Church and State

Although this issue is not normally associated with extremism, advocacy of separation of church and state provides an excellent example of a cause in which all the above characteristics may be found, especially:

- Belief in a good value.
- Belief that you can never have enough of the value.
- Failure to acknowledge competing good values.
- The ignoring of consequences.
- An inability to compromise.

Belief in a Good Value

Separation of church and state is an important value; without it, a society would have neither tolerance nor democracy. When a government legislates religion, or allows only one faith (or one form of a religion), both the state and the religion will be corrupted, no matter how good and noble that religion is.

Yet, like patriotism, the good value of secular government can be taken to an extreme. Unfortunately, though, while most people fear patriotic or religious extremists, most people do not even acknowledge the existence of, let alone fear, secular extremists.

You Can Never Have Too Much of Your Value

Regarding separation of church and state, the American Civil Liberties Union is an example of an organization that possesses the characteristics of an extremist movement. Just as religious zealots believe that there can never be too much religion, secular extremists believe that there can never be too much secularism. Thus, the ACLU opposes every public manifestation of religion in America. It opposes invocations in Congress and at high school graduations (that the latter has been upheld by Supreme Court decisions does not diminish the ACLU's secular extremism, it only illustrates how normative this extremism has become); it wants the words "In God we trust" removed from American currency; it advocates that military chaplains no longer be funded; it supports the withdrawal of tax-exempt status from religious institutions; and it wants the oath to God removed from the Boy Scouts. If this is not too much secularization, what would be?

No Acknowledgment of Competing Good Values

Moderates who want secular government acknowledge the existence of competing values, such as the need to raise a generation of citizens with awareness of God and religious moral values. Secular extremists acknowledge no such need.

Extremists Ignore Consequences

The value of church-state separation is more important to them than the consequence to a society of having no public acknowledgment of God- and religion-based ethics. Better that the ship be secular and sink than that it support any religiosity and float.

Extremists Cannot Compromise

Secular extremists seem purer in their idealism than the rest of us who also believe in secular government. Those of us who care about the separation of church and state, but who *also* know how much good Jewish and Christian values and organizations have accomplished, appear as compromisers in comparison to the secular extremists. The moment we say, "Wait, you've gone too far"— since we believe that there is now too *little* reference to God in young people's minds—it appears as if we have weakened our support for the separation of church and state.

Abortion

Both pro-choice and pro-life positions possess extremist characteristics.

Each is based on a good value: Pro-life argues for the sanctity of nascent human life; pro-choice argues that pregnant women have greater rights than fetuses.

It is therefore very difficult to argue against either side without sounding like the other. If you argue with pro-life advocates that abortion sometimes can be morally justified or that abortion is not the moral equivalent of murder, most pro-life advocates will lump you with the opposition. On the other hand, if you argue that most abortions are immoral, since they destroy nascent human life for no good reason—there is, after all, a couple waiting to adopt every newborn child—pro-choice activists depict you as anti–women's rights.

For each side, there is no recognition of a competing value. Pro-lifers recognize no woman's right to choice and no moral differences between a microscopic embryo and a born person; pro-choice advocates recognize no rights for the unborn.

To those who want abortion made illegal, it is morally insignificant that many women will do anything to get an abortion, that many children will be born only to suffer with mothers who will not love and care for them, that some of these fetuses have been diagnosed with terrible diseases, and that in the first weeks of life, a fetus is a microscopic creature with little in common with human beings.

To those who want no restrictions on abortion, it is morally insignificant that over a million abortions take place annually, that virtually none of them has anything to do with saving the mother's life or with preserving her health, and that most abortions are simply acts of birth control.

WHY EXTREMISM IS HERE TO STAY

Given the appeal of extremism, it is very unlikely that it will ever disappear.

One reason is that extremism is self-perpetuating—one extreme breeds the other. Right-wing extremists breed left-wing extremists who in turn breed more right-wing extremists. The czarist government helped breed Communists, while the left in the German Weimar Republic helped engender the Nazi reaction. Every leftist flag-burner in America helps create a right-winger. Every shooting of an abortion doctor breeds another pro-choice activist.

Many people do not realize that the real adversary of extremism is not its opposite, but moderation. That is why people who reject the religious extremism of their youth often become secular extremists rather than religious moderates; and people who are raised in thoroughly secular homes and become religious rarely become moderately religious. Similarly, many Americans who hated the tactics of Senator Joseph McCarthy did not conclude that baseless accusations are wrong, but rather that opposing Communism was wrong.

The major reason for extremism's durability, however, is simply that it is much easier than moderation. Extremists portray themselves as selfless idealists, but the real struggle with oneself takes place among idealistic moderates. It is they who have to constantly wrestle with and weigh competing values. And they don't have at least one major advantage enjoyed by extremists—a community of same-thinking people.

29

MURDER IN THE NAME OF GOD

AN ISLAMIC EXAMPLE

With all the talk about freedom of expression on the one hand and the hurt to Muslim sensitivities on the other, it has been easy to lose sight of the most important—and frightening—aspects of the late Ayatollah Ruhollah Khomeini's 1989 call to Muslims to murder Salman Rushdie for writing *The Satanic Verses*.

First, a renowned religious leader called for the murder of a man who had neither committed nor incited any violence.

Second, a religious leader offered one million dollars to anyone who would commit murder.

Third, even though this call to murder and the offer of payment is an act more representative of the leader of an organized crime syndicate than of a leader of a world religion, millions of Muslims have agreed with it in the name of God.

The Issue Is Murder, not Muslims' Feelings

The call to murder a man must overshadow the hurt feelings of many Muslims, because actions are far more important to God—and should be to people—than feelings.

This is not to say that Muslims' feelings are not important, only that murdering writers is considerably more important. Had Khomeini not made the death threat, and had Muslims vented their anger at the Rushdie book in a nonviolent manner, I, and millions of other non-Muslims, would have listened sympathetically to their anger and pain. And if the book would have been made into a popular film, non-Muslims might have joined with Muslims in peaceful protest just as some of us non-Christians joined Christians in a peaceful protest against *The Last Temptation of Christ*.

But until Iran rescinds the death threat to Salman Rushdie, the moral problem of Muslims' sense of outrage must pale in comparison to the moral problem presented by the Khomeini death threat.

The death threat jeopardizes three of our most precious values—freedom to write anything that does not incite violence, the abolition of the death penalty for all offenses except murder, and the dispensing of punishment only after a fair trial.

Those whose values prevent them from condemning Khomeini's call to murder reject these three foundational values of what we regard as higher civilization. That is why such people merit fear and opposition rather than sympathy.

Muslim Reactions

Well-meaning Jews, Christians, and Muslims who have focused on Muslim pain and rage rather than on the death threat contend that the threat represents only Khomeini and a small minority of Muslims.

I pray that is so. But based on the Muslim responses that I read, on the numerous calls that I received at the time on my radio talk show, and a dialogue I held with a prominent moderate Muslim leader, I was forced to conclude that many Muslims—even among those living in the tolerant West—agreed with the Ayatollah Khomeini's call to murder Salman Rushdie, and that many more do not particularly disagree.

Some evidence:

- "A leading Muslim figure in New Delhi, Syed Abdullah Bukhari, the chief cleric at the city's largest mosque, has endorsed Iran's condemnation of Mr. Rushdie and the calls for his killing" (*New York Times*, February 25, 1989).
- Shahid F. Khalid, secretary of the Islamic Center of Conejo Valley, California, wrote: "Our organization condemns all forms of terrorism including the writing of this book. The civilized world believes that terrorists should be appropriately punished. We feel the same way about this author" (letter published in the *Los Angeles Times*, February 25, 1989).

- Muzammil Siddiqi, director of the Islamic Society of Orange County, California, "asked whether he personally thinks capital punishment would be appropriate in Rushdie's case, was noncommittal. . . . " (*Los Angeles Times,* February 22, 1989).
- In Pakistan, former religious affairs minister Kausar Niazi said, "'The people are after his [Rushdie's] blood. My prediction is that he will be eliminated in the coming few months.' This chilling prediction was repeated *matter-of-factly* today in interviews with other Islamic leaders, some of them regarded as moderate or progressive in their social views" (*New York Times,* February 15, 1989; emphasis added). ·

Perhaps in recognition of the damage done to the good name of Islam, some American Muslim organizations subsequently issued stronger condemnatory statements. The president of the Council of Mosques said, "The Muslim leadership condemns the Khomeini death threats," and the Muslim Political Action Committee on March 7, 1989, said it "rejects any threats or death sentences."

One conclusion, however, seems inescapable: Either there are relatively few moderate Muslim believers, or they are numerous (which I believe) but are very afraid of antagonizing their violence-prone coreligionists. Neither scenario is comforting.

Christian and Jewish Reactions

The relative lack of response among Christian and Jewish religious leaders to the Khomeini death threat was also discouraging for those of us who look to religion for moral guidance.

Just as liberals need to condemn the left for its evils to maintain their moral credibility, so religious people need to condemn religious evil to maintain their moral credibility.

Interestingly, though unfortunately not surprisingly, those Christian leaders who condemned the death threat tended to be religious conservatives. As the *New York Times* reported (February 26, 1989), "Liberals appeared less inclined to give unqualified rejection of the Muslim reaction than were more Conservative Christians." The article cited as examples the contrasting reactions of two prominent Christians, conservative Richard Land, executive director of the Southern Baptist Christian Life Commission, and liberal Harvey Cox, the Harvard theologian.

Cox suggested that writers who protested the Khomeini death

threat "don't really seem to engage the actual hurt and rage of the [Muslim] people." On the other hand, Land "repeatedly said he was 'appalled' by this savage attempt to attack the First Amendment rights of American citizens and by what he considered a weak reaction by President Bush and 'the abject cowardice of the booksellers [who had stopped selling the book].'"

Cox the liberal focused on Muslims' feelings. The conservative focused on the threat to a man's freedom to live and write. The first spoke as a social worker, the second as if he were guarding Western values. He was.

Many Jewish and Christian leaders do not seem to understand the harm done to *their* religions when God's name is attached to evil. The Vatican newspaper's refusal to cite Khomeini by name while dwelling on Muslim sensitivity, and the tepid Jewish religious responses, left it to nonreligious and antireligious figures such as Norman Mailer to lead what should have been a religious protest against the desecration of God's name, not to mention the violation of the Sixth Commandment.

One commentator, Anthony Lewis of the *New York Times*, actually likened the Khomeini death threat to Christian protests against the film *The Last Temptation of Christ*. He was largely alone in finding a moral equivalence between peaceful protest and a death threat (that's what happens when anger [at the Christian right] overwhelms rational inquiry). Virtually all those who commented on this affair either refrained from mentioning the Christian opposition to *The Last Temptation of Christ* or noted how instructive those differences were. Not one Christian leader called for the murder of Martin Scorsese or anyone else who made the film. More significantly, had a Christian leader actually done so, he or she would have been censured by Christians throughout the world. Likewise, imagine the chief rabbi of Israel announcing a million-dollar reward to anyone who would murder Jewish author Philip Roth for his scathing depictions of Jewish life. Such a rabbi would be drummed out of Jewish life.

SALMAN RUSHDIE

The positions expressed here in no way imply admiration for Salman Rushdie. He is no moral hero, no latter-day Thomas More. In fact, Rushdie is somewhat of a moral idiot. Prior to the publication of *The Satanic Verses*, he had a long record of praise for Third World leftist dictators and for those, such as the Irish Republican Army, who terrorize democracies. Perhaps this terrible episode has led him to rethink his oft-expressed contempt for the Western democracies.

But contempt for Rushdie cannot be an issue here. His right to live and to write is the issue.

A war is taking place between Western values and the anti-Western elements within fundamentalist Islam. The price paid to protect Rushdie is minor in comparison to that we'll have to pay if we don't protect him and confront his would-be murderers. It is sad that many people in the Western world have not understood this.

ETHICAL MONOTHEISM VINDICATED

The Iranian clerics' use of God and religion for evil dramatically underscores the need for ethical monotheism.

That message, first proclaimed in the Hebrew Bible, is that belief in God and acting ethically must be inextricably linked; that God demands right behavior more than anything else, including right ritual and right belief; and that faith in a universal God without universal ethical standards is a false faith.

Belief in God without belief in the primacy and universality of ethics leads to murder in the name of God, from the Crusades to the Khomeini edict.

The Ayatollah Khomeini may have been a monotheist, but he was not an *ethical monotheist*, not only because he was unethical—an understatement given his persecution of the Baha'i faith in Iran, his support of terrorism, and his call to exterminate the nation of Israel—but because he believed that God judges people by their beliefs rather than by their ethical treatment of others. That is why it made sense to him to offer money to anyone who would kill a man solely because that man had written a novel that offended the Ayatollah's beliefs. According to Khomeini and the millions who agreed with him, God is offended more by a novel that treats Muslim beliefs lightly than He is by the murder of the novelist.

For all those who believe that faith in God ensures goodness, the Khomeini episode provides an important lesson in the necessity of *ethical* monotheism.

A JEWISH EXAMPLE: SHOULD BARUCH GOLDSTEIN BE UNDERSTOOD OR CONDEMNED?

In February 1994, Dr. Baruch Goldstein, a follower of the late Rabbi Meir Kahane, burst into a Muslim religious service in Hebron and machine-gunned thirty people to death. Goldstein was himself immediately killed. Shortly thereafter the following dialogue took place between Isaac, who identified himself as an Orthodox Jew, age thirty-five, and me on my radio show.

Isaac: As far as the motivations that would lead Dr. Goldstein to commit an act as you described, "mowing down innocent people in a mosque," I don't think we can understand it in a vacuum.

Just go over a little bit of history. From what I understand, the Thursday night prayer services on Purim [a Jewish holiday, the day before Goldstein carried out his attack] had to be interrupted because there were Arabs screaming "Massacre the Jews!"

According to a fax that I received from Israel, in the streets of Hebron there were a number of Arabs—Palestinians with axes in their hands—screaming en masse at the Jews. And, in fact, I think a week before that, a number of settlers in the community met with army officials and told them, "You have to protect us from this. Otherwise something very serious is going to happen."

According to this transmission, the Jews were apparently communicating with the authorities, and they wished to just get this horrible, horrendous situation out of their minds. But I guess push came to shove, and I think Dr. Goldstein just took so much. I mean, he was actually decorated as quite an accomplished physician. He was known in the Hebron-Judea-Samaria area as quite a healer, and so I don't believe that he was led because of any misinterpretation of any biblical text about wiping out the Amalekites [as the ancient Israelites were commanded in Deuteronomy 25:19], but rather because he just found he was at the brink of sanity, and there was not enough protection by the authorities.

Dennis: If a Palestinian, sick of twenty-seven years of Israeli occupation, just started mowing down Jews, I assume that you would also call up a radio show to explain the context.

Isaac: Well, I don't think that twenty-seven years of occupation has anything to do with it. The 1929 Hebron massacre against the Jews had nothing to do with occupation.

Dennis: Wait, wait.

Isaac: So what are you saying?

Dennis: I'll tell you what I'm saying. I sat here shaking my head that a man calls up and basically offers an understanding of evil rather than a condemnation of it. That's what you did. It comes from some on the left on behalf of violent criminals [such as rioters, see Chapter 22], and now it's coming from some Jews on the right.

Isaac: Well, what can I say?

Dennis: I'll tell you one thing you *should* say. Next Yom Kippur, you should bang your chest hard and ask God, "How did I, Isaac, get from the beauty of the Torah to saying before hundreds of thousands of people on the radio, as a religious Jew, that I understand and don't condemn a Jewish mass murderer?"

Isaac: Well, terrorism, hijackings, bombings, and deliberate targeting of civilians is the daily fanfare that's being served up for fifty years by those who wish our destruction. I think it's very difficult for us to judge over here, from the comfort of our Beverly Hills and Los Angeles homes, a person living in that environment.

Dennis: That's exactly the argument of Damian Williams and his supporters [Williams was one of the black youths who beat white truck driver Reginald Denny almost to death at the beginning of the Los Angeles riots in 1992]: "Who are you in West Los Angeles to judge us blacks who rioted? You don't live our life." Everybody now has these excuses.

Isaac: We're not empowered to judge.

Dennis: We're not empowered to judge? Really! We're not empowered to make moral judgments of behavior?

Isaac: I don't think we can judge a person until we stand in his shoes.

Dennis: I didn't say a person, I said *behavior*.

Isaac: You couldn't judge him until you sit there, living in the West Bank right now.

Dennis: I said *behavior*. You defended his behavior.

Isaac: Let me ask you, if instead of being in Hebron, we're talking about some African-American in South Central and the KKK are walking down the street and saying, "Kill the black, kill the black—"

Dennis: And the next day, a black walks into a white church and mows the people down because they're white? I'd think he's scum.

CONCLUDING THOUGHTS ON AIR

My deepest belief is ethical monotheism, the belief in one God, and therefore one morality, for all people. This is the most revolutionary idea in human history, but it is almost as far from being lived today as it was when Abraham helped develop it four thousand years ago.

The unfortunate tendency of most people is to divide morality by "team." "If my team does it, it's okay." "If their team does it, it's bad." When you judge behavior in terms of race, religion, nationality, or anything other than a universal moral code, good ceases to be transcendent. As long as our guys did it, it's okay.

Historically, this thinking started out as family-based—"I support my family, right or wrong." Once, on the talk show preceding mine, a woman whose husband was serving a life sentence for first-degree murder, said, "These people [murderers] should just be reeducated and sent back into society." This woman saw the issue not in moral terms, but in family terms. If her husband had been the victim rather than the murderer, she would have a very different view of what ought to be done with murderers. The desire to think in family, group, ethnic, and/or racial terms, and not in universal moral ones, is very deep in the human species.

In addition to that, we have another factor at work here—the argument by some people that since their group has been a victim of injustice for so long, its members should be forgiven for almost anything they do. There are blacks who feel that "Because of all this racism and slavery, you can't make moral demands on us." And, as shown here, there are Jews who say, "Given the Arab pogrom against Jews in Hebron in 1929, the Holocaust, and all the other sufferings we've experienced, you have to understand that you have no right to make normal moral demands of us."

It is generally believed that people who have suffered become more empathetic with other people's suffering. Apparently there are people for whom the opposite is true.

30

WHEN RELIGION MAKES PEOPLE CRUEL

I have devoted much of my life to making the case for religion- and God-based ethics. But I have never for a moment denied the existence of bad religious people or the ability of religion to be used for evil.

I would now like to go one step further. The problem of religious evil exists not only because there are bad religious people, and not only because religion can be used for evil. Unfortunately, religion itself can be a source of cruelty. There are doctrines in every religion that, if unchanged or followed literally, make some people meaner than if they had not been religious. I will give examples from the three monotheistic faiths.

ISLAM

Kind and good Muslims have to confront their religion's insistence that the only true Islam is a theocracy, i.e., a state governed solely by Muslim law. My Muslim friends who loathe the terror, cruelty, and totalitarianism of Muslim governments in Iran and the Sudan, and who are unhappy with the lack of freedom, suppression of non-Islamic faiths, and oppression of women in Saudi Arabia, nevertheless continue to yearn for a state ruled entirely by the sharia (Muslim law). For that is what their religion teaches them.

Yet a state ruled by Muslim religious law, enforced by its police, must by definition be nondemocratic and persecute those who believe "incorrectly." To cite a few of many examples, a state ruled by Islamic law punishes a Muslim who drinks liquor in his own home, or who smokes in public during the holy month of Ramadan; it punishes a Muslim woman who doesn't dress according to Islamic law; and it *puts to death* any Muslim who forsakes Islam for another religion.

To those of us who believe in personal freedom, these are examples of religion causing people to act cruelly.

Then there are those relatively few religious Muslims who murder as many non-Muslims as they can, and who are then honored by more than a few Muslim religious leaders from mosques in Gaza to some mosques in Brooklyn or Algiers.

Muslims who are repulsed by such behavior will argue that these people are not doing what Islam demands. And we can only wish that more leading Muslims speak out against such evil in the name of Allah.

But many learned Muslims do support such behavior, and they can cite religious texts to back up this support. Certainly, there is widespread theological justification for—as well as opposition to—the late Ayatollah Ruhollah Khomeini's call to murder Muslim writer Salman Rushdie for heresy.

JUDAISM

Many Orthodox Jews yearn for a state ruled by halakha (Jewish law), just as orthodox Muslims yearn for an Islamic state. But such a state, if it ever came into being, would cause many otherwise fine observant Jews to become cruel, freedom-denying human beings. The late Rabbi Meir Kahane introduced a bill in the Israeli Parliament calling for the state's implementation of such halakhic rules as long imprisonment for any Jew who engaged in sexual relations with a non-Jew (the non-Jew was to receive an even longer prison sentence), the banning of mixed-religion beaches, and many other laws that would destroy democracy and radically curtail personal freedom. Indeed, he and more than a few other Orthodox Jews have frequently stated that Orthodox Judaism and Western democracy are not compatible in a halakhic Jewish state. They are right.

The ability of Judaism to make a person meaner is demonstrated by the behavior of some religious Jewish parents who give Down's syndrome children to institutions with the proviso that those institutions keep the child if no Jewish family can be found to adopt the child. Better that the child have no family than be raised in a non-Jewish family. This is because these Jews believe that the souls of Jews and non-Jews are different. It is, therefore, better to ruin a child's life than to have a child born to Jewish parents raised by loving non-Jews. Religion can make a person meaner.

To cite another example, some right-wing Orthodox rabbis and laymen—not all, I hasten to add—have told me in private that they would not save a non-Jew's life on the Sabbath if it meant violating the Sabbath (unless, they add, if it were known that they refused to intervene, because that would lead to giving Judaism a bad name and to Jew-hatred). This is another example of religion making a person worse. Were it not for this halakha, these Jews would do what their values and human instinct called for—saving the non-Jewish person.

Arguments that these rabbis and laypeople are incorrectly citing the halakha are disingenuous. They *are* citing the halakha. There may be more than one way of interpreting this halakha, but their way is not necessarily halakhically wrong; it is morally wrong.

It is very sad for me personally to note the ability of Judaism to engender cruelty and totalitarianism because I have always identified Judaism with kindness, and I continue to do so. Over the course of millennia, the record of Judaism in making people kinder has been awe-inspiring—from its concern with hurtful speech to its concern with the suffering of animals.

But there are some beliefs and practices that can make a Jew less noble. The great rabbi, the Gaon of Vilna, correctly observed that the Torah is like rain—it gives growth to both poisonous weeds and beautiful flowers.

CHRISTIANITY

Historically, the greatest evidence of the ability of religion to make a person cruel can be found among believing Christians; Christian treatment of non-Christians was often evil. For example, otherwise law-abiding people could tolerate or even participate in atrocities against Jews, because the Christian Bible blamed Jews for killing Jesus.

The record of Christianity in America has generally been a humane and tolerant one, but an American Christian can also become a meaner person because of religion.

This was brought home to me when a Christian caller to my radio show told me that "According to Christianity, it is a sin to divorce." With the exception of adultery, no matter how tortured a couple's life is, the Christian position, as he and many other Protestants and Catholics teach it—and they have a Christian biblical source for this position—is that it is better to live a life of misery than ever to divorce. An Evangelical Christian pastor friend of mine has related to me how he was thoroughly ostracized by his Christian community after he and his wife divorced. Even the fact that she alone pushed for the divorce made no difference. This doctrine is quite simply a cruel one that leads otherwise fine people into advocating and practicing cruelty.

When the world's best-known Protestant, the Reverend Billy Graham, went to the Soviet Union, his sole message was one of salvation and the need to obey the constituted authorities. He said nothing about the suffering of fellow Christians, even when KGB agents dragged away Christians protesting Soviet persecution from the very church in which he preached. The Reverend Graham's emphasis on obeying the authorities, even when they are vicious, has Protestant Christian bases.

One final example: To non-Christians, the most obvious way in which Christianity can make a Christian less kind is the belief that *all* non-Christians, no matter how moral and kind, will suffer eternal torment, while all believers in Jesus Christ, no matter what their behavior, will have eternal salvation.

I have never been particularly distressed by this belief because I know many kind Christians who hold it (and I measure people by their behavior, not by their theology). Nevertheless, to the extent that beliefs do shape behavior, the belief that all the goodness of a non-Christian does not add up to a hill of beans in God's eyes must inevitably minimize the importance of goodness to many devout Christians.

ALL RELIGIONS

There is another way that religion can provoke cruelty. When religion becomes obsessed with sexual matters, it inevitably conveys the message to many of its adherents that God cares more about premarital sex, or women covering their hair, or masturbation, or pornography than about anything else, even murder.

I draw the following conclusions from the realization that religion can cause a diminution in an adherent's goodness:

1: Ethical monotheism is the only antidote to religion causing evil. The central teaching of all faiths must be that God's primary demand is that we be good people.

2: The separation of religion and government is a moral necessity. The ideal is a secular government and a religious population.

3: Each religion needs a reformation—forcing the religion to make peace with, and craft a productive religious response to, secular governmental authority. Christianity had it and gave birth to Protestantism, which, by acknowledging secular authority, enabled the growth of democracy and personal freedom. Judaism has had it, giving birth to non-Orthodox denominations and to Orthodox Jews who do not yearn for a theocracy.

Islam has not had it, and therefore some of its more fundamentalist parts are at war with the West, specifically the West's separation of church and state and its nearly total personal freedom. If Islam does not undergo a reformation, this war could become worldwide and deadly.

4: The Achilles' heel of the three monotheistic faiths is their attitudes toward those, within and outside their faith, who believe differently. Some classic Jewish attitudes toward non-Jews, Christian attitudes toward non-Christians, and Muslim attitudes toward non-Muslims need to be rejected.

5: Finally, the Gaon of Vilna was right; religion is like rain; it does bring forth both beautiful flowers and poisonous weeds. Two lessons are to be learned from this.

The lesson for the religious is that they must plant only beautiful flowers. The belief that practicing one's religion will automatically make one a good person is absolutely wrong. Religion will make people good only if they want it to.

The lesson for the nonreligious is that since religion is like rain, we cannot live without it. The response to religion-induced evil must therefore be religion-induced goodness, not no religion. There is no exclusively secular route to a good world.

31

WHEN ANGER OVERWHELMS LOVE: REFLECTIONS ON FEMINIST AND CIVIL RIGHTS ORGANIZATIONS

Do most Americans know that:

- Nearly one hundred million women worldwide have been sexually mutilated by having their clitoris cut off, usually with crude cutting tools?
- In China, millions of girls are aborted, countless others are murdered at birth, and millions more are sold to brothels or to men who cannot otherwise marry?
- In India, thousands of women are burned to death by husbands and families seeking larger dowries?
- In Pakistan, according to that country's Commission on the Status of Women, "nearly 30 million [are] born in near slavery, and die invariably in oblivion"?

Probably not.

But nearly every American knows that a professor named Anita Hill claimed that unwanted sex-related words were once spoken to her, and that one must say "chairperson" rather than "chairman."

Do most Americans know that:

- In 1972, more than two hundred thousand blacks of the Hutu nation in Africa were systematically murdered by the Tutsis? And that in 1988, another twenty thousand were murdered? (Finally, the 1994 Rwanda massacres were publicized.)

- In the late 1980s, each year, thousands of black African children were taken against their will to be indoctrinated in Cuba?
- In the first decade of its independence, one-third of all the citizens of the black African nation of Equatorial Guinea were forced into exile? (Do most Americans even know that Equatorial Guinea exists?)
- Between 1982 and 1985, approximately three hundred thousand blacks Africans in Uganda were slaughtered? And that this followed Idi Amin's murder of approximately five hundred thousand black Africans?
- Hundreds of thousands of black Africans have already been killed, and more are being killed at this moment, by the Arab Islamic fundamentalist regime of the Sudan? And that this regime also flogs, amputates the limbs of, and crucifies blacks?
- In 1989, the Islamic government of Mauritania expelled approximately one thousand blacks a day from that country?
- Despite the large number of black children in orphanages, black organizations in the United States have made it almost impossible for white parents to adopt black babies?

Probably not.

But tens of millions of Americans were quite familiar with the miseries of apartheid and knew when a single black protester was killed in South Africa.

Why?

Why so much knowledge about lesser evils, sometimes even trivial annoyances, and so little knowledge about immense evils?

The primary reason, I believe, is that, contrary to their declared goals, it is not the welfare of blacks that most preoccupies black and civil rights organizations; it is anger at whites. And it is not the welfare of the mass of women that preoccupies feminist organizations; it is political power and anger at men.

It is anger at men that explains why feminist leaders can become livid over relatively minor matters, such as the accusations against Justice Clarence Thomas or the greater funding for men's sports at a college, while generally ignoring the nightmares endured by hundreds of millions of women around the world.

Political power explains why feminist organizations and their supporters in the media declared 1992, not 1990, the "Year of the Woman"—although only two more women ran for the United States Senate in 1992 than in 1990. But in 1990, all the women candidates but one were Republican; in 1992, all the women candidates but one were Democrats.

In the 1970s, during the years when Idi Amin and his followers were butchering about a half-million black Africans, almost the only news the world heard from Africa concerned South Africa and the evils of apartheid. To this day, mention evil inflicted upon black Africans to university students and you will be told—and rightly so—about apartheid. But it is questionable whether one out of ten university students who can tell you about apartheid can identify Idi Amin, the greatest murderer of blacks in this century.

Given their proclaimed concern with black people's suffering, why was it that so few antiapartheid forces called the world's attention to the mass murder of blacks in Africa? Why is this all but ignored on campuses that otherwise are so concerned with black issues? As I write these words, a slaughter of black people is taking place in the Sudan. Why does this information come as a revelation to the great majority of people?

The reason, I am afraid, is this: Civil rights and feminist groups are animated more by anger at those they oppose than by concern for those groups in whose names they speak. Their members, and especially their leaders, are angry people—and their movements reflect that fact. Some are angry at Christianity (for slavery and patriarchy); some at the West, especially the United States (for historic racism and sexism); some at men; and some at whites.

To illustrate the feminist preoccupation with anything hinting at sexism more than with female suffering, I recall an incident with a nationally renowned feminist attorney. She had guest-hosted the radio talk show before mine, and near the end of her broadcast, she asked me on air what I was going to discuss on my show. I told her that my lead commentary would be about clitoridectomies. She responded that this was sexist; equal time should be devoted to condemning male circumcision!

Only someone more interested in sexism than in minimizing the torture of women could morally equate male circumcision, the harmless removal of a newborn boy's useless foreskin, with clitoridectomies, the horribly painful removal of a maturing girl's clitoris, an essential component of a woman's ability to experience sexual pleasure. One would think that this is rather obvious. As I told her, although I am circumcised, I don't miss my foreskin, whereas I suspect that she would feel differently if she had no clitoris.

Of course, feminist organizations might respond that the reason they do little about the mass mutilation of African girls is because their concerns are with the problems of American women. This is probably true, and if it is, it only confirms my thesis. What would people think of American Jewish organizations, for example, if they had ignored the Jews of the Soviet Union, Ethiopia, and Syria, while concerning themselves with the defacing of American Jewish cemeteries and discrimination against Jews in some American country clubs?

As for black and civil rights organizations, they cannot respond that they are concerned only with American blacks; for decades, they were enormously preoccupied with blacks abroad, in South Africa.

The reason, of course, was that the blacks in South Africa were persecuted by whites, while the murder and torture of millions of blacks has been perpetrated by blacks and other nonwhites (e.g., Arabs).

The black *Washington Post* columnist William Raspberry has written that "Black Americans don't want to hear—are almost incapable of hearing" about evils perpetrated in Africa. He cites the Ghanaian-born economist, George B. N. Ayittey:

> Many Africans have no difficulty condemning apartheid and condemning the tyranny in the rest of Africa. But it seems that Americans have this particular difficulty—especially African-Americans—that if you criticize black African leaders, then you must be either a racist if you are white, or a traitor if you're black. . . .
>
> When Idi Amin was slaughtering Ugandans at the rate of 150 a day [ed. note: the actual rate was much higher], the world did nothing. Why? Because he was black.
>
> We *[blacks] seem blind to oppression unless it wears a white face.* . . . [Emphasis added.]

Though they enjoy more freedom, affluence, and rights than blacks and women almost anywhere else on earth, many American blacks and women are angry people. They are angry in part because they were taught to associate personal unhappiness with racism and sexism. (One radical physician, Peter Breggin, devotes his life to convincing women not to take psychiatric drugs such as Prozac because, he contends, female depression emanates from sexism. Some women believe him.) As long as women continue to blame men, and blacks continue to blame whites, for their unhappiness in life, women and blacks will vigilantly search for every vestige of sexism and racism. For only when they are removed, then and only then, they believe, will they finally be able to attain some happiness.

The movement for blacks' and women's equality is one of the great developments of our time; all good people, by definition, support it. But it is one thing to support an ideal and quite another to support all the groups that claim to fight on its behalf. It is time to cease identifying the interests of women with feminist groups and the interests of blacks with civil rights groups. They are not the same.

32

FIRST, TAKE CARE OF YOUR OWN

On my radio talk show some time ago, a caller of Armenian descent posed the following question: "How come Jews always talk about the Holocaust, but seem to almost never mention the Armenian genocide?"

"With all respect, and with tremendous sympathy for the suffering of the Armenian people," I responded, "it seems to me that it is the Jews' task to remind the world about the Holocaust and that it is your task as an Armenian to tell the world about the sufferings of your people."

After some silence on the other end of the line, the man said, "You're right."

That call made as much of an impression on me as it apparently had on that Armenian-American. It started me thinking about an issue that has wide ramifications—groups taking care of their own. I have come to realize that as important as universalist ideals are, concern for one's own group is also significant.

How a group treats its own members reveals a great deal about its moral level. Those who treat their own decently will not necessarily treat others decently, but those who are cruel to their own are certain to be cruel to others.

Examples abound:

The major reason that the Soviet Union elicited so much mistrust from outsiders was how the Soviet government treated its own citizens. As Aleksandr Solzhenitsyn pointed out, if a state confines its own dissenting citizens in mental asylums, it obviously would treat citizens of other countries equally badly, if not worse.

Or consider the government of Syria. As active as it has been in sponsoring international terrorism, the Syrian government's greatest victims have been Syrians themselves. In 1982, for example, the Syrian government slaughtered fifteen thousand of its citizens in the city of Hama. The day the Syrian government begins treating its own people decently, there will be reason to hope that it will keep peace with its neighbors as well.

In fact, the twentieth century has not seen a democracy go to war against another democracy. All of the century's wars have involved police states that torture their own citizens against either other police states or democracies.

A third example strikes closer to home: During the Holocaust in Europe, there were proportionately more rescuers among Catholic clergy than among the general population. But the Vatican itself was largely silent during the most systematic slaughter in history, one that took place in the heart of Christian civilization. Many people attribute this silence to anti-Semitism. While that was a factor in some cases, I do not believe that it was the primary factor— because the Church has also been largely silent about evils committed against Catholics and other Christians. The Vatican was timid in speaking out on behalf of dissident Catholic priests put in Nazi concentration camps.

During the 1970s and 1980s, Lebanon, until then a peaceful and democratic island in the Arab world, was almost decimated. Once governed by Maronite Christians, the country was brought to ruin by anti-Christian and antidemocratic groups, ranging from the Palestine Liberation Organization to a multitude of pro-Iran organizations. The Catholics of Lebanon were severely hurt during that time, yet aside from ritual calls for peace, the Vatican said little about the sufferings of its fellow Christians. A church that had been used to speaking out against evil perpetrated against its own would have been far more likely to speak out against the evil perpetrated against the Jews during the Holocaust.

Protestants have a similar record of not fighting on behalf of their own. The remarkable behavior of the world's most famous Protestant, the Reverend Billy Graham, in the Soviet Union provided a good example. The Reverend Graham was visiting a country where Christians had been viciously persecuted, where Christians were serving long sentences in Soviet prison camps merely for printing Bibles. Many were Baptists whom Soviet authorities treated particularly cruelly. Yet the Baptist leader not only abandoned persecuted Baptists, he actually spoke as if he sided with their Soviet persecutors.

By late 1987, there were no longer any Jewish political prisoners in the Soviet Gulag. Yet the day before the Soviet Union's then-leader Mikhail Gorbachev arrived in the United States, 250,000 Jews from all over the United States converged on Washington to protest Soviet persecution of Soviet Jews. Had the same percentage of American Christians gathered in Washington to protest the many Christians who were still languishing in Soviet prisons, over ten million Christians would have made this the largest protest in history. What a powerful message that would have sent to Christians throughout the world, especially the lonely persecuted Christians in the Soviet Union who felt abandoned by their coreligionists. Why was there no such Christian protest on behalf of fellow Christians?

This problem continues. The Christians of the Sudan face horrific persecution from the Muslim authorities in that country. Yet one can probably count on the fingers of one hand the number of Christian clergy who have spoken on this issue to their congregations, let alone organized a movement to help their fellow Christians' plight. This is not intended as an indictment of either Christians or Christianity. It is meant to show the consequences of the problem of not taking care of one's own.[1]

In general, the people who have the most important things to say to the world—and who receive the most respectful attention from it—are people who are rooted in a particular group. To cite but a few modern examples, the world has paid attention to Mahatma Gandhi, who was first a Hindu; to Elie Wiesel, first a Jew; to the Dalai Lama, first a Buddhist; and to Mother Teresa, first a Catholic. The rule is simple: Before you can be a universalist, you have be a particularist. But that is only the first part of the rule: While it is good and proper to care for your own first, those who care *only* for their own do no good for the world. These chauvinists are the mirror image of the radical universalists who care about everyone except their own. Once again, the middle road is the only road to a better world.

---

[1] Among Jews, there is often the opposite problem. In the twentieth century, many Jews who fled from their Jewish origins have devoted their lives to taking care of everyone *except their own*. The famous German Jewish revolutionary thinker and activist Rosa Luxembourg once said that she would sooner involve herself in the problems of the most distant tribe before concerning herself with Jews' sufferings. These self-hating Jews affirmed allegiance only to "humanity," and ended up doing harm not only to Jews but to humanity.

It was all summarized two thousand years ago in a famous statement by the Talmudic sage Hillel: "If I am not for myself, who will be for me? But if I am only for myself, what am I?"

One can put it another way, "If I am not for my own, I probably won't be for anybody else, either."

33

THE IMMORALITY OF PACIFIST THINKING

Since the 1960s, pacifist doctrines once associated with isolated individuals and religious fringe groups have become quite popular.

Although few refer to themselves as pacifist—"antiwar," "peace activist," and "nonviolent" are among the preferred self-descriptions—millions of people living in democracies have in fact come to sympathize with a doctrine that would lead to widespread cruelty and the triumph of evil. If, during the Nazi era, democratic societies had practiced pacifism and nonviolence, democracy and human rights would have disappeared, the Jews of the world would have been annihilated, and far more than the fifty-five million killed in World War II would have been killed.

Yet despite all this, the pacifist belief that killing, war, and violence are always immoral has spread through the Western world.

To begin with religious examples: During the Cold War against Communist tyranny, the Presbyterian Church, the United Church of Christ, the Disciples of Christ, the United Methodist Church, and the Episcopal Church all made "peace" their priority program. By "peace," such groups meant anything from unilateral disarmament to outright pacifism. Thus, thirty-five of the thirty-seven organizations on the peace resource list of the Episcopal Church promoted unilateral disarmament, while the other two denominations, the American Friends Service Committee and the Fellowship of Reconciliation, have actually proclaimed adherence to pacifism.

Catholic leaders, too, moved in that direction. The National Catholic Educational Association has made "peace" (read disarmament, nonviolence, antinuclear arms) a cornerstone of Catholic education. The Catholic trend, according to Vanderbilt University social critic Chester E. Finn Jr., was toward teaching unilateral disarmament; Seattle's Bishop Hunthausen called Puget Sound "Auschwitz" because nuclear submarines dock there. (This morally perverse equation of submarines that protect democracy and have not killed a single soul with the Nazi death camp where over a million Jews and hundreds of thousands of non-Jews were gassed to death offers a good illustration of the immoral thinking to which pacifism can lead.)

Even some Reform rabbis, spokesmen for a religion that deems pacifism a sin—Judaism demands that a Jew kill a murderer if that is the only way to stop him—have said on my radio show, not simply in private conversation, that they would respect an individual who during World War II could have killed Hitler but refused to do so because of pacifist principles.

Outside religion, there are many indicators of growing sympathy with pacifist thinking. Many journalists, politicians, and intellectuals routinely condemn virtually any use of force by democracies; and groups such as the British Labor Party and the Left and the Greens in Germany supported unilateral disarmament during the latter part of the Cold War. Providing additional intellectual, moral, and financial support for the spread of pacifism have been organizations such as Physicians for Social Responsibility.

How do otherwise decent people justify embracing or even respecting a doctrine that leads to limitless cruelty?

When challenged, pacifists and their sympathizers generally offer one or more of the these arguments:

1. It is always wrong to kill another human being.
2. The Ten Commandments state, "Thou shall not kill."
3. Human life is the supreme value.
4. The best answer to the problem of combating evil is the doctrine of nonviolence as practiced by Mahatma Gandhi and Martin Luther King.
5. You can't fight violence with violence.
6. Nuclear weapons have made pacifism a moral imperative. Thus, when Russia was still Communist and militarily strong, pacifists argued that no matter how much we may deplore Gulags and the spread of totalitarianism, it is better

Red than dead (a phrase associated with the British philosopher Bertrand Russell).

It is necessary to show why these arguments are not moral. Only then can we remove the mantle of morality from the pacifists and return it to those who believe that being a good person means that sometimes you must kill.

PACIFIST ARGUMENT 1:
IT IS ALWAYS WRONG TO KILL ANOTHER HUMAN BEING

The key word here is "always." The moment you do not mean "always," you are no longer a pacifist, but are, like the rest of us, a proponent of the moral use of violence and, thus, an opponent of pacifism.

The moment you affirm the morality of killing Hitler during World War II or killing a sniper who is shooting schoolchildren, you are an opponent of pacifism and an advocate of the moral use of violence.

The question is, therefore, not whether killing is ever moral, but *when* killing is moral.

Sometimes the answer is perfectly clear, such as when there is no other way to protect an innocent human life. Sometimes the answer is less clear, e.g., the Allied bombing of Dresden during World War II. But one thing is entirely clear: By prohibiting moral killing, *pacifism ensures immoral killing, i.e., murder.* If we do not kill the sniper who is shooting at schoolchildren, he will murder them. If men had not killed Nazis, virtually every Jew in the world would have been gassed. And if someone had killed Lenin in 1917, or Stalin ten years later, over forty million Russians and other Soviet citizens would not have been murdered.

There is, in sum, moral killing and immoral killing. The latter is known as murder, which is why we have two words for the taking of human life.

PACIFIST ARGUMENT 2:
"THOU SHALL NOT KILL"

Now we can understand why the above is not what the Ten Commandments command. It is an erroneous translation; the sixth commandment reads, "Thou shall not *murder*." Like English, Hebrew distinguishes between killing and murder. According to the Bible, killing can sometimes be justifiable, even virtuous, whereas murder, the deliberate killing of an innocent person, is deemed the most evil of acts.

It is sad when clergy misquote the Ten Commandments, but it is much worse than sad when they denounce all violence equally in the name of religion. The first is excusable when the reason is ignorance of Hebrew, but the second is inexcusable. All decent people long for Isaiah's vision of the time when "nation shall not lift up sword against nation" (2:4), but the way to hasten Isaiah's messianic vision is to fight evil, not to allow it to proliferate.

Moses, the greatest human in the Bible, killed a slave master who was beating a slave (Exodus 2:12). This biblical hero deliberately killed a man, an act that God, who thereafter chose Moses as his prophet, apparently deemed virtuous.

PACIFIST ARGUMENT 3:
HUMAN LIFE IS THE SUPREME VALUE

This is pacifism's fundamental tenet—and its fatal flaw. It is this belief that enables pacifists to avoid confronting the cruel consequences of their beliefs.

The belief that life is the supreme value is contrary to the normative moral codes that are the bases of our civilization, from Judaism and Christianity to democracy and national independence. These codes and ideals, as well as common sense, hold that at times life must be sacrificed for the sake of morality. Pacifism, however, holds the direct opposite: Morality must be sacrificed for the sake of life. Pacifists believe that it would have been immoral to take the lives of the German and Japanese doctors who during World War II performed grotesque experiments on human beings, even though that was the only way to stop them from dissecting conscious people with no anesthetic.

If life is the highest value, everything else is, by definition, of lower value. Justice, decency, morality, kindness, and all other noble values are rendered less important than life. Pacifism means biology takes precedence over morality: Long lives are more valuable than good lives.

The belief that human life is the supreme value fails not only on moral grounds, it fails even on its own terms of preserving life. By prohibiting the killing of murderers, when only killing them will stop them, pacifism actually increases death.

It is not surprising that secular ideals, because they reject a reality beyond life, should lead to the veneration of life—after all, what else is there but life? But it is quite shocking that religious Christians or Jews should flirt with, let alone embrace, the idea that life is always higher than all other values. The essential message of Judaism and Christianity is that life is not an end in itself. Life is to be a means—to goodness, to sanctity, and to God. The belief in life as an end in itself is a form of idolatry.

PACIFIST ARGUMENT 4:
NONVIOLENCE IS THE BEST WAY TO RESIST EVIL

The nonviolent resistance espoused and practiced by Mahatma Gandhi and Martin Luther King in their respective struggles against British imperialism and American racist institutions was a major moral achievement: It attained its moral ends without recourse to killing. In many instances, however, nonviolence would not attain its moral ends and would lead to the triumph of the evil it wished to resist.

When a Winston Churchill is the enemy, nonviolence is an appropriate moral response. But when Stalin, Hitler, Pol Pot, Idi Amin, Saddam Hussein, a death squad, or Charles Manson is the enemy, nonviolence is suicidal for the innocent and ensures victory for the evil. Against Nazism, Communism, terrorism, or murderers in crime-infested cities, "nonviolent resistance" is literally meaningless. All it does is increase violence.

The naïveté inherent in the doctrine of nonviolence, no matter who is doing the evil, is nowhere more clearly revealed than in the words of Gandhi himself. In 1938, after the Nazis had already carried out the Kristallnacht pogrom, he directed the following words of advice to the suffering Jews of Germany:

> I am as certain as I am dictating these lines that the stoniest German heart will melt [if only the Jews] adopt active non-violence . . . I do not despair of his [Hitler's] responding to human suffering even though caused by him.

In 1942, Gandhi directed similarly pacifistic advice to the British. He published an open letter, "Non-Violence in Peace and War," in which he wrote:

> I would like you [the British] to lay down the arms you have as being useless for saving you or humanity. You will invite Herr Hitler and Signor Mussolini to take what they want of the countries you call your possessions. . . . If these gentlemen choose to occupy your homes, you will vacate them. If they do not give you free passage out, you will allow yourselves, man, woman and child to be slaughtered, but you will refuse to owe allegiance to them.

I shudder to think what the world would be like if the pacifist Mahatma Gandhi had been the leader of England, and not the proponent of moral violence, Winston Churchill.

PACIFIST ARGUMENT 5:
YOU CAN'T FIGHT VIOLENCE WITH VIOLENCE

The essence of this argument is that when you use violence to fight evil, you are fighting evil with evil, and you become the moral equivalent of the evil you are fighting. This pacifist contention that fighting violence with violence is always wrong is an example of the pernicious doctrine of moral equivalence—all violence is morally equivalent; the person who kills a murderer is morally equated with the murderer.

The idea that violence can sometimes be used to achieve good has become foreign to the mind blunted by the pacifist notion that it is always wrong.

But, of course, the most obvious rejoinder to the argument that you can't fight violence with violence is: With what then will you fight criminal violence?

PACIFIST ARGUMENT 6:
NUCLEAR WEAPONS NECESSITATE PACIFISM

One reason often offered for the increased respect for doctrines of nonviolence is the threat of nuclear war. Granted that nuclear war does challenge previous theories of just wars. In conventional war, good could vanquish evil. But in a nuclear war, it is conceivable that no one, neither the good nor the evil, would survive.

But this fact doesn't render pacifism moral. It was an immoral doctrine when humanity's survival was not at stake, and it remains so in the nuclear age. Even if one believes that the use of any nuclear weapons will lead to the end of the human race, there is no reason we should be absolved from fighting evil whenever possible with *nonnuclear* weapons.

A moral case can be made for an individual's refusal to use nuclear weapons in time of war on the grounds that it can lead to the end of humanity. But this has nothing to do with pacifism, or with the doctrine of nonviolence; it is the refusal to fight in a *specific* war on moral grounds. Such a position should be honored. That pacifism is immoral hardly renders fighting in all wars moral. Killing without moral questioning is no more moral than never killing without moral questioning.

Pacifist opposition to all wars, even conventional ones to save innocent Cambodians, Jews, Ugandans, or oneself, remains as immoral in the nuclear age as it was before. It still involves acquiescence in evil.

Killing must always be the last resort. Every nonviolent attempt to stop evil must be made first. But "last resort" means just that: When all other attempts fail, moral violence must be used to fight immoral violence.

PART THREE

THERE IS A SOLUTION TO EVIL

34

WHY AREN'T PEOPLE PREOCCUPIED WITH GOOD AND EVIL?

I am a Jew who was born three years after the Holocaust, and although no relative of mine was murdered (all were living in America), ever since I can remember, I have thought about the Holocaust almost every day of my life. I even have recurring nightmares about being rounded up for a death transport or actually being in a Nazi death camp. Perhaps, then, it is the Holocaust—and the realization that but for my grandparents' decision to emigrate to America, my family would have been murdered—which accounts for my lifelong preoccupation with fighting evil.

Of course, not every Jew is obsessed with good and evil, so I suspect there are additional factors. One is that whenever I imagine being terribly hurt and no one coming to my aid, I am overwhelmed with despair and anger.

Is there anyone who does not fear that he, she, or a loved one will be hurt by someone? Is there an American city-dweller who does not fear being robbed, beaten, or murdered, or a woman who does not fear also being raped? Given humanity's history of enslavement and mass murder (especially in our century when well *over one hundred million people* have been killed by other people), is there anyone who doesn't fear evil?

One would think that in addition to all their other concerns, people would be preoccupied with relentlessly promoting good and fighting evil. That many other concerns take precedence is truly a riddle. One would think that enlightened self-interest, if not morality, would prevail. Yet it doesn't. For this reason, before discussing whether a solution to evil exists, we first need to answer the question: Why aren't people preoccupied with fighting evil?

LACK OF EMPATHY

Many people lack the character trait most needed to treat others decently—empathy. While a minority of people seem to have an innate capacity to empathize with others' suffering, most people need to learn it. *It does not come naturally to see others as equally real or as fully human.* That is why most people need to learn that people of different races, creeds, and nationalities are just as human as they. Most men and women, even within the same group, need to learn that the other sex is composed of real people, not just members of the opposite sex.

Yet, while it is quite difficult to become empathetic, it is quite easy to learn that others are *not* fully human. It did not take much to teach Europeans, Americans, and Arabs that black people were born to be slaves, nor was it particularly difficult for Germans to learn to regard Jews as subhuman.

WEAKNESS

Humans also tend to be weak. Even when people do know right from wrong, they may do the wrong thing because it is often more difficult, sometimes dangerous, to do what is right. You don't have to be evil to commit evil. It is enough, for example, merely to be lazy; it is easier to drive by a person lying in the street than to stop and offer help. At other times, it is enough merely to lack courage; it is easier to call for peace than to confront Nazism, Communism, international terrorism and aggression, and other evils.

To do good often necessitates suppressing fear, acting courageously, and overcoming laziness—quite a large order.

PERSONAL PROBLEMS

To varying degrees, all people have emotional and psychological problems. Nearly all people also have economic problems and family difficulties. These burdens can easily preoccupy a person—and when they do, it is the rare person who can find time and energy to fight for others: "I've got my own problems; the last thing I need to worry about are Tibetans."

IT MEANS MAKING MORAL JUDGMENTS

Another reason many people don't concern themselves with issues of good and evil is that the moment you take ethical issues seriously, you must begin to make moral judgments—both of yourself and of others. This has two unpleasant consequences: subjecting yourself to constant moral scrutiny and publicly opposing other people's immoral behavior.

Since making moral judgments means that some people will hate you and fight you and that others will pass judgment on you, it is much easier not to make moral judgments.

IT MEANS CONFRONTING EVIL

Many people do not preoccupy themselves with moral issues because doing so forces them to confront evil. Once you judge a person, government, group, or action as evil, you have to do something about it or live with a guilty conscience. Neither is a pleasant prospect. Confronting evil is unpleasant and possibly dangerous; and a guilty conscience is a source of misery.

IT MEANS BELIEVING IN A HIGHER MORAL LAW

To make moral judgments, you have to posit a universal moral code. If you do not, then the students are right who contend that whether you choose to save your dog or a person is entirely a matter of personal opinion. Only if you posit a code that is higher than personal or societal opinion, which says that human life is more sacred than animal life, can you say that it is wrong to save the dog you love rather than the stranger whom you don't love.

Unfortunately, many members of this past generation of Americans and other Westerners have been raised not to believe in a higher moral law, but only to believe that there are differing personal opinions, all valid.

MORAL JUDGMENTS ARE DIFFICULT

Another obstacle to people's preoccupation with good and evil is the difficulty involved in having to morally assess every action *in every circumstance*. It is easier to label certain actions as always right or always wrong than to have to judge each action within its context.

It is easier to say, "Invasions are wrong" than to assess the morality of every invasion. Some invasions are moral (e.g., the D-Day invasion at Normandy) and some are immoral (e.g., the Soviet invasions of Czechoslovakia and Afghanistan). And some are morally ambiguous (e.g., the American invasion of Panama). No specific action is always wrong—we always need to know the context to make a moral judgment.

To cite another common example, people routinely condemn hatred. Yet hatred is not always wrong. I once participated in a national television show devoted to the subject of hate. At one point, the moderator stated that all hatred is wrong. Not surprisingly, the audience agreed—who defends hate? I did, noting that I hated Nazis, Charles Manson, and many other murderers and torturers. I argued that one has to distinguish between moral hatred and immoral hatred. To my pleasant surprise, the moment the audience heard that distinction, most of them agreed (it was a good example of the power of thinking a second time).

Although many of the obstacles to preoccupation with goodness are created by those who believe in moral relativism (good is relative to the individual, not universal), this particular obstacle is created by the *opponents* of moral relativism. The people who fight moral relativism often believe that situational ethics (determining what is right by the situation or context) is identical with moral relativism (morality as a matter of opinion). It isn't. If situational ethics means determining the ethics of an act by its context, that is a moral position, not moral relativism.

The way to fight moral relativism is with *universal* morality, meaning that a given act is *wrong for everyone* in that situation (and therefore not a matter of personal opinion). It is wrong for everyone to save the pet he loves before a human stranger. But it is not wrong for *anyone* to save his pet (or pen, for that matter) before a drowning Nazi mass murderer during World War II.

PREOCCUPATION WITH OTHER VALUES

The final, and perhaps most important, reason for many people's lack of preoccupation with goodness is that other concerns, frequently even honorable ones, divert their attention from moral issues.

People's attention is seduced by countless other worthwhile interests and values, which frequently are more glamorous and compelling than goodness. The most important of these are discussed in Chapter 36, "How Good and Evil Become Irrelevant."

35

THE ONLY SOLUTION TO EVIL: ETHICAL MONOTHEISM

Ethical monotheism means two things:

1. There is one God from whom emanates one morality for all humanity.
2. God's primary demand of people is that they act decently toward one another.

If all people subscribed to this simple belief—which does not entail leaving, or joining, any specific religion, or giving up any national identity—the world would experience far less evil.

Let me explain the components of ethical monotheism.

GOD

Monotheism means belief in "one God." Before discussing the importance of the "mono," or God's oneness, we need a basic understanding of the nature of God.

The God of ethical monotheism is the God first revealed to the world in the Hebrew Bible. Through it, we can establish God's four primary characteristics:

1. God is supranatural.
2. God is personal.
3. God is good.
4. God is holy.

Dropping any one of the first three attributes invalidates ethical monotheism (it is possible, though difficult, to ignore holiness and still lead an ethical life).

Supranatural

God is supranatural, meaning "above nature" (I do not use the more common term "supernatural" because it is less precise and conjures up irrationality). This is why Genesis, the Bible's first book, opens with, "In the beginning, God created the heavens and the earth." In a world in which nearly all people worshiped nature, the Bible's intention was to emphasize that nature is utterly subservient to God who made it. Obviously, therefore, God is not a part of nature, and nature is not God.

It is not possible for God to be part of nature for two reasons.

First, nature is finite and God is infinite. If God were within nature, He would be limited, and God, who is not physical, has no limits (I use the pronoun "He" not because I believe God is a male, but because the neuter pronoun "It" depersonalizes God. You cannot talk to, relate to, love, or obey an "It.").

Second, and more important, *nature is amoral*. Nature knows nothing of good and evil. In nature there is one rule—survival of the fittest. There is no right, only might. If a creature is weak, kill it. Only human beings could have moral rules such as, "If it is weak, protect it." Only human beings can feel themselves ethically obligated to strangers.

Thus, nature worship is very dangerous. When people idolize nature, they can easily arrive at the ethics of Nazism. It was the law of nature that Adolf Hitler sought to emulate—the strong shall conquer the weak. Nazism and other ideologies that are hostile to ethical monotheism and venerate nature are very tempting. *Nature allows you to act naturally, i.e., do only what you want you to do, without moral restraints; God does not.* Nature lets you act *naturally*—and it is as natural to kill, rape, and enslave as it is to love.

In light of all this, it is alarming that many people today virtually venerate nature. It can only have terrible moral ramifications.

One of the vital elements in the ethical monotheist revolution was its repudiation of nature-as-god. The evolution of civilization and morality have depended in large part on desanctifying nature.

Civilizations that equated gods with nature—a characteristic of all primitive societies—or that worshiped nature did not evolve.

If nature is divine, and has a will of its own, the only way for human beings to conquer disease or obtain sustenance is to placate it—through witchcraft, magic, voodoo, and/or human sacrifice.

One of ethical monotheism's greatest battles today is against the increasing deification of nature, movements that are generally led (as were most radical ideologies) by well-educated, secularized individuals.

Personal

The second essential characteristic is that God is personal.

The God of ethical monotheism is not some depersonalized force: God cares about His creations. As University of Chicago historian William A. Irwin wrote in a 1947 essay on ethical monotheism: "The world was to be understood in terms of personality. Its center and essence was not blind force or some sort of cold, inert reality but a personal God." God is not an Unmoved Mover, not a watchmaker who abandoned His watch after making it, as the Enlightenment Deists would have it. God knows each of us. We are, after all, "created in His image." This is not merely wishful thinking—why would God create a being capable of knowing Him, yet choose not to know that being?

This does not mean that God necessarily answers prayers or even that God intervenes in all or even any of our lives. It means that He knows us and cares about us. Caring beings are not created by an uncaring being.

The whole point of ethical monotheism is that God's greatest desire is that we act toward one another with justice and mercy. An Unmoved Mover who didn't know His human creatures couldn't care less how they treat one another.

Goodness

A third characteristic of God is goodness. If God weren't moral, ethical monotheism would be an oxymoron: A God who is not good cannot demand goodness. Unlike all other gods believed in prior to monotheism, the biblical God rules by moral standards. Thus, in the Babylonian version of the flood story, the gods, led by Enlil, sent a flood to destroy mankind, saving only Utnapishtim and his wife—because Enlil personally liked Utnapishtim. It is an act of caprice, not morality. In the biblical story, God also sends a flood, saving only Noah and his wife and family. The stories are almost identical except for one overwhelming difference: The entire Hebrew story is animated by ethical/moral concerns. God brings the flood solely because people treat one another, *not God*, badly, and God saves Noah solely because he was "the most righteous person in his generation."

Words cannot convey the magnitude of the change wrought by the Hebrew Bible's introduction into the world of a God who rules the universe morally.

One ramification is that despite the victories of evil people and the sufferings of good people, a moral God rules the world, and ultimately the good and the evil will receive their just deserts. I have never understood how a good secular individual can avoid debilitating despair. To care about goodness, yet to witness the unbearable torments of the good and the innocent, and to see many of the evil go unpunished—all the while believing that this life is all there is, that we are alone in a universe that hears no child's cry and sees no person's tears—has to be a recipe for despair. I would be overwhelmed with sadness if I did not believe that there is a good God who somehow—in this life or an afterlife—ensures that justice prevails.

Holiness

As primary as ethics are, man cannot live by morality alone. We are also instructed to lead holy lives: "You shall be holy because I the Lord your God am holy" (Leviticus 19:2). God is more than the source of morality, He is the source of holiness.

Ethics enables life; holiness ennobles it. Holiness is the elevation of the human being from his animal nature to his being created in the image of God. To cite a simple example, we can eat like an animal—with our fingers, belching, from the floor, while relieving ourselves–or elevate ourselves to eat from a table, with utensils and napkins, keeping our digestive sounds quiet. It is, however, very important to note that a person who eats like an animal is doing something unholy, not immoral. The distinction, lost upon many religious people, is an important one.

ONE GOD AND ONE MORALITY

The oneness of God is an indispensable component of ethical monotheism. Only if there is one God is there one morality. Two or more gods mean two or more divine wills, and therefore two or more moral codes. That is why ethical polytheism is unlikely. Once God told Abraham that human sacrifice is wrong, it was wrong. There was no competing god to teach otherwise.

One morality also means one moral code *for all humanity.* "Thou shall not murder" means that murder is wrong for everyone, not just for one culture. It means that *suttee*, the now-rare but once widespread Hindu practice of burning widows with their husband's body, is wrong. It means the killing of a daughter or sister who lost her virginity prior to marriage, practiced to this day in parts of the Arab world, is immoral. It means that clitoridectomies, the cutting off of a girl's clitoris (and sometimes more), a ritual practiced on almost one hundred million women living today mostly in Africa, is immoral.

While, in theory, the celebration of multiculturalism is neither offensive nor original, in actuality multiculturalism is yet another attempt to undermine ethical monotheism. Its underlying assumption is that there is no one universal moral code; all cultures are morally equal. As a professor wrote to the *New York Times* after that newspaper came out against clitoridectomies, who are we in the West to condemn anyone else's cultural practice?

ONE HUMANITY

One God who created human beings of all races means that all of humanity are related. Only if there is one Father are all of us brothers and sisters.

HUMAN LIFE IS SACRED

Another critical moral ramification of ethical monotheism is the sanctity of human life. Only if there is a God in whose image human beings are created is human life sacred. If human beings do not contain an element of the divine, they are merely intelligent animals.

For many years, I have been warning that a totally secular world-view will erode the distinction between humans and animals. The popular contemporary expression "All life is sacred" is an example of what secularism leads to. It means that all life is *equally* sacred, that people and chickens are equally valuable. That is why the head of a leading animal rights group, People for the Ethical Treatment of Animals (PETA), has likened the barbecuing of six billion chickens a year to the slaughter of six million Jews in the Holocaust; and that is how PETA could take out a full-page ad in the *Des Moines Register* equating the slaughter of animals with the murder of people.

Such views don't so much enhance the value of animal life as they reduce the value of human life.

GOD'S PRIMARY DEMAND IS GOODNESS

Of course, the clearest teaching of ethical monotheism is that God demands ethical behavior. As Ernest van den Haag described it: "[The Jews'] invisible God not only insisted on being the only and all-powerful God . . . He also developed into a moral God."

But ethical monotheism suggests more than that God demands ethical behavior; it means that God's *primary* demand is ethical behavior. It means that God cares about how we treat one another *more* than He cares about anything else.

Thus, ethical monotheism's message remains as radical today as when it was first promulgated. The secular world has looked elsewhere for its values, while even many religious Jews, Christians, and Muslims believe that God's primary demand is something other than ethics.

JEWS AND ETHICAL MONOTHEISM

Since Judaism gave the world ethical monotheism, one would expect that Jews would come closest to holding its values. In some important ways, this is true. Jews do hold that God judges everyone, Jew or Gentile, by his or her behavior. This is a major reason that Jews do not proselytize (though it is not an argument against Jews proselytizing; indeed, they ought to): Judaism has never believed that non-Jews have to embrace Judaism to attain salvation or any other reward in the afterlife.

But *within* Jewish religious life, the picture changes. The more observant a Jew is, the more he or she is likely to assume that God considers ritual observances to be at least as important as God's ethical demands.

This erroneous belief is as old as the Jewish people, and one against which the prophets passionately railed: "Do I [God] need your many sacrifices?" cried out Isaiah (Isaiah 1:11). The question is rhetorical. What God does demand is justice and goodness based on faith in God: "Oh, man," taught the prophet Micah, "God has told you what is good and what God requires of you—*only* that you act justly, love goodness and walk humbly with your God" (Micah 6:8, emphasis added).

In Judaism, the commandments between human beings and God are extremely significant. *But they are not as important as ethical behavior.* The prophets, Judaism's most direct messengers of God, affirmed this view repeatedly, and the Talmudic rabbis later echoed it. "Love your neighbor as yourself is the greatest principle in the Torah," said Rabbi Akiva (Palestinian Talmud, Nedarim 9:4).

That is why when the great Rabbi Hillel was asked by a pagan to summarize all of Judaism "while standing on one leg," he was able to do so: "What is hateful to you, do not do to others; the rest is commentary; now go and study" (Babylonian Talmud, Shabbat 31a). Hillel could have said, "Keep the 613 commandments of the Torah; now go and do them," but he didn't. In fact, he went further. After enunciating his ethical principle, he concluded, *"The rest is commentary."* In other words, the rest of Judaism is essentially a commentary on how to lead an ethical life.

Unfortunately, with no more direct messages from God, and few Hillels, the notion that the laws between man and God and the laws between people are equally important gained ever wider acceptance in religious Jewish life.

Perhaps there are three reasons for this:

1: It is much more difficult to be completely ethical than to completely observe the ritual laws. While one can master the laws between people and God, no one can fully master human decency.

2: While ethical principles are more or less universal, the laws between people and God are uniquely Jewish. Therefore, that which most distinguishes observant Jews from nonobservant Jews and from non-Jews are Judaism's ritual laws, not its ethical laws. Thus it was easy for a mind-set to develop which held that whatever is most distinctively Jewish—i.e., the laws between people and God—is more Jewishly important than whatever is universal.

3: Observance of many laws between people and God is public and obvious. Other Jews can see how you pray, how diligently you learn Talmud and Torah, and if you dress in the modest manner dictated by Jewish law. Few people know how you conduct your business affairs, how you treat your employees, how you talk behind others' backs, or how you treat your spouse. Therefore, the easiest way to demonstrate the depth of your religiosity is through observance of the laws between man and God, especially the ones that are most public.

Yet, while observant Jews may overstress the "monotheism" in "ethical monotheism," the fact is that they believe the entire doctrine to be true. Secular Jews, on the other hand, believe that ethics can be separated from God and religion. The results have not been positive. The ethical record of Jews and non-Jews involved in causes that abandoned ethical monotheism has included involvement in moral relativism, Marxism, and the worship of art, education, law, etc. (see the next chapter).

The lessons for religious Jews are never to forget the primacy of ethics and not to abandon the ethical monotheist mission of Judaism. The lesson for secular Jews is to realize that ethics cannot long survive the death of monotheism.

CHRISTIANS AND ETHICAL MONOTHEISM

While the challenge to making ethics primary in Judaism is largely one of Jews rather than of Judaism, the challenge to Christianity is more rooted in the religion itself. Within Christianity, the doctrine developed that correct faith, not correct works, is God's primary concern.

Paul articulated this view in the New Testament: If good deeds could lead to salvation, he reasoned, "Christ would have died in vain" (Galatians 2:21). For that reason, he continued, "We conclude that a man is put right with God only through faith, and not by doing what the law commands" (Romans 3:28).

True, Catholicism holds that faith alone is not sufficient, that some works, too, are necessary for salvation. But between faith in Christ and goodness in behavior, the Church has, until recently, nearly always taught that faith is more important. Thus the Church held for nearly two millennia that even the kindest non-Christians were all doomed: "Outside of the Church there is no salvation." In a major move toward ethical monotheism, the twentieth-century Catholic Church has reinterpreted this statement, and now teaches that while salvation will come through Jesus, it is not necessary for an individual to assert belief in Jesus by name in order to be saved; only God judges who is saved, and Catholics cannot declare who they are.

Historically, the thrust of Church teachings has not been that cruelty or unethical behavior is the greatest sin. As historian Norman Cohn wrote:

> The sins to which the Devil of Christian tradition has tempted human beings are varied indeed: apostasy, idolatry, heresy, fornication, gluttony, vanity, using cosmetics, dressing luxuriously, going to the theater, gambling, avarice, quarreling, spiritual sloth have all, at times, figured in the list. . . . I have looked in vain for a single instance . . . of the Devil tempting a human being to cruelty.[1]

Some statements attributed to Jesus can lead a Christian to abandon the fight against evil: "Resist not evil" is the prime example. Others include: "Pray for those who persecute you," "Love your enemies" (Matthew 5:44), and Jesus' prayer on the cross beseeching God to forgive his murderers. Christians can interpret each of these verses in a way that does not detract from a Christian's duty to fight evil. For example, the verses can be explained as applying only to an individual—i.e., the ideal individual Christian will not resist evil done to *him*, will love those who hurt *her*, etc., but this shouldn't be taken to mean that believers won't resist evil done to others. Such interpretations are certainly welcome. But it is difficult to imagine that the ideal Christian will lead a life of nonresistance to evil directed to self, and then strongly resist evil when it is done to others.

These verses of Jesus may explain why as prominent and personally fine a Christian as the Reverend Billy Graham, the most widely listened to Protestant in the world, failed to call evil by its name when he visited the Soviet Union in 1982. Indeed, true to Martin Luther's teachings, Graham called on Soviet Christians to obey the Soviet authorities, and did not publicly side with perse-

[1] *The New York Review of Books*, April 25, 1985.

cuted Christians. Rather than refer to the Soviet Union as an enemy of Christianity, the Reverend Graham only referred to the "common enemy" of nuclear war. At the time of the visit, George Will wrote:

> Graham's delicacy [about the Soviet Union] is less interesting than his "common enemy" formulation. . . . His language suggests a moral symmetry between his country and the Soviet Union.
>
> The *Washington Post* reports that when Graham spoke in two churches, both "were heavily guarded, with police sealing off all roads leading to them. Hundreds of KGB security agents . . . were in the congregation." Graham told one congregation that God "gives you the power to be a better worker, a more loyal citizen because in Romans 13 we are told to obey the authorities." How is that for a message from America?
>
> Graham is America's most famous Christian. Solzhenitsyn is Russia's. The contrast is instructive.[2]

Another area of Christian theology that undermines ethical monotheism is the belief that God saves human beings irrespective of how they act toward one another, just as long as they have the right faith. Millions of Protestants hold that believers in Jesus, no matter how many cruel acts they may perform, attain salvation, while nonbelievers in Jesus, no matter how much good they do and how much they may love God, are doomed to eternal damnation.

In spite of these teachings, two points need to be emphasized.

First, it is Christianity, more than any other religion, including Judaism, that has carried the message of the Jewish prophets, the clearest voices of ethical monotheism, to the world.

Second, Christianity, though not theologically pure in its ethical monotheism, can and does lead millions of people to more ethical lives. People do not live by theology alone. Theological teachings aside, the kindness and selflessness often associated with religious Christians and with charitable Christian institutions are rarely paralleled anywhere in the secular world—and infrequently in the religious world, either.

I yearn for the day when Christians will emphasize ethical monotheism as the most important part of their commitment to Christianity. I know from years of work and friendship with Chris-

---

[2]George Will, "Churches in Politics: Pray for Skepticism," *Los Angeles Times*, May 13, 1982.

tians of all persuasions that ethical monotheism is a value that many of them can easily and passionately affirm.

MUSLIMS AND ETHICAL MONOTHEISM

During some of the Western world's darkest periods, Islam was a religious light in the monotheistic world. The seeds of ethical monotheism are deeply rooted in Islam. For whatever reason, however, the soil for their nourishment has, over the last several hundred years, been depleted of necessary nutrients. Islam could be a world force for ethical monotheism, but in its present state, the outlook is problematic.

The Quran has numerous verses that emphasize belief in the one universal God who judges people according to their behavior. Like all religions, however, Islam contains xenophobic elements and doctrines that are incompatible with ethical monotheism. Unlike some other religions today, however, within Islam, xenophobia and hostility to ethical monotheism too often seem to prevail. For example, though the Quran states explicitly that in matters of faith there shall be no coercion, almost everywhere Islam dominates there is considerable religious coercion, whether by the state or by the community.

An example of such state-sponsored coercion is Saudi Arabia, where religious police monitor what Muslims drink and reduce women to childlike status by forbidding them, for example, to drive cars. Saudi Arabia also severely restricts the religious freedom of other faiths.

The Sudan, too, is ruled by devout Muslims, and it is one of the most cruel states in the world, especially to its large black non-Muslim minority.

Muslims need what most Christians and Jews have experienced—separation of church and state; interaction with other faiths and with modernity; and reform. Islam needs to compete with secularism, not outlaw it, and to allow competing ideologies within Islam. In religion, as in politics, when there is no competition, there is corruption and intolerance.

There are some Muslim voices crying for reform and for ethical monotheism, such as that of Dr. Fathi Osman, the former Princeton historian of Islam and editor of *Arabia*. When their influence increases, Islam will be a world force for ethical monotheism.

CONCLUSION

In his essay "The Hebrews" in the seminal 1947 work *The Intellectual Adventure of Ancient Man: An Essay on Speculative Thought in the Ancient Near East*, Professor William A. Irwin writes:

> Israel's great achievement, so apparent that mention of it is almost trite, was monotheism. It was an achievement that transformed subsequent history.
>
> One may raise the question whether any other single contribution from whatever source since human culture emerged from the stone ages has had the far-reaching effect upon history that Israel in this regard has exerted both through the mediums of Christianity and Islam and directly through the world of Jewish thinkers themselves.
>
> The nations are condemned [by the Prophets] for the depravity of their morals. And here is the point: they are so condemned by the God of Israel! It is His righteousness, be it observed, not His might or His glory or any other of the divine qualities prized at the time, which provides the ground of his supremacy. Here we see the meaning of that phrase so commonly employed in the study of Hebrew history: Israel's monotheism was an ethical monotheism.

As the twentieth century ends, most people have still not learned its most obvious lesson—that attempts to change the world that do not place God and goodness at their center will make this world worse. Is it not time to try ethical monotheism?

It is the only truly effective answer to moral relativism, to racism, to nationalism, to worshiping art or law or success. All one needs to do is live by the simple and revolutionary message of Micah, "to do justice, love goodness, and walk humbly with your God."

36

HOW GOOD AND EVIL BECOME IRRELEVANT: THE OTHER GODS WE WORSHIP

The most fundamental teaching of ethical monotheism is that any value, *no matter how meaningful or beautiful,* when divorced from goodness and God, can easily lead to evil. Put in theological terms, any value that becomes an end in itself can easily become a false god.

What follows are widely held *good* values that easily become ends in themselves and can then lead to evil.

ART

It is very tempting to adulate beauty. That is why art is one of humanity's oldest gods. To some of the ancient Greeks, for example, no value surpassed beauty. In contrast, biblical ethical monotheism prohibited the making of graven images. As a result, in the words of one scholar, "To the Greeks, the beautiful was holy, and to the Jews the holy was beautiful." That is why the Greeks, for all their magnificent artistic and philosophical achievements—and we owe the Greeks an enormous debt—could abandon ugly and sick infants to die on hilltops. They deemed beauty more important than morality—or, more accurately, beauty *was* a form of morality.

To this day, the power and appeal of art are so great that art can easily become a supreme value in an individual's life. But artistic values are not necessarily moral ones. Ethical monotheists must constantly remind people that art is value-neutral. While art can be aesthetically and emotionally uplifting, not to mention a source of profound personal gratification—it certainly is in my life (I conduct classical music as an avocation)—it can also morally desensitize its devotees.

A person may be moved to tears when listening to a Brahms symphony or standing before a Matisse painting. But neither the symphony nor the painting has an impact on ethics (unless the person wants it to, but that is true of gardening, sports, and any other human endeavor). The relationship between art and morality is the same as between football and morality. The greatest artist or art connoisseur is no more likely to be a good person than the greatest football player or fan.

This may seem obvious, but Western culture has a way of hiding this truth. Many parents take much more pride in their children's flute playing or ballet dancing than in their goodness. And it is usually considerably more prestigious to be a member of a museum's or orchestra's board of directors than to serve on the board of Big Brothers or of a church or synagogue.

One of the Holocaust's most important lessons is that the most cultured nation in Europe produced the death camps and gas chambers. People often ask how the nation that produced Goethe, Schiller, and Beethoven could produce Auschwitz. But the question betrays the questioner's belief in art as a generator of morality. A nation that produces great artists is no less likely to commit atrocities than one that produces great athletes.

The ability of great art and evil to coexist was exemplified in the life of Richard Wagner, a musical genius who embodied both traits. Those who identify art with human decency must confront the fact that Auschwitz had a resident orchestra and that its commandant was an accomplished pianist who would spend his nights playing Schubert after having supervised the torture and gassing of thousands of people during the day.

The amorality of art was likewise illustrated by the life of one of the greatest conductors of the postwar era, the German Herbert von Karajan. Throughout his postwar life, he never repented for joining the Nazi Party or serving as *Kapellmeister*, chief musician, under Hitler. He simply stated whenever the question was raised— and few in the music world ever raised this issue with the maestro—that his only concern was making beautiful music. Karajan personified the rule that *the moment anything other than goodness becomes your most important concern, good and evil become irrelevant.*

One does not have to go back to World War II for examples of artists placing art over decency. Witness this front-page story in the *New York Times* of August 10, 1984: "Malaysia, a Moslem country, has asked the New York Philharmonic to replace a work by a Jewish composer on a concert program there. *The orchestra has agreed to comply.*" (Emphasis added.)

Only after adverse publicity, and under great pressure, did the New York Philharmonic change its mind and refuse to perform in Malaysia.

Examples of artistic beauty coexisting with moral ugliness can be found in all the arts. For example, Norman Mailer, who is considered among America's greatest novelists, has glorified both criminals and murder. This is how he once described the act of murder:

> It means that one human being has determined to extinguish the life of another human being. It means that two people are engaged in a dialogue with eternity. . . . What happened is that the killer is becoming . . . a little more ready to love someone.[1]

Mailer's belief that murderers are loving types—in addition to his belief that blacks who murder are essentially victims themselves—led him to work for the release of Jack Abbot, a convicted murderer, from prison. Mailer was deeply impressed with the literary quality of Abbot's writings, which held American society in contempt, defended violent criminals, and praised Communist societies. In his introduction to Abbot's book, the novelist wrote: "The proudest, the bravest, the most daring, the most enterprising, and the most undefeated of the poor . . . are drawn to crime . . . " After *The New York Review of Books* printed Mailer's introduction, and literary critics praised Abbot's book, Mailer and Abbot were featured on national American television ("Good Morning America"). Shortly thereafter, Abbot murdered another man. Mailer's reaction was that we have to take risks for the sake of culture, and that "If society is willing to invest in nuclear weapons, we should be willing to invest in people like Jack Abbot."

[1] *Mademoiselle*, February 1961.

Music and other artistic talents are great gifts from God. But unless accompanied by a higher regard for goodness, no one becomes a kinder or more just human being after playing Mozart.

This is something that ethical monotheists need to remind the art world, a world too often intoxicated with its own importance. In repeated battles in the United States over government funding of the arts, the art world has repeatedly taken the position that one of the truest indicators of a society's level of development is its artistic development and, of course, the degree to which it funds its artists. Both positions are untrue, because neither necessarily says anything about a society's moral development.

Ironically, the battle over funding was engendered by the very sorts of works that prove that art, unaccompanied by higher values, can lead to a degradation of the human spirit. One of the works that prompted the controversy was an exhibit of photographs by Robert Mapplethorpe. Among them were photographs of a naked man in boots, bent over, a bullwhip protruding from his anus. Another photo showed a young girl spreading her legs, wearing nothing underneath her skirt.

The spiritual state of the art world was demonstrated by its widespread defense of Mapplethorpe's photographs as fine art. It is only when the notion of the holy is dead that people can find beauty in a photograph of a man urinating into another man's mouth. During a Cincinnati trial, convened to rule whether the Mapplethorpe exhibit constituted obscenity, the curator of another art museum was shown this photo and asked if she considered it good art. "Yes," she replied. "Why?" asked the lawyer. "Because of the lighting and composition," responded the art curator.

Only when nothing is more important than art can museum curators fixate on the "lighting and composition" in such photos. Few groups in Western life need ethical monotheism more than artists.

EDUCATION

One of these groups is academia.

Even more than art, education is widely regarded, especially by the well-educated, as a great good in and of itself; and the well-educated are regarded as society's most likely saviors. These notions are as mistaken as the belief in art's moral qualities. Education as an end in itself is a false god that is no more likely to produce a good person than is baseball.

Of course education can lead to goodness, but only when it is not divorced from good and evil and from God. That, unfortunately, is generally the case in the modern secular world, which is why a person with a doctorate is no more likely to be moral or kind than one with only a high school diploma. In fact, higher education in the twentieth century has often meant a particular attraction to evil or, at the very least, an extraordinary inability to recognize it.

- In the West, it was intellectuals, far more than blue-collar workers or high school dropouts, who were most likely to be attracted to the greatest mass murderer in history, Joseph Stalin.
- The Anti-Defamation League reports that blacks at American universities are more likely to be anti-Semitic than blacks who never attend college.
- The architects of the poison gas attack on the Tokyo subway were the most highly educated of Japan's young people— young men who held doctorates from Japan's equivalent of Harvard and Stanford.

None of this is new.

Professor Peter Merkl of the University of California, Santa Barbara, studied 581 Nazis and found that Germans with a high school education or "even university study" were *more likely* to be anti-Semitic than those with less education.[2] A study of twenty-four leaders of the *Einsatzgruppen* (the mobile killing units that murdered more than a million and a half Jews prior to the use of gas chambers) indicated that the majority were highly educated professionals: "One of the most striking things . . . is the prevalence of educated people, professionals, especially lawyers, Ph.D.s . . . "[3]

Of course, there are many highly moral academics and other well-educated people. In fact, many of the finest works critical of academic amorality and immorality have been written by professors. But there are also many highly moral uneducated people. In other words, there is no link between having a good education and being a good person. This should come as sobering news to the large number of parents who view education as the most important

[2]Peter Merkl, *Political Violence Under the Swastika*, p. 503.
[3]Irving Greenberg in Eva Fleishner, ed. *Auschwitz: Beginning of a New Era*, p. 17.

value in their children's lives. To make a living and to get ahead, education is very important. To become a proficient doctor or lawyer, college and graduate school are essential. But to become a good person, modern secular education is largely irrelevant. Given the moral relativism and hostility to religious morality that characterize contemporary higher education, it is frequently a handicap.

It is primarily for this reason that I am so partial to religious schooling for Jews and Christians; though unless ethical monotheism—i.e., the centrality of ethics—is taught, religious education, too, does not guarantee moral graduates.

When I was a young child in a Jewish day school, we recited the biblical verse "Wisdom begins with awe of God" (Psalms 111:10) during the morning prayer service. Seeing the magnitude of moral foolishness that has emanated from secular universities in this century—e.g., widespread attraction to Marxism and fascism; the reduction of values to race, gender, and class; and moral relativism—I again think of this verse daily. Belief in God certainly doesn't guarantee wisdom, but the death of God seems to guarantee foolishness.

LAW

Nothing is more important to the creation of a better world than societies based on law. Law is indispensable to goodness and to ethical monotheism. Yet law, too, is a value-neutral tool and can become an end in itself. When it does, it ceases to be a vehicle for goodness.

This is true for both religious and secular law. To cite a religious example, in both Judaism and Catholicism, laws of marriage and divorce, when unbending, can lead to injustice. In Judaism, they can lead to the *agunah*, a woman who cannot remarry because her husband refuses to grant her a divorce (Deuteronomy 24:1-2 are understood as vesting the right of divorce solely in the husband's hands). In Catholicism, the injustice is considerably more widespread, as it affects all divorcing individuals. No matter how miserable a Catholic's marriage may be, once it is entered into, divorce is unacceptable. If divorce is obtained civilly, the divorced parties are never permitted to remarry within the Church and are expected to remain chaste and celibate for the rest of their lives.

Belief in law as an end in itself is also widespread in the secular world. Increasingly, attorneys and judges ask not "What is moral or right?" but "What is the law?" In the American criminal justice system, lawyers typically use the law to win, not as a vehicle for justice or morality. And when state supreme court justices order that children be permanently taken away from every person they love and given to "birth fathers" who never had seen them, they use law as a vehicle to evil.

Examples of the law being used to frustrate justice abound. The Miranda law is frequently used this way. The Miranda ruling stipulates that, at the moment of arrest, suspects must be read their rights, including the right to remain silent until a lawyer is present. Seeing this law as an end in itself, a United States federal district court disqualified the confession of a terrorist who blew up an airplane because the Miranda warning presented to him at the time of arrest had three words misspelled in Arabic.[4] For that judge, the Miranda law, not justice, was what mattered.

To cite one other example, the American Civil Liberties Union, basing its argument on the legal principle that people are free to do whatever they want unless engaged in criminal activity, argued against a mayoral directive to the New York City police to take homeless people off the street when the temperature dropped below freezing. As the *Wall Street Journal* (January 14, 1986) reported: "The New York Civil Liberties Union is so affronted that it sends out its own 'freeze patrol' to advise the mentally ill of their 'right' to refuse the city's benevolence." This is what can happen when one loves laws more than people.

As indispensable as laws are, they are only a means. Law, like art and education, is value-neutral. Laws can be used to lead to goodness and to God. They can also be used for evil. Indeed, at Nuremberg, after the war, there was a special trial for Nazi judges, and their well-articulated defense was that they only judged according to the law of their society.

Finally, a life devoted to law assures no more decency than a life devoted to art. According to the study of the twenty-four Nazi mass murderers cited above, *nine were lawyers*. The lawyer who introduced me before I delivered a lecture to the Beverly Hills Bar Association told the group, "In order to be a good lawyer, you must first be a good person." His heart was in the right place, but he was wrong. It is very possible to be a bad person and a good lawyer.

[4]L. Gordon Crovitz, "How Law Destroys Order," *National Review*, February 11, 1991.

LOVE

In 1989, a group of youths attacked a woman jogging in New York's Central Park; raped her; beat her with rocks, bricks, fists, and an iron bar; and left her to die. New York's archbishop, John Cardinal O'Connor, visited the injured woman in the hospital, and then visited the boys arrested for the rape, to tell them, according to his own report in *Catholic New York*, "that God loves you."

"God is love" reads the title on the cover of one of my copies of the New Testament. "God is love" proclaimed minister after minister during the ten years I hosted a weekly interreligious dialogue on radio.

But if God is love, it is equally correct to say that God is justice, or God is truth, or, for that matter, God is punishment. God has many qualities; love is only one of them.

The equation of love and God is morally and theologically dangerous. If love is the supreme value, all other values are, by definition, subordinate to it, and among those values is morality.

Declaring love to be the supreme value is meaningless. Does it refer to love as a feeling or love as an act? If it means a feeling, then am I sinning if I do not love a torturer as much as the person he tortured? On the other hand, if love is defined by action and I am supposed to love everyone, then I must *act* equally loving toward everyone. But this is immoral. Anyone who acts with equal love toward torturers and their victims is rewarding evil.

"Hate the sin, love the sinner," is the response of many Christians to this challenge. But when evil is involved, it doesn't work. Those who love Hitler are less likely to fight him than those who hate him.

Finally, I do not believe that God equally loves Hitler and Raoul Wallenberg, the Swedish diplomat who saved tens of thousands of Jews from Hitler. Therefore, I certainly don't believe that any human being should love them equally. To ask that I love them both is to play with the word "love" and literally to de-moralize it. Surely, no Christian can possibly desire that anyone actively or emotionally respond to Charles Manson and Mother Teresa equally. Unless one answers that by punishing Manson with life in prison and by hugging Mother Teresa one is showing them "equal love"—a response that stretches love to the point of meaninglessness—there is no moral way to bestow love equally on all people. Nor should there be.

Love is beautiful, and it is a very high value. But it is not the highest value. Goodness is higher, and love should be a means to it. When it becomes an absolute value in itself, love easily ends up tolerating evil. Some hatred, morally based, is necessary for a good world.

COMPASSION

Another tempting distraction from making goodness one's primary concern is compassion. For some people, especially in contemporary America, compassion is a higher value than goodness, or, to be more precise, is considered identical with goodness (in the way some religious people equate "religious" with "good").

Yet even compassion, like love and all the other values cited here, is value-free. Unlike love, however, which can be dispensed equally to both healthy and sick people, compassion is by definition selective: For example, one cannot show equal compassion to both the healthy and the sick. The question must always be: To which party do we dispense compassion? The answer must be guided by ethical values. But in our time, with its ethical relativism, compassion is frequently dispensed to the wrong parties.

Compassion is a beautiful trait, but only when morally focused. That is why the Hebrew Bible warns people against unjust compassion—judges are instructed not to favor poor people against rich people. (It also warns judges against favoring the rich, but that is a warning against being intimidated by wealth and status, not a warning against misplaced compassion—Leviticus 19:15.) And the prophet Isaiah declared that Israel will be "redeemed through justice"—through justice, not compassion (Isaiah 1:27).

Truth, too, is at risk when compassion becomes the highest value. As Bernard Goldberg, a CBS News correspondent, has noted, many media people are governed more by compassion than by truth:

> There was a lot of bad, irresponsible reporting on AIDS. . . . The real reason journalists got this story so wrong, I think, is much more subtle than circulation and ratings competition—and much more insidious. It is what we might call journalism-by-sentiment. And it applies to far more than just the AIDS story. . . . In 1987, David Wilson wrote in the *Boston Globe*: "The media don't mind having their chains pulled by the homeless. Sanctimonious com-

passion, someone once said, is a key element in media self-defini-
tion and self-promotion."[5]

Compassion for AIDS victims has led many media people to
greatly overstate the likelihood of middle-class heterosexual
non–intravenous drug users to contract AIDS—because they fear
that if people knew that AIDS in America is far more likely to strike
gay men, IV drug users and their partners, and inner-city blacks
and Hispanics, the great majority of the society would not care
much about funding research into the disease. So, too, compassion
for the homeless has dictated that journalists portray them as folks
like you and me who have been hurt by hard luck and a callous
society. That the large majority are individuals with a history of
drug, alcohol, or mental problems is rarely noted—lest people not
respond generously.

Editor-in-chief of *U.S. News and World Report* Mortimer B.
Zuckerman has pointed out what colleges' misdirected compassion
toward blacks has led to:

> To show compassion and to avoid confrontation, academic leaders
> who would never have given whites separate dorms have given
> them to blacks, along with their own student unions, homecoming
> dances, yearbooks and the like. Thus has the noble cause of civil
> rights been corrupted by the arrogant gods of social engineering.
>
> Nor are the special programs working for black students.
> They have the lowest college completion rate—only thirty percent
> obtained a bachelors degree in 5 years.[6]

George Will summarized the invidiousness of inappropriate
compassion in these words:

> Conspicuous consumption has been supplanted by a new vulgarity
> conspicuous compassion (Allan Bloom's phrase). It is flaunted by
> people too exquisitely even-handed to "single out" the raped from
> the rapists [referring to Cardinal O'Connor's previously discussed
> action]. . . ."[7]

If we wish to *feel* good, compassion is excellent. But if we want
to *do* good, our compassion must be guided by moral standards.

[5]"No Place for Sentimental Journalism on AIDS," *New York Times*, February 2,
1990.
[6]*U.S. News and World Report*, July 29, 1991.
[7]*Washington Post*, May 16, 1989.

REASON

Ethical monotheism means that God demands ethical conduct from us. To secular thinkers, God is unnecessary to ethics, since reason alone can distinguish good from evil.

Reason therefore becomes the humanists' substitute for God and religion. As Yale philosopher Brand Blanshard wrote, "Rationality takes the place of faith. . . . Take reason seriously . . . Let it shape belief and conduct freely. It will shape them aright if anything can."[8]

Without detracting from the need for reason, which is invaluable to morality and which too many religious people have insufficiently used, we have to recognize reason's moral limitations:

1.   Reason can justify virtually any behavior.
2.   Reason does not demand moral behavior.
3.   Reason does not spur moral passion.

Morally speaking, reason suggests only means, not goals. If you want to be good, reason will be indispensable in helping you to achieve it. But reason alone does not suggest that you be good. Acting immorally can be at least as reasonable as acting morally. The decision to be good is not a reason-based one; it is an act of *faith*, even by an atheist, namely that acting good is more important than anything else.

If reason were one's only guide, on what purely rational basis could slavery have been opposed during the long time that it was economically advantageous? If reason had been their only guide, no non-Jews would have risked their lives to save a Jew during the Holocaust. Was the German or Polish non-Jew who did nothing on behalf of a Jewish neighbor acting rationally? More so than the non-Jew who risked his or her life to save a Jew. Reason without ethical monotheism is an amoral tool, one that can as easily be used for evil as for good.

When great moral figures have been asked why they acted as they did, none of whom I am aware responded that it was reason that impelled them to make the sacrifices they did. Often religious in nature, the value may also have been a secular one such as love of one's country, freedom, or humanity, but never "reason." How could reason compel a person to sacrifice his or her life when reason argues at least as persuasively for self-survival?

[8]*The Humanist*, November–December 1974.

Finally, reason doesn't induce passion. Neither Moses nor Jesus, nor Muhammad nor the Buddha, was motivated by reason alone. Nor, in our century, were people like Martin Luther King Jr. or Aleksandr Solzhenitsyn. Moreover, the institutions and individuals most committed to reason—Western universities and intellectuals—have had a particularly unimpressive moral record.

Reason and ethical monotheism constitute the most effective combination for achieving good.

The belief that reason alone leads to morality is a secular myth, just as the belief that faith alone leads to morality is a religious myth.

BLOOD AND NATIONALISM

Perhaps the most widely worshiped false god in history has been blood—the denial of value to individuals unrelated by blood, and the valuing of race. To the great majority of human beings who have lived on this planet, standards of good and evil were always second to considerations of blood—I owe my family, my tribe, and my race (or ethnicity) a certain level of behavior, but not others.

The Japanese treatment of non-Japanese and the German treatment of non-"Aryans" in World War II, the ethnic cleansing in Bosnia, and the ethnic mass slaughter in Rwanda are only a few twentieth-century examples of the consequences of the belief that moral concerns are secondary to ties of race and blood.

Such beliefs animate policy in modern democracies such as the United States as well. Some people believe that it is better for a child to be raised by a blood-related single parent who has never met the child than by the loving adoptive couple whom the child has considered as mother and father from birth. The majority of justices on the Illinois Supreme Court ruled in 1995 that the fate of a four-year-old child is of no concern, only the claims of a biological father who had never seen the child mattered. They ruled that no hearing to determine Baby Richard's best interests be allowed. Better to ruin the lives of a young boy, his seven-year-old brother, and the mother and father who were his parents than to leave him with this nonblood family.

So, too, the National Association of Black Social Workers and the community of social workers that supports this decision hold that it is better for a black child, even a half-black child, to have no family than to have a nonblack family. Similarly, children are sometimes taken from their families if they are found to have as little as one-sixteenth Indian blood, and are given to Indian tribes (not even birth parents) to be raised. The government of Rwanda has ruled that it is better for hundreds of thousands of its orphaned children to have no family, indeed almost no food or clothing or human contact, than to be adopted by non-Rwandan families.

These are a few of countless examples, in the micro realm, of the belief that moral concerns are secondary to racial or blood ones.

Then there is nationalism.

With the decline of belief in God and religion in the Western world, many well-educated people adopted reason and humanism as their guiding values. Many others, however, adopted a far less abstract and far more dangerous value—the nation or state. In its most virulent forms—fascism, Nazism, and Communism—the state became an end in itself. In such instances, good was defined as that which serves the state (fascism), the race (Nazism), or the party (Communism).

One does not have to be a fascist or Communist, however, to allow nationalism to obscure good and evil. Conservatives in democracies who ask only "Is it good for my country?" rather than "Is it good?" also place country above morality. That is why the motto of American conservative Pat Buchanan, "America first," is, as another conservative, William Bennett, described it, "flirting with fascism."

The same holds true for gender and race. Women's groups that ask only "Is it good for women?" and racial or ethnic groups that ask only "Is it good for my race or ethnic group?" are on the same moral plane as rightist groups that ask only "Is it good for my country?" They all elevate kinship over decency.

LIFE

Another possible consequence of secularism is the idealization of life as the highest good. Life should be very close to the highest value (if it isn't, the consequences, as Japanese kamikazes and Islamic suicide bombers have shown, are frightening). But life cannot be the highest value. Life, like all the other wonderful values noted here, is not to be an end in itself, but a means to goodness and God.

For many individuals, however, life has become an end in itself, and therefore never to be relinquished for a higher good because there is no higher good than living. Living has become the purpose of life.

One consequence of this belief is the widespread belief in pacifism, the belief that it is always wrong to kill. Pacifism is a product of the collapse of ethical monotheism among both secular and religious individuals. Since secularism means that this life is all there is, life is understandably the greatest value to many secular people. As for religious pacifists (a term that ought to be an oxymoron), they affirm a God whose primary demand is life, not goodness.

Life *is* sacred, but a good life is more sacred.

RELIGION AND FAITH IN GOD

Although religion ultimately provides the best vehicle for a good world, *religion, too, can become a false god and lead to evil.*

It does so when it:

1:   Becomes an end in itself and not a means to goodness.

2:   Holds some value other than goodness to be God's primary demand ("primary" does not mean "only"; God also demands holiness). Examples include faith, as when Christians teach that proper faith is more important to God than proper actions, and religious law, as when Jews and Muslims regard religious law as an end in itself rather than as a means to goodness.

Religion without goodness as its central demand is among the most dangerous of all humanity's false gods. People who appear to be religious but act immorally may be the greatest threats to a better world. No atheist damages ethical monotheism as much as a religious person who acts immorally, because the evil religious person convinces other people that religion and God are irrelevant or even a barrier to leading a moral life.

Religious people must confront the fact that it is possible to believe fervently in God and to commit evil. The argument that a person who commits evil obviously does not believe in God—"Anyone who does something like that cannot possibly be religious"—is merely self-serving.

This argument is also destructive. People who believe that "religious" and "good" are synonymous (incidentally, these people believe this only about members of their own religion!) will never recognize the need for their religion to emphasize the teaching of goodness.

Finally, since the moral record of religions that have achieved political power is awful (although not as bad as secular antireligious ideologies that have attained power), the ideal society is one with a secular government and a religious (ethical monotheism–based) population.

PROFITS AND SUCCESS

When profits are given a higher priority than ethics, the result is cooperation with evil: I. G. Farben and the other German firms that helped the Nazis gas Jews; Pepsi-Cola's business dealings with Leonid Brezhnev's totalitarian USSR and its past support for the Arab economic boycott of Israel; the German, French, and American firms that supplied Iraq's Saddam Hussein with the means to manufacture chemical and biological weapons; and companies that market music and rap albums that condone violence against police and women are among the innumerable examples of businesses placing a value higher than goodness.

The depiction of big business as a foe of the Left is a myth. The goal of businesses is to make money, and some will do it no matter what moral compromises it entails, and therefore ally themselves with anyone of any political persuasion. Lenin was right when he said that capitalists would vie with one another to sell the rope by which they themselves would ultimately be hanged.

While the pursuit of profits is obviously value-neutral, the pursuit of success seems perfectly fine. Yet the pursuit of success for its own sake is as morally dangerous as Herbert von Karajan's pursuit of music with no moral considerations was. In my media life, I often see what the pursuit of success as the highest goal leads to— the daily compromising of people's integrity for ratings and profits. Likewise, there are too many lawyers who will morally compromise themselves to win cases. The raising of our children to be successful as their primary goal in life is a major factor in the widely perceived decline of American life.

PSYCHOLOGY

One contemporary phenomenon that often undermines goodness is the substitution of psychology for morality. Instead of good and evil, many people now speak of "healthy" and "sick."

As a result, many people aspire far more to psychological health than to moral health. The two are not necessarily related, and they are certainly not the same. People who do bad are not necessarily characterized by psychopathology, and those who do good are not necessarily psychologically healthy.

It is very tempting to dismiss evil as sick, but that is often false, and the longer people believe in this falsehood, the longer we delay the arrival of a more moral world. We have no reason to believe that Adolf Eichmann, an architect of the Holocaust, was a particularly sick man, nor do we have reason to assume that Raoul Wallenberg, Eichmann's moral opposite, was particularly healthy. What differed most were not their psyches, but their values. Values. Always values.

None of this is meant to deny the immense importance of psychology to a happier life. We deeply need the insights of psychology. But we also deeply need God and religious values. That is why I believe that every clergyman should go through psychotherapy and every psychotherapist should attend church or synagogue. Unfortunately, while the majority of clergy recognizes the importance of psychotherapy, few psychotherapists recognize the importance of God and religion.

That is very sad. Psychotherapists who believe that people are curable through psychology alone are as mistaken as clergy who believe religion alone can guarantee a happy and healthy individual.

At its best, psychotherapy enables us to know what is blocking our ability to function healthfully, especially lovingly. But even at its best, psychology cannot tell us why to live and how to behave. That is the province of religion—at *its* best.

PROGRESS

Economics

During the Cold War, when I debated opponents of anti-Communism, they often conceded that Communist regimes deny their people some liberties, but, these people argued, at least they fed and educated their people.

As it happens, Communist regimes generally did an awful job of feeding their people, which is one of the reasons so many people wanted to flee Communist countries. Many Communist takeovers have led to the worst famines in their countries' histories. The Soviet Union, Tibet, and Ethiopia are three such examples.

But even to the extent that the argument that "They feed their people" was true, it betrayed an absence of moral thinking. Black slaves in the United States were generally adequately fed, yet who could defend slavery on those or any other grounds? Likewise, blacks living under apartheid in South Africa were better fed than nearly all other Africans. Did that make apartheid morally defensible?

The substitution of economic for ethical concerns has been one of the most powerful tools employed by those opposed to ethical monotheism.

Literacy

Defenders of Communist regimes did cite one valid statistic—literacy rates generally rose under Communism. This was, however, *morally* insignificant. If the only literature one is allowed to read is Communist Party lies, what good is literacy? I know that I would much rather be free and illiterate than literate and a slave.

Of course, literacy is desirable, but it is not an absolute good. Only those who value it as an end in itself, rather than as a means to goodness, can find totalitarian literacy rates admirable.

CONCLUSION

It is extremely easy to be distracted from the question, "Do my actions result in goodness?" Regarding any of the aforementioned values as ends in themselves does that. In fact, holding any of these values as supreme makes a person *worse*.

A religious person who does not affirm ethical monotheism will use religiosity to deflect attention from ethics. Such a person will tell others that what matters most to God is faith or rituals, not goodness.

An artist who does not affirm ethical monotheism can regard

his art as so important that he and it are beyond moral considerations.

A scholar who does not affirm ethical monotheism can easily use her knowledge and intelligence to support evil.

It is one of life's ironies that once a person dies, most of these accomplishments mean little to others. Every eulogy I have heard emphasized, when possible, the goodness of the deceased far more than professional achievements. It's sad that it usually takes death to clarify what is most important in life.

37

WHY NOT LOOT? AN EXAMPLE OF WHY ETHICAL MONOTHEISM IS NECESSARY

During the riots in Los Angeles, my family and I watched what was happening to our city on television (and through our window). At one point, as we watched yet another store being looted by young people, I turned to my eldest son, who was then nine, and asked him if he would loot something he really wanted if he were certain he wouldn't get caught.

"No," he answered.

I expected this answer. It was the answer to the next question that most interested me.

"Why not?" I asked.

"Because it's against the Ten Commandments."

That was precisely what I wanted to hear.

I suspect, however, that this is not what most well-educated Americans would want to hear. For them, the preferred response would be, "Because I think it's wrong."

WHICH RESPONSE IS PREFERABLE?

Which response a person prefers goes to the heart of what divides the religious viewpoint from the secular. Secularists generally believe that, ideally, people shouldn't loot because they think it is wrong to do so, period. In their view, to invoke God is not only unnecessary, it actually represents an inferior morality—"You mean you need to believe in God in order not to steal?"

Thus, when the late moral philosopher Lawrence Kohlberg of Harvard constructed a list of possible reasons to do what is right, he put believing that it was right as the highest reason, and belief in God as among the lowest. And he ranked belief in divine reward and punishment lowest of all.

Do *I* need God in order not to steal?

I don't know exactly how my behavior would change if I were absolutely convinced that there was no God. I do know that I would despair if I believed that the universe was deaf to all goodness and to all cruelty, that torturers and their victims, the cruel and the kind, all have the same fate. But I don't know precisely how the realization that morality was entirely a human construct would affect my *conduct*. By now, in middle age, with my morals from religion and childhood so deeply entrenched and with my self-image as an honest person, I certainly wouldn't begin to hurt people. I *emotionally*, not only morally or religiously, hate to see people suffer. But what about padding insurance claims and being otherwise dishonest with large impersonal institutions?

Belief in God is not the only reason I don't cheat, but my belief in a God who knows my behavior matters. While I don't think that I will go to hell if I cheat a store, I do believe in ultimate reward and punishment; in some cosmic sense I do believe that all my actions matter.

The secular belief that God and religions are primitive props for morality emanates from a greater faith in human nature than my religion or I have. If you believe that people are by nature good and honest, then neither God nor religion is necessary to ensure decent behavior. But if you don't believe that people are basically good—and neither reason nor religion believes we are—then conscience alone won't guide most people to do what is right. A conscience that is unaccountable to God may produce consistently good behavior in a few people, but conscience unaccountable to God and without a religious code is only a subjective, often transient, *feeling*.

Our secular age has raised a generation that believes that *feelings* should be the primary guide to one's behavior. That is why, in the relatively rare instances that secular schools have decided to make values a part of their curriculum, they never actually teach values. Rather they have offered courses in "values clarification," which consist of students sitting around *clarifying their feelings* about stealing, looting, etc. The substitution of feelings for standards also explains why so many people (not only students) would not save a human stranger before their dog whom they love.

Thank God my son answered, "Because it's against the Ten Commandments." If all our children did, we could look to the future with far greater optimism. I would like all young people to think that stealing is wrong. But I would sooner trust those who also believe that God thinks it is wrong.

IS THIS LIFE ALL THERE IS?
THOUGHTS ON GOD

38

IS THIS LIFE ALL THERE IS?

I once attended a funeral at which a prominent rabbi officiated. To probably everyone present, nothing unusual occurred; the service was traditional Conservative and the rabbi's remarks about the deceased were moving.

Then, at the grave, the rabbi spoke about Judaism's attitude toward death. "Judaism does not believe in a life after death," he said. "Rather, we live on in the good works we do and in the memories of those we leave behind."

Because this is what most contemporary Jews believe, few people at the funeral found reason to take particular notice of these remarks. But I was furious. The rabbi had told Jews a profound untruth at a moment of deep impressionability.

For ten years, I hosted a two-hour interreligious radio dialogue, "Religion on the Line." Each week, I moderated a panel consisting of a minister, a priest, and a rabbi, and often a fourth religious representative. Callers frequently asked questions concerning the afterlife, and nearly every non-Orthodox rabbi who participated said that Judaism does not believe in an afterlife.

Jews who believe that there is no reality beyond death are certainly entitled to hold such a belief. They may even be right. But that is their belief, not Judaism's. Judaism is unambiguous in its affirmation of a hereafter (see, for example, the eleventh chapter of the Talmudic tractate Sanhedrin and the Thirteen Principles of Faith of Maimonides). The entry under "Afterlife" in the scholarly and secular *Encyclopedia Judaica* begins, "Judaism has always maintained a belief in an afterlife."

True, Judaism gives no details about what happens after death—because it wants its adherents to focus on this world, "to repair the world under the rule of God." One reason that Judaism prohibits its priests from coming into contact with the dead—a prohibition that may be unique among the world's religions—is that a Jewish priest's focus must be on this world and life, not the next world and death.

But the affirmation of this world in no way implies that this life is all that there is.

Since Judaism and all monotheistic religions are predicated upon the existence of a God who is nonphysical and beyond nature, and who is just and loving, our physical existence cannot be the only reality. It defies logic to hold that the nonphysical God would create a world whose only reality is physical. And it is illogical that a just and loving God would create a world wherein the sum total of the existence of any of His creations is often cruel suffering. To state this case as starkly as possible, if there is nothing after this life, then the Nazis and the children they threw alive into furnaces have identical fates. If I believed such a thing, I would either become an atheist or hate the God who had created such a cruel and absurd universe.

Furthermore, those who believe that this life is the only reality are likely to be led to one or more of three negative conclusions about life:

1: *Hedonism.* If this life is all one has, then it is quite logical to live a life devoted to self-gratification. If the physical is the only reality, we should experience as much physical pleasure as possible. To paraphrase the old beer slogan, the message today is, "You only go around once in life, so get all the gusto you can."

2: *Utopianism.* Idealistic people who believe that this life is all there is reject hedonism. But they may embrace a far more dangerous ideology—utopianism, the desire to make heaven on earth. Hence the attraction of utopianism to so many twentieth-century radicals who have rejected Judaism and Christianity.

In light of the hells on earth that secular utopians have produced, it is clear just how important the deferring of utopia to a future world is. Had people like the Bolsheviks and millions of other secular radicals not tried to create heaven on earth, they would not have created hell here.

3: *Despair.* In light of the great physical and emotional pain that so many people experience, what is more likely to induce despondency than believing that this life is all there is? The malaise felt by so many people living in modern Western society is not traceable to material deprivation but, at least in part, to the despair induced by secularism and its belief that this world is all there is. That is why peasants with religious faith are probably happier than affluent people who have no faith (and why more affluent secularists, not the poor, are generally the ones who start radical revolutions).

As for the rabbi's statement that we live on through the memories of loved ones, what would the rabbi say about the millions of Jews, *every one* of whose loved ones also died during the Holocaust? If people live on solely through the memories of their loved ones, then many of the six million are forgotten smoke.

Those who wish to believe that this life is all there is are certainly welcome to do so. But they should be honest enough to acknowledge that this belief renders the lives of most people little more than a cruel joke.

39

CAN I BELIEVE IN GOD AFTER THE HOLOCAUST?

"How can I believe in God after the Holocaust?"

Anyone who speaks to Jews hears this question more than any other.

Yet, no matter how often the question is posed, it almost seems as if there has been a ban on offering an answer. The Holocaust has been so traumatic to the Jewish soul that as the preeminent Holocaust writer Elie Wiesel has often stated, the most appropriate response to this question is silence.

In some ways, that is true. But even if there was a time when the question of believing in God after the Holocaust had to be greeted with silence, that time has long since passed. We have done contemporary Jews, *particularly* Holocaust survivors, and all the non-Jews who ask such a thing a grave disservice by not attempting to answer the question, "How can I believe in God after the Holocaust?" When survivors say that their faith in God died along with members of their families, people usually offer sympathy. But fifty years after the liberation of the death camps, survivors, their children, and many others need and want answers much more than sympathy.

Why else would people still be asking the question fifty years after the end of the Holocaust? Are rabbis or Jewish philosophers helping people by only empathizing with them or, even worse, agreeing with their doubts, rather than attempting to answer them?

One of the greatest services one can render contemporary Jewry, particularly Holocaust survivors, is a convincing argument on behalf of continuing faith in God.

WHAT DOES THE QUESTION REALLY MEAN?

To answer the question, we first have to truly understand it.

It means, first, that the person who says, "I cannot believe in God because of the Holocaust," would in fact believe in God were it not for the Holocaust. If a person cannot believe in God for other reasons, the question, "How can I believe in God after the Holocaust?" is an emotional outcry, not a real question. The question is meaningful only if the questioner knows that, were it not for the Holocaust, he or she would believe in God.

I don't doubt that there are people who are nonbelievers because of the Holocaust, particularly some survivors and their children, but I suspect that such people are rare. In a lifetime of involvement in Jewish life, I have never met a Jew (who didn't go through the Holocaust) who believed in God prior to the Holocaust and who stopped believing because of it. Even among Jews who experienced the Nazi terror, nearly all Jews who were religious prior to the Holocaust retained their religiosity after it. Additionally, for every religious Jew who lost faith, there was an irreligious Jew for whom the Holocaust actually served as a catalyst to believing in God and Judaism.

Therefore, Jews who say that they cannot believe in God after the Holocaust should honestly confront the question of whether the Holocaust is actually what caused the disbelief.

"How can I believe in God after the Holocaust?" means one of two things: either that the Holocaust shows that there is no God, or that God simply stood by and therefore there is no point in believing in Him.

I believe that both meanings are Jewishly and logically untenable. The Holocaust does not present any new arguments against belief in God. Nothing about the Holocaust renders it, as opposed to all other unjust suffering in history, an argument against belief in God.

THE ARGUMENTS FOR REJECTING BELIEF IN GOD BECAUSE OF THE HOLOCAUST

Six Million

The first argument concerns the number six million. Its magnitude, it is argued, renders the Holocaust a unique challenge to God's existence.

The Holocaust *was* unique. The systematic attempt to murder every person belonging to an ethnic group has no parallel in recorded history (a major work of scholarship explains why the Holocaust is the one true genocide—the multivolume work of Professor Steven Katz, *The Holocaust in Historical Context*, Oxford University Press).

But though the Holocaust was unique, this in no way reflects on the question of God's existence. Why would one believe that there is a God when thousands of innocent Jews were murdered in Russian pogroms, but not when six million were murdered by the Nazis? At what number does faith become impossible? At three million? At 265,000? At one? How does a person hold that if a Jewish family was killed by the Nazis between 1939 to 1945, God does not exist, but if the same family was killed by other anti-Semites, then God does exist?

Either a Jew's faith is destroyed the moment one innocent Jew (or any other person) is killed, or it is not undone at any number—provided that, speaking only from a Jewish perspective, the Jewish people survive. Obviously, if a holocaust were to kill so many Jews that the Jewish people died out, the question of faith in God for a Jew would be moot.

Finally, in terms of percentage of Jews murdered, the Holocaust is not as unique as those who raise the number six million believe it is. For example, nearly one out of every three Jews was murdered in the 1648 pogroms in Eastern Europe.

Six Million Jews

A second argument—held by Jews alone—against faith in God after the Holocaust is, "How can one believe in a God who allowed *six million Jews* to be slaughtered?"

There are a number of responses.

First, no Jewish source holds that God has ever saved, or promised to save, every Jew from persecution. God has only promised that the Jewish *people* will survive all attempts to destroy them. Any Jew who believes that God took the Jews out of Egypt can also believe that God took the Jews out of Hitler's Europe. According to the Bible, God did not take all the Jews out of Egypt—Jews had been tortured, enslaved, and killed there for hundreds of years. But the Jewish *people* did escape Egypt. So, too, one may argue that while few Jews got out of Europe, the Jewish people did.

Second, only if people are unaware of how horribly Jews suffered at the hands of Jew-haters in the past can they maintain that the Holocaust makes belief in God impossible. The following is a contemporaneous description of one day during the 1648 pogroms:

> Some of the Jews had their skins flayed off them and their flesh flung to the dogs. The hands and feet of others were cut off and they were flung onto the roadway where carts ran over them and they were trodden under foot by horse. . . . And many were buried alive. Children were slaughtered in their mother's bosoms, and many children were torn apart like fish. They ripped open the bellies of pregnant women, took out the unborn children, and flung them in their faces. They tore open the bellies of some of them and placed a living cat within the belly and left them alive thus, first cutting off their hands so that they should not be able to take the living cat out of the belly. . . . And there was never an unnatural death in the world that they did not inflict upon them.

Why does this challenge God's existence less than the Holocaust does? Jews who point to the Holocaust as the source of their atheism are either ignorant of the other mass horrors in Jewish history or are reacting emotionally to the horror that took place in their own lifetimes.

Third, the Cambodian Communists murdered nearly one out of every three Cambodians, just as the Nazis murdered one out of every three Jews. Yet I have never heard a Jew say, "I cannot believe in God because He allowed two million Cambodians to be murdered." A Jew who specifically cites the murder of Jews as the reason not to believe that there is a God smacks of racism. Why does the murder of millions of innocent Jews challenge the existence of God more than the murders of millions of non-Jews? Does a Jew believe in a God who allowed the Soviets to deliberately starve nearly ten million Ukrainians to death but not in one who allowed the Nazis to murder six million Jews?

God Stood By

Of course, many people will respond that, indeed, it is not the Holocaust alone that causes them not to believe in God. They may single out the Holocaust because of its awesome horror and its proximity to our time, but *all* these horrendous evils argue against God's existence.

Do they really?

Only if one believes that, by definition, God must stop all evil. But that is not the Jewish (or any other mainstream religious) understanding of God. The God of biblical monotheism allows people to commit evil. God permitted the Nazis to murder six million Jews because it is a fundamental tenet of Judaism that God gives people moral freedom. Human beings are as free to build gas chambers as they are to build hospitals.

That may leave us emotionally unsatisfied, but the only alternative is that God would prevent any bad act from ever taking place. Would we really want to live in a world where people had no moral freedom?

If God should have stopped the Nazis from murdering Jews, should He not also stop the murders on America's streets? And what about rapes and child abuse? Would we really prefer to live in a world where all evil was impossible? Is being a good automaton preferable to being a free human being? Would we rather be loved by freely choosing people or by love-robots?

God constructed a world in which people choose to do good or evil. To construct one in which people could do only good, God would have to destroy the world in which we now live and create something entirely different. This may explain a remarkable passage in the Yom Kippur liturgy, which tells the story of the ten Talmudic sages who were tortured to death by the Romans. During their horrible ordeal, a voice called out from heaven, "Is this the Torah and its reward?" And God answers, "Keep quiet, or I will destroy the world!" God was right. If we want a world in which hurting innocent people is impossible, the world in which we live would have to be destroyed, and an entirely different one created.

We live in a world in which people can do unbelievably beautiful or unbelievably horrible things to other people. *And if those horrible acts argue against the existence of God, then the beautiful acts must argue for God's existence.*

If one is to abandon faith in anything after the Holocaust, it would be far more rational to abandon faith in the inherent good-ness of mankind. To abandon faith in God while retaining faith in humanity may be emotionally satisfying, but it is not logically com-pelling. God never built a gas chamber, and He has told us not to. Humans who loathed this God built the gas chambers—to destroy the people who revealed this God to mankind.

40

IS GOD LOVABLE?

I have long argued the case for belief in God. On purely rational grounds, the arguments for God's existence strike me as far stronger than the arguments against it. The real problem, when one really thinks the issue through, is not believing in God, it is loving God.

The problem is not really how do you believe that there is a God when so many children die from natural causes, or when so many innocents die at the hands of other people. The problem is, how do you *love* such a God?

Several years ago, while driving home right before the holiest day of the Jewish calendar, Yom Kippur, was about to begin, I heard a radio report about a disorder in children that causes them to mutilate themselves; for example, they put their hands into fire. As I listened, I thought about the holy day that was about to commence, and I wondered whether God ought to have His own Day of Atonement on which to ask human beings to forgive Him.

When I read Holocaust memoirs, hear stories of families that lose their children to hereditary diseases, and witness the immensity of human suffering in the world at large, I frequently fill up with anger at God. He can have my faith, and He can have my obedience, but why should I love Him?

During an extended dialogue I had with Rabbi Harold Kushner, author of *When Bad Things Happen to Good People*, I commented that I believed the most difficult commandment in the Torah is the one commanding us to love God—"And you shall love the Lord your God with all your heart" (Deuteronomy 6:5).

Kushner: Why do you think the commandment to love God is the hardest?

Prager: Because with either the traditional theology that I advocate or yours [Kushner has argued that God is not all-powerful], God isn't lovable. Certainly not in yours; God deserves no love for creating a universe wherein such terrible, unjust suffering would take place. That merits love?

Kushner: What does it mean, to merit love? If you're talking about esteem . . .

Prager: Oh, no. He has my esteem. It's a major achievement to create the universe. But He doesn't have my love.

Kushner: Why?

Prager: Why would I love Him? He's not lovable. That's why. My child does not have to merit my love; such love is innate. But there's no innate tendency to love God. It's something one works at. If it were innate, there wouldn't be a commandment ordering it. Do you love God?

Kushner: I think I do. Archibald MacLeish says that if God deserved love, then we wouldn't be doing anything for Him by loving Him. Love is something which has to be freely given and not earned. God has everything else. The one thing we can do for God is love Him without having to.

Prager: Agreed. I have always considered it a credit to God that He wants us to love Him. But I still don't understand why you find the Creator of the world, a world filled with inevitable, horrible, unjust, and unbalanced suffering, lovable?

Kushner: I love God because of what it does for me, not for what it does for Him. Maybe I want to love Him so I'm not alone. Maybe I want to forgive God in the hope that He will forgive me.

Prager: Forgive you for what?

Kushner: For being imperfect. As I forgive Him for not always being in control.

After pondering this question for some time, I have concluded that we ought to love God—for these reasons:

First, God created us out of love. The proof is that we love life. Why else would He have created us? God after all does not need us—and if He did, He would even be more lovable.

Second, God created us with the ability and deep desire to experience love. Only a lovable God would do that.

Third, only a lovable God would command us to love Him. Why else would He want our love and be sensitive enough to understand that without such a commandment, we might not be so predisposed?

Finally, Kushner was right—we need to love God; otherwise, life is lonely and depressing.

Nevertheless, it sometimes remains difficult to love both people and God simultaneously. It is very hard to witness the horrible suffering that people endure and at the same time love the God who made a world in which such suffering is built-in. We can blame man-made evils on man (though it remains difficult to love a God who created creatures capable of torturing and murdering), but we can't blame people for deformed babies or genetic diseases. The God who made Alzheimer's isn't easily loved.

So where do I stand?

I still have problems with loving God. But I am thankful for a religion that allows me to have such ambivalence, and to express it without guilt. It is comforting to know that the biblical name for the Jewish people, Israel, means "struggle with God."

41

WHY GOD MUST BE DEPICTED AS
A FATHER AND NOT AS A MOTHER

Most people believe that the Bible, the book that introduced humanity to God, refers to God in the masculine because of the patriarchy and sexism of the ancient world.

It is true that the Bible was written within a patriarchal context, and it is true that there is sexism in Bible-based religion. But I do not believe that these facts explain why God is depicted as a "father" rather than as a "parent" or "mother" (a neutered "It" would be unacceptable because the biblical God is a personal God).

The depiction of God in masculine terms, I believe, is essential to the Bible's fundamental moral purposes. To understand why, one must posit two premises: that the Hebrew Bible's primary concern is promoting good behavior, and that the primary perpetrators of evil behavior, such as violence against innocents, are males, especially young males.

From these facts I derive three reasons that it is in men's *and women's* best interests to depict God in the masculine.

Before offering these reasons, a personal note is in order: I strongly support women's equality, and I strongly affirm that God is neither male nor female and that both men and women are created in God's image (Genesis 1:27). In addition, my own religious life is quite egalitarian, and I regard the notion that either sex is superior as nonsense.

BOYS TAKE RULES FROM MEN

When males are young, they need to feel accountable to a male authority figure. Without a father or some other male rule giver, young men are likely to do great harm. Almost any mother will tell you that if there is no male authority figure to give a growing boy rules, it is very difficult for her to control his wilder impulses. For this reason, a God depicted in masculine terms, not a goddess, not a "Mother in heaven," must be the source of such commandments as "Thou shall not murder" and "Thou shall not steal."

Women who feel discriminated against because of the male depiction of God should reflect on the consequences of a goddess- or mother-based religious/ethical code. Any discomfort they feel because of a masculine depiction of God is not comparable to the pain they will endure if boys are not civilized into good men.

The need for male authority figures is illustrated by the current criminal population in the United States. The absence of a father or other male authority in the formative years of a boy's life is the most important contributing factor to his turning to criminal behavior. A widely accepted figure is that *70 percent* of the violent criminals in American prisons did not grow up with a father.

If the father figure/rule giver that boys need is not on earth, a loving and morally authoritative Father in heaven can often serve as an effective substitute.

But the last thing that a boy growing up without a father needs is a female figure to worship. He already has one—his mother—and to develop healthfully, he needs to separate from her, not bond with another mother figure. Otherwise, he will spend his life expressing his masculinity in ways that are destructive to women and men.

MALES NEED A MALE ROLE MODEL

To transform a wild boy into a good man, a male model is as necessary as a male rule giver.

When the Bible depicts God as merciful, caring for the poor and the widow, and as a lover of justice, it is not so much interested in describing God, who is, after all, largely indescribable, but in providing a model for human emulation. Especially male emulation.

If God were depicted as female, young men would deem traits such as compassion, mercy, and care for the downtrodden as femi-

nine, and, in their pursuit of their masculinity, reject them. But if God, i.e., our Father in heaven, who is, on occasion, even a warrior, cares for the poor and loves justice, mercy, and kindness, then these traits are also masculine, and to be emulated.

The argument that this is sexist, since girls need moral female models, is both irrelevant and untrue. It is irrelevant because the problem of mayhem and violence is overwhelmingly a male one—and this is the problem with which the Bible is most concerned. It is untrue because girls are able to retain their femininity and their decency with a male-depicted God. Girls, too, view their fathers as rule givers. Of course, girls need female role models—but not to avoid violence.

THE MALE IS MORE RULE-ORIENTED

A third reason for depicting God in masculine terms is the indispensability of law to a just and humane society.

"Law and order" can be code words for repression, but they are in fact the building blocks of a decent society. It is therefore natural and desirable that God be identified with the gender that is more naturally disposed to rules and justice—males. Females are more naturally inclined toward feelings and compassion, two essential qualities for a decent *personal* life, but not for the governance of *society.* A male depiction of God helps makes a law-based society possible. And the Hebrew Bible is nothing if not law-based.

It is ironic that some women, in the name of feminism, are attempting to emasculate the God of Western religious morality. For if their goal is achieved, it is women who will suffer most from lawless males.

We have too many absent fathers on earth to begin to even entertain the thought of having no Father in heaven.

42

CAN WE MAKE DEALS WITH GOD?

Once, after I gave a lecture at a synagogue in London, a man in the audience asked me to reconcile the existence of God with the fact that good people suffer.

Whenever I am asked this, I usually talk about the inscrutability of God's ways, about Judaism's desire that people work on reducing suffering, and about the biblical book of Job. But this time I decided to approach the subject more directly.

"Why *shouldn't* good people suffer?" I responded, and then paraphrased a question I first heard asked by Harold Kushner: "Should a pious person be able to go out on a freezing night without a jacket and not get sick?"

"But what about those who keep all the Torah's commandments?" the man, an Orthodox Jew, responded.

"What about them?" I asked.

"How do you explain their unjust suffering?" he countered.

"I don't understand," I said. "Do you believe that observing the Torah's commandments should safeguard you from suffering and evil?"

"Yes, of course I do."

I then asked the audience, composed primarily of Orthodox Jews, if others felt the same way. Most did.

I was stunned. I had never realized how widespread deal making with God is. I have come to realize that many religious people, of all faiths, believe that they should be able to avoid the calamities that afflict the less pious. They believe, in effect, that they can make a deal with God—"I'll do what You want so that You do what I want."

If this is true, it helps to explain why the problem of unjust suffering can be so devastating to people's faith. The problem is not merely that of reconciling the terrible injustices of this world with a just Creator—a problem that I and many others have. For countless religious people, this issue is compounded by their belief that God has reneged on a deal with them.

While I don't expect religious people to be immune to childish images of God, the fact that many religious people seem to be religious in part, or even entirely, because of having made a deal with God—"I'll be religious, You keep me safe"—*was* surprising.

I have never believed that there is a connection between my religious observance and God's granting me anything in this world. I have always assumed that the purpose of religious practice is to affect *my* behavior, not God's. The purpose of leading a religious life is to make us better human beings, to bring us closer to God, to add holiness to our lives, and to make a just society. *These are all rewards in and of themselves.* To expect an additional reward for being religious is analogous to expecting an additional reward for following the rules in learning how to use a computer—your reward is that you can now use the computer. That is precisely what the Talmud means when it says, "the reward of fulfilling a commandment is the fulfillment of the commandment."

Judaism does believe that God rewards the good and punishes the evil—but that is in the *afterlife* (this belief is one of Maimonides' Thirteen Principles of the Jewish Faith). It would be ludicrous for God to reward the individual for keeping His laws. If observing the laws led to rewards from God, everyone would have long ago started to observe them—who doesn't want to be protected from cancer?

Nor are these the only wrongheaded beliefs to which such thinking leads. For example, if God provides this-worldly rewards for keeping His laws, then the converse must also be true—all suffering is a punishment from God. I have seen this cruel belief at work. I witnessed a particularly fine Orthodox Jew slowly waste away from a tumor while a member of his family told him that if he engaged in enough repentance for his past sins, God would remove the tumor.

Such thinking is not only cruel (instead of offering compassion to the suffering, we imply that they have somehow earned their plight) but also a desecration of God's name in that it depicts God as vindictive: "Moshe didn't observe the Sabbath as he should have, so I'll give him a tumor."

The final proof of this belief's foolishness is that it renders the question, "Why do good people suffer?" self-contradictory. People who believe that keeping God's laws will protect them from suffering have already answered their question. If you suffer, you're clearly not a good person!

Given the irrational and cruel ramifications of the belief that religious observance protects us, I have come to think that there is another reason that some religious people espouse it.

When religious people expect rewards in this world for their religiosity, I suspect that they really do not want to be as religiously observant as they are. If they truly enjoyed and benefited from living a religious life, they wouldn't be so concerned with additional rewards. Therefore, it may very well be that these individuals are forcing themselves to be religious lest they lose their health and life insurance policies with God.

That is why, whenever I meet joyless, angry, or stern religious people, of whatever religion, I assume that they really don't want to be doing what they are doing. I assume that they are engaged in a life of ever-increasing, all-enveloping, and restrictive laws and dogmas not because they want to, but out of fear of God's punishment if they don't live at their present level of religiosity.

You can tell when people love what they are doing and derive pleasure from it, just as you can tell when they don't.

One solution to this problem lies in having different attitudes toward the two basic types of religious laws, those between people and God (laws of holiness) and those between people (laws of ethics). It doesn't matter if people are ethical because they have made a deal with God, but it does matter if people observe the rituals because of a deal. What matters in ethics is behavior more than motives. The downtrodden do not care why people help them; they only care *that* people do so. We would have a considerably finer world if all people feared God's wrath for stealing, cheating, raping, murdering, or ignoring evil inflicted on others.

But when it comes to the laws between man and God, motives are very important. It doesn't matter why you give charity, but it does matter why a Jew keeps the Sabbath, why a Christian regularly attends church, or why a Muslim observes the laws of Ramadan. If one gives charity solely out of fear of God, the act is still entirely beneficial. But if one observes the ritual practices solely out of fear of God (and/or the community, which is often the case), the act eventually becomes almost meaningless and can even become ugly.

Religious life would be greatly enriched if people who were religiously observant would drop their belief in deals with God. If they then observed fewer rituals, but observed them because they believed in the *intrinsic* worth of these practices, they would radiate a joy and kindness that would make religion the beautiful way of life it can be, but so often is not.

43

—

A JEW'S THOUGHTS ON CHRISTMAS

Christmas is not my holiday. For a practicing Jew, the twenty-fifth of December is no more significant than the twenty-fifth of any other month. But I enjoy the Christmas season a great deal. I appreciate the spirit of generosity and the reflection on religious themes that the holiday engenders, and I love the mood, the music, and even the decorations.

Many Jews and other non-Christians may feel a bit "out of it" during the Christmas season, but I have absolutely no problem with such a feeling. For one thing, as a Jew who lives Judaism, I feel no void during Christmastime. A Jew who celebrates Purim in March, Passover in April, Shabuoth (Pentecost) in May or June, Rosh Hashanah in September, Sukkoth (Tabernacles) in October, and Hanukkah in December—not to mention the Sabbath every week—hardly lacks for festive occasions. Non-Christians who feel pangs of regret for a "missed holiday" during the Christmas season are individuals who, for whatever reason, do not celebrate religious holidays of their own.

Moreover, I enjoy observing Christians celebrate their Christianity. For a Jew rooted in Judaism, Christians rooted in their identity are a blessing, not a problem. In the religious Jewish home in which I grew up, my family sat, the males wearing our yarmulkes (skullcaps), and watched the midnight Mass televised from the Vatican every Christmas Eve. The more secure a Jew is in his Judaism, the less likely he is to feel threatened by Christians practicing their Christianity.

And what is wrong with being reminded that because we are members of a minority religion, we are a bit "out of it"? I like being different, and I bless America for enabling me to celebrate my distinctiveness.

Hanukkah is not nearly as important to Judaism as Christmas is to Christianity (if Jesus' birth were celebrated in October, Jews would celebrate Sukkoth, a far more important holiday than Hanukkah). But I deeply appreciate Christian America's attempt, which has been incredibly successful, to elevate Hanukkah to a status alongside that of Christmas. That is a very touching tribute to the fact that Christians recognize that although Jews are numerically small, Judaism is the mother religion of Christianity and its partner in shaping the Western world's values.

For these reasons, rather than dread the Christmas season, I welcome it. What this Jew does dread is an America that ceases to celebrate Christmas.